BRITISH COLUMBIA
ALBERTA
SAS
CANA
WASHINGTON
Glacier N. P.
15
Missouri
River
MONTANA
90
Yellowstone
Billings
IDAHO
Yellowstone N. P.
Boise
Grand Teton N. P.
Snake
River
WYOMING
80
Great Salt Lake
Salt Lake City
NEVADA
UTAH
Green
River
15

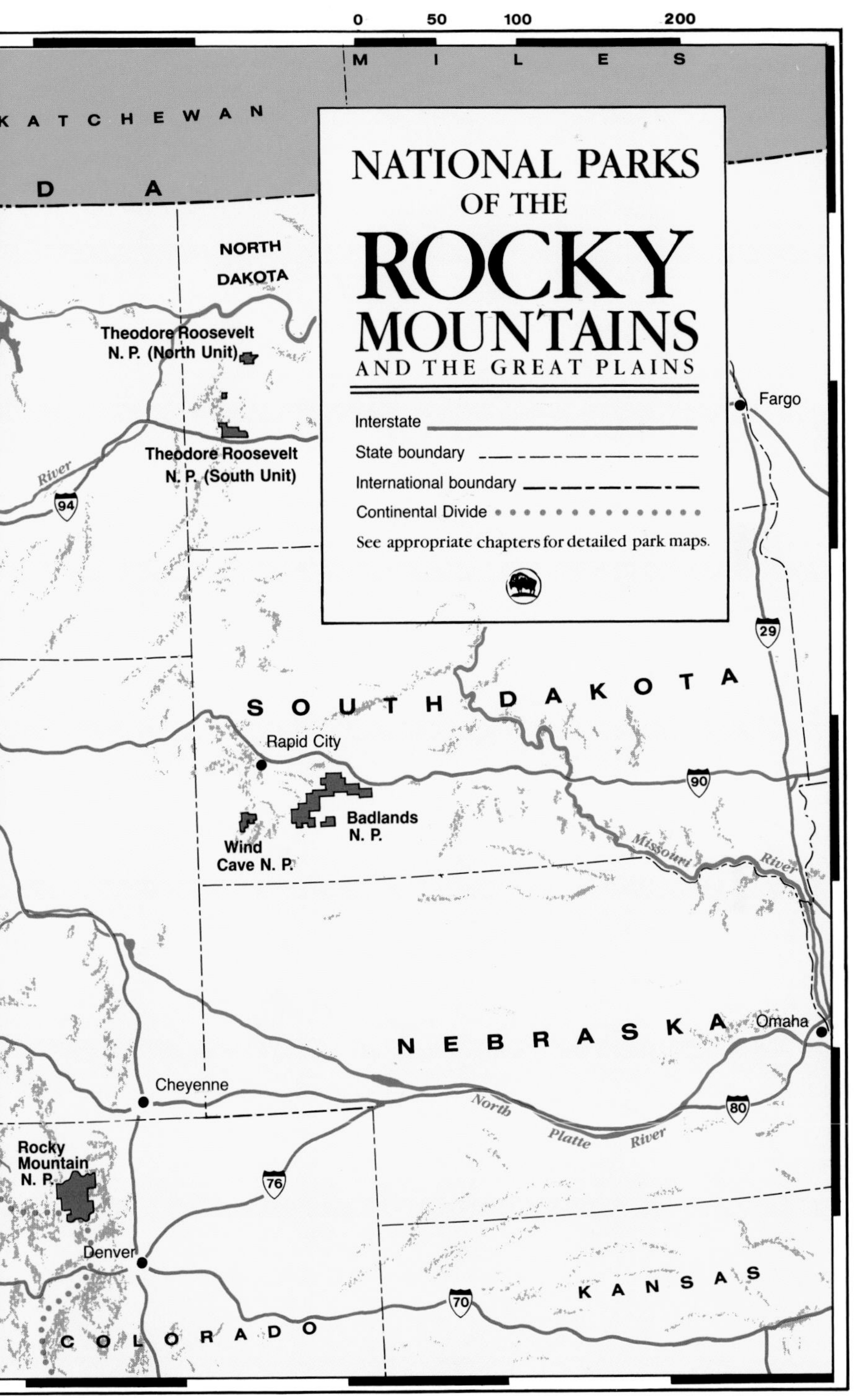
NATIONAL PARKS
OF THE
ROCKY
MOUNTAINS
AND THE GREAT PLAINS
Interstate
State boundary
International boundary
Continental Divide
See appropriate chapters for detailed park maps.
0
50
100
200
M I L E S
KATCHEWAN
D A
NORTH
DAKOTA
Theodore Roosevelt
N. P. (North Unit)
Theodore Roosevelt
N. P. (South Unit)
River
94
Fargo
29
SOUTH DAKOTA
Rapid City
90
Badlands
N. P.
Wind
Cave N. P.
Missouri
River
NEBRASKA
Omaha
Cheyenne
North
Platte
River
80
Rocky
Mountain
N. P.
76
Denver
70
KANSAS
COLORADO

THE SIERRA CLUB GUIDES TO THE NATIONAL PARKS OF THE ROCKY MOUNTAINS AND THE GREAT PLAINS

Published by
Stewart, Tabori & Chang

Distributed by
RANDOM HOUSE

Front cover: Cathedral Group, Grand Teton National Park
(©David Muench)

Frontispiece: Winter sunrise, Grand Teton National Park
(©David Muench)

Back cover: Lower Falls, Yellowstone National Park
(©Manuel Rodriguez)

Text by:

Conger Beasley, Jr.—Badlands and Wind Cave
C. W. Buchholtz—Glacier
Paul Schullery—Grand Teton and Yellowstone
Stephen Trimble—Rocky Mountain and Theodore Roosevelt

Consulting Editor: James V. Murfin

Project Editors: Irene Pavitt and Donald Young

Designer: J.C. Suarès

Photo Editor: Christine A. Pullo

Illustrations and maps © Bill Russell

Library of Congress Cataloging in Publication Data
Main entry under title:

The Sierra Club guide to the national parks of the
Rocky Mountains and the Great Plains.

Includes index.
1. National parks and reserves—Rocky Mountains Region
—Guide-books. 2. Rocky Mountains Region—Description and
travel—Guide-books. I. Beasley, Conger. II. Sierra Club.
F721.S58 1984 917.8 84-2539
ISBN 0-394-72754-1 (Random House)

Created and published by Stewart, Tabori & Chang, Inc.

300 Park Avenue South, New York, N.Y. 10010.

Photo credits are on pp. 263–264.

Distributed by Random House, Inc.
201 East 50 Street, New York, N.Y., 10022.

Printed and bound in Japan.

PREFACE

THIS COUNTRY'S FORTY-EIGHT NATIONAL PARKS CONtain natural wonders more varied and extraordinary than those found in any other nation on earth. Embodied and preserved in them is the beauty of a vast land, which only a few centuries ago was wilderness. Every year, 50 million people visit these parks, testifying to a deep appreciation of the treasures they offer.

Recognizing the need for park guide books that are practical as well as beautiful, Stewart, Tabori & Chang is proud to present *The Sierra Club Guides to the National Parks*. These books have been created with the cooperation of the Sierra Club, which has been committed to conservation since 1892, and with the participation of the National Park Service and Random House. The five regional guides planned for the series—the Desert Southwest, the Pacific Southwest and Hawaii, the Rocky Mountains and the Great Plains, the Pacific Northwest, and the Midwest and East—take you through each of the national parks of the United States.

Leading nature writers and photographers, experts in their fields, have provided text and photographs that work together as a tour of the parks. One chapter is devoted to each park, beginning with its discovery and use by man, moving on to its natural and geological history, its animal and plant life, and finally exploring its sites, trails, and trips. Each chapter also includes an up-to-date facilities chart, trail guides, and park and trail maps created especially for the book. An extensive full-color appendix of the most commonly seen animals and plants is included at the end of each book.

M A P S

C O N T E N T S

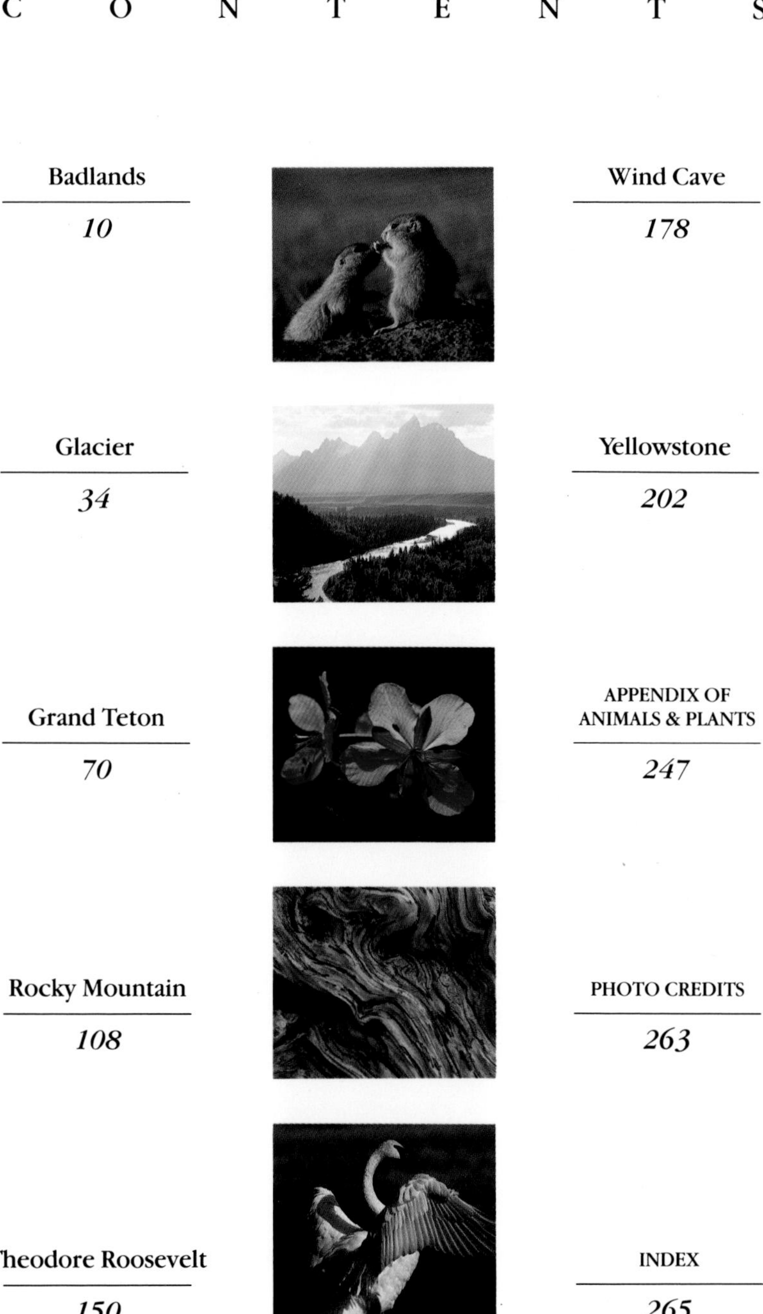

BADLANDS NATIONAL PARK

Bright yellow soil near Dillon Pass contains sediments laid down by an ancient sea.

BADLANDS NATIONAL PARK
P.O. BOX 6, INTERIOR, SOUTH DAKOTA 57750
TEL.: (605) 433-5361

Highlights: The Wall □ Windows □ Cliff Shelf □ Bison Herd □ Fossil Exhibit Trail □ Sage Creek Wilderness Area □ Prairie Dog Town

Access: From Kadoka, take I–90 west 27 miles; from Wall, take I–90 for 30 miles. From Interior, take South Dakota 377 off South Dakota 44 for 2 miles.

Hours: Open year-round, 24 hours daily; Visitor Center closed Thanksgiving, Christmas Day, and New Year's Day.

Fees: Entrance, $1/car; 50¢/person in commercial vehicle. Camping, $6/unit.

Parking: Ample throughout park.

Gas, food: In Interior, Cactus Flats, Wall, and Kadoka. In park at Cedar Pass Lodge (food only).

Lodging: In park at Cedar Pass Lodge between May 1 and October 15. Also in Kadoka and Wall.

Visitor Center: Cedar Pass, 7 A.M.–8 P.M. during summer; 8 A.M.–4:30 P.M. thereafter. White River, 8 A.M.–4:30 P.M.

Museum: Exhibits in Cedar Pass Visitor Center.

Gift shop: At Cedar Pass Lodge.

Pets: Permitted on leashes, except in backcountry, on trails, or in public buildings.

Picnicking: At Cedar Pass Campground, Sage Creek Campground, and Conata Picnic Site.

Hiking: Throughout park; carry water.

Backpacking: Permitted, but no camping within .5 mile of any road. Carry water.

Campgrounds: 110 campsites; 4 group campsites, reservations needed. Cedar Pass Campground has water, restrooms, RV dump stations.

Tours: During June, July, and August.

Other activities: Naturalist programs, horseback riding from mid-June through August.

Facilities for disabled: Cedar Pass Visitor Center, amphitheater, some cabins at lodge, and many wayside trails accessible.

For additional information, see also Sites, Trails, and Trips on pages 29–32 and the map on pages 14–15.

THE MISSOURI RIVER—THE MAJOR RIVER OF THE NORTHern Great Plains—divides South Dakota into contrasting sections. To the west of the river, the climate is dry; the rainfall, sparse; the land, carved by wind and water into remarkable shapes. Badlands National Park, comprising 380 square miles at an elevation of 2,443 to 3,255 feet, is located in the southwestern part of the state between the White and Cheyenne rivers, tributaries of the Missouri. The backbone of the park—the geological feature from which it derives its name—is a ridge, or "wall," that stretches 100 miles south into the Nebraska panhandle. Formed by sedimentary deposits, the land has been cut and eroded over the millennia into a variety of configurations, and its lush, rolling grasslands nourish sizable populations of large grazing and small burrowing animals.

In the Sage Creek Basin, 64,250 acres have been designated as a wilderness area.

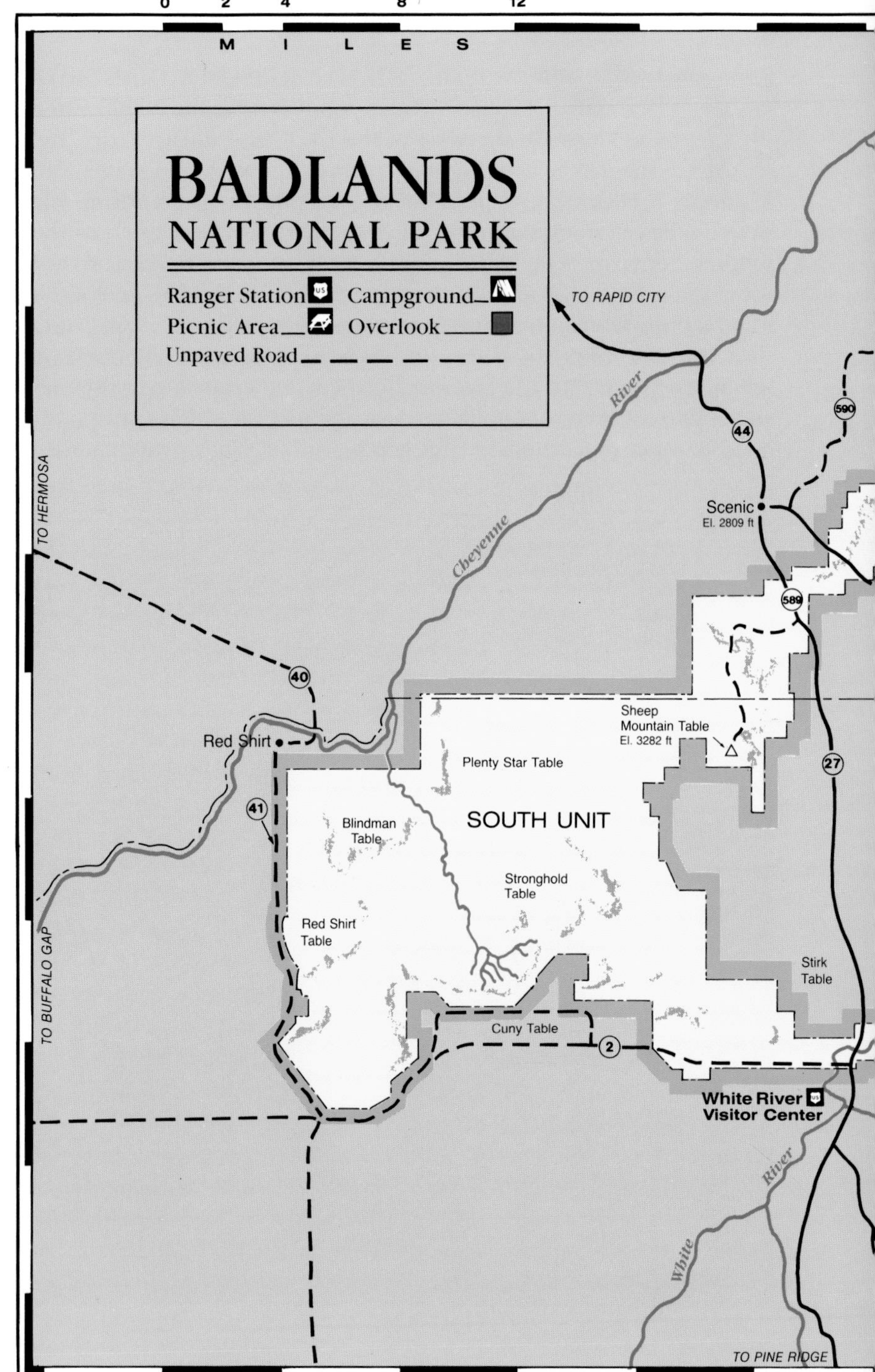
0 2 4 8 12
MILES
BADLANDS
NATIONAL PARK
Ranger Station
Campground
Picnic Area
Overlook
Unpaved Road
TO RAPID CITY
Cheyenne River
TO HERMOSA
44
590
Scenic
El. 2809 ft
589
40
Red Shirt
Sheep Mountain Table
El. 3282 ft
Plenty Star Table
27
41
Blindman Table
SOUTH UNIT
Stronghold Table
Red Shirt Table
TO BUFFALO GAP
Stirk Table
Cuny Table
2
White River Visitor Center
White River
TO PINE RIDGE

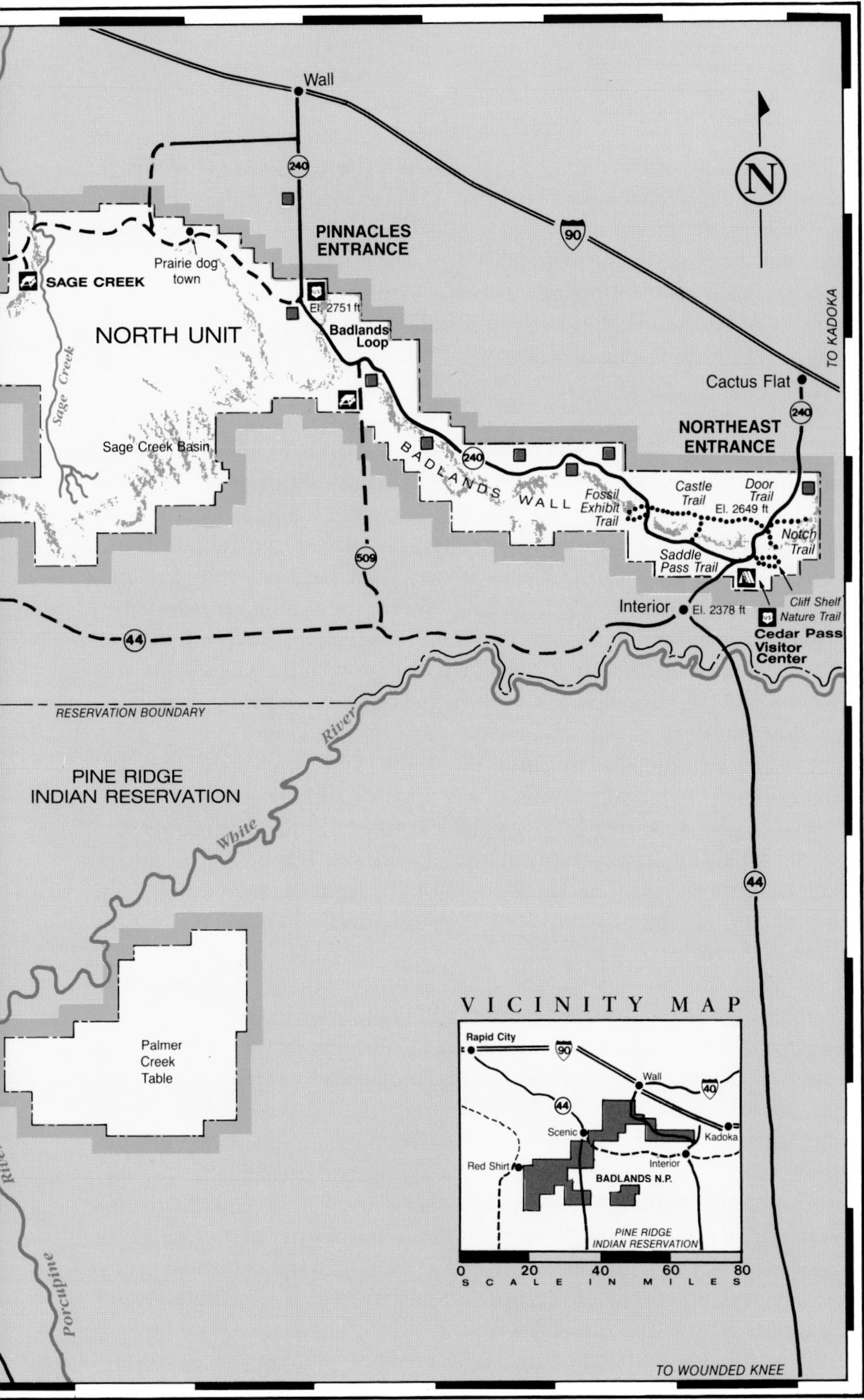
Wall
240
PINNACLES ENTRANCE
90
SAGE CREEK
Prairie dog town
El. 2751 ft
NORTH UNIT
Badlands Loop
TO KADOKA
Sage Creek
Cactus Flat
240
NORTHEAST ENTRANCE
Sage Creek Basin
BADLANDS WALL
240
Fossil Exhibit Trail
Castle Trail
Door Trail
El. 2649 ft
Notch Trail
Saddle Pass Trail
509
Interior
El. 2378 ft
Cliff Shelf Nature Trail
Cedar Pass Visitor Center
44
RESERVATION BOUNDARY
White River
PINE RIDGE INDIAN RESERVATION
44
Palmer Creek Table
VICINITY MAP
Rapid City
90
Wall
90
44
Scenic
Kadoka
Interior
Red Shirt
BADLANDS N.P.
PINE RIDGE INDIAN RESERVATION
0 20 40 60 80
SCALE IN MILES
Porcupine
TO WOUNDED KNEE

H I S T O R Y

Early Inhabitants

The exact time of the entry of humans into the Badlands is unknown. More than 80 archeological sites have been located within the park boundaries, the oldest dating back 7,000 years. Radiocarbon tests indicate that fire pits in the Pinnacles area were used around A.D. 900. A hundred years later, nomadic tribes roamed the territory. Primarily hunters and gatherers, they belonged to the Caddoan, Athapaskan, Kiowa, and Shoshonean linguistic groups.

The Sioux

The preeminent Native Americans in the Badlands in historical times have been the Dakota, more commonly called the Sioux. When Columbus first arrived on these shores, the Sioux were living in what is now North Carolina. A migration that lasted almost 300 years took them from North Carolina through present-day West Virginia, Ohio, Indiana, Illinois, and Wisconsin, to Minnesota. There, they came up against the Chippewa. Supplied with guns by French traders, the Chippewa drove the Sioux west and south onto the Great Plains. In the late 1700s, the Sioux acquired horses. Their culture changed dramatically, and they became fierce warriors.

A division of the Sioux Nation, the Teton, first crossed the Missouri River about 1775. They chased away Spanish and French traders and displaced the Arikaree. In 1804 the explorers in the first Lewis and Clark Expedition had a tense encounter with the Teton near the site of Pierre, South Dakota. The Teton sought to prevent the expedition from proceeding up the Missouri, but they relented when the Americans threatened to use force.

By 1840, the Sioux were the masters of the northern Great Plains, dominating the territory from the Canadian border to the Platte River, and from the eastern Dakotas to the Rocky Mountains. The Oglala Sioux, a branch of the Teton division, hunted buffalo and antelope throughout the Badlands. When whites first invaded the Dakotas, the Sioux fought back valiantly. Led by warriors like Red Cloud, Sitting Bull, and Crazy Horse, they inflicted sharp defeats on the cavalry, the most famous occurring in 1876, when General George Custer and his troops were wiped out at the Little Bighorn River. In the late 1880s, the Sioux embraced the religious movement called the Ghost Dance, which promised that the buffalo would return and that the white Americans would disappear. The Sioux danced without interference in remote strongholds within the Badlands. Faced with growing militancy by the Sioux,

U.S. Army troops entered the area. In 1890, Chief Big Foot and his band passed through the present-day park and were detained at Wounded Knee, just to the south. Tension led to shooting, and Big Foot and more than 150 of his followers were killed.

Explorers, Scientists, and Settlers

Fur trapper and mountain man Jedediah Smith led an expedition through the Badlands in 1823. Although Smith had been preceded by French-Canadian trappers, his was the first recorded trip, and due to the lack of potable water, it nearly ended in disaster. Twenty years later, Alexander Culbertson, chief agent for the American Fur Company, collected several wagonloads of fossilized bones and teeth in the Badlands and shipped them back east to the Smithsonian Institution. The paleontologist Hiram A. Prout wrote a monograph about them, which was the first publication of what was to become an extensive literature on the subject. In 1849, a scientific party under John Evans was sent to the Badlands by the federal government to collect more fossil specimens.

Texas cattlemen, attracted by federal government leasing of Indian lands in the 1880s, drove huge herds up to the Dakotas. In 1890, President Benjamin Harrison signed a proclamation that took more lands away from the Sioux and opened the Badlands to homesteading. Settlers, brought in by railroad, arrived in large numbers; by the first decade of the new century, sod huts and dugouts dotted every section of western South Dakota. Heavy plowing took away the topsoil, and the droughts of 1911 and of the 1930s forced many farmers to abandon their lands.

Through the 1880s, Texas cattlemen drove great herds to the plains, including the Badlands.

Establishment of the Park

In 1922, Senator Peter Norbeck introduced the first bill in Congress to set aside the Badlands as a national park. Badlands National Monument, an area of 50,830 acres, was authorized by Congress in 1929. In 1936, by presidential proclamation, the area was enlarged; three years later, President Franklin Roosevelt formally established Badlands National Monument. In 1976, the South Unit and the Palmer Creek Area were added, bringing the total acreage up to 244,300; this addition, while still owned by the Oglala Sioux, is administered by the National Park Service. Two years later, Congress upgraded the monument to Badlands National Park.

G E O L O G Y

Early inhabitants of and travelers in present-day southwestern South Dakota were struck by the aridity of the terrain and the peculiarity of the land formations. The Sioux referred to the place as *mako sica*, or

The steep slopes of the Brule Formation contain rhinoceros and protoceras fossils.

"land bad." French-Canadian trappers described it as *les mauvaises terres à traverser*, or "bad lands to travel across." But not all the impressions of early visitors were negative. In 1848, Fray Pierre-Jean DeSmet penned this fanciful description: "Viewed at a distance, these lands exhibit the appearance of extensive villages and ancient castles, but under forms so extraordinary, and so capricious a style of architecture, that we might consider them as appertaining to some new world, or ages far remote."

Sedimentation

During the late Cretaceous period, about 80 million years ago, the northern Great Plains were inundated by an extensive sea. North America was located closer to the equator than it is now, and the climate was humid and tropical, supporting a variety of primitive creatures and vegetation. It was a time of tremendous sedimentary deposition, during which the Pierre Shale—the bottom rung of the Badlands geological ladder—was laid down.

About 70 million years ago, at the close of the Cretaceous, the continent buckled in a north–south direction, and the Rocky Mountains and the Black Hills were uplifted. The land to the east of the new mountain chain formed a gradual slope that funneled water through clearly defined channels, and the shallow, inland sea was transformed into a muddy plain. The rejuvenation of the landscape during the Oligocene epoch (32 to 23 million years ago) resulted in the deposition of a layer of sediment known as the Chadron Formation.

Two more formations date from the Oligocene: the Brule Formation (visible in the beige and pinkish red bands of the jagged-shaped pinnacles) and the Sharps Formation. Swampy flood plains again soaked the area; the warm, humid climate provided a fertile ecosystem for such animals as the mesohippus (small horse), entelodont (giant pig), and saber-toothed cat. Toward the end of the epoch, the climate became cooler and drier.

At the beginning of the Miocene epoch (23 to 10 million years ago), volcanic activity, probably from the Rockies, resulted in an outpouring of ash that was carried eastward and that dropped in tremendous quantities on western South Dakota. The remains of this ash are visible in the chalk-gray coloring that overlies the land around the towns of Cedar Pass and Rockyford, as well as other places along the Badlands Wall. Additional layers, which were laid down afterward, have long since eroded away.

Erosion

After the Miocene epoch ended, little sediment accumulated in the Badlands. Then began the relatively rapid erosion that continues to this day. Water is the main sculpting tool, assisted by "airborne sandpaper": wind carrying dust and grit. Although averaging only 13 to 15 inches, the annual rainfall is concentrated in a few heavy thunderstorms, which erode the land into ridges, pillars, overhangs, shelves, chimneys, and toadstool-shaped hoodoos. The freeze–thaw cycle is also a contributor, especially on the north-facing slopes. The surface of the Badlands Wall wears away at a rate of as much as 1 inch a year. Photographs taken of specific sites fifty years ago show different configurations from those of today as a result of rapid weathering. The Wall divides the upper, or northern, grasslands—those "above the Wall" —from those to the south. The latter, on average, are 200 feet lower in elevation. The grasslands below the Wall are drained by tributaries of the White River.

Opposite: Pounded by rain in heavy storms, soft Badlands soils have been deeply eroded.

Top: Bison bull. Bottom: Prickly pear cactus.

NATURAL HISTORY

The richest Oligocene fossil beds in the world are located in the South Dakota Badlands. Almost every important natural-history museum in the world possesses some of the White River fossils.

Prehistoric Animals: Fossils

Fossils are traces of prehistoric life, be they animal tracks, leaf impressions, shells, bones, or teeth. Only a few plants and animals become fossilized after they die. Usually, they decay into the earth. Rapid burial is necessary for fossilization to occur. It did occur when remains of animals and plants were trapped and buried under sediments of streams, marshes, flood plains, and lakes. Later sediments buried these remains even deeper. Ground water seeping through the sediments deposited calcium and silica in the spaces within the organism, fossilizing it. Fossils in the park date from about 38 million to 25 million years ago, during the so-called Age of Mammals. Dinosaurs, which lived in an earlier era, are not found in the park.

A common fossil in Badlands National Park is the stylemys, or turtle. The Pierre Shale (the floor of the Cretaceous period sea) has yielded many sea-turtle fossils. Oreodonts, which may have looked like pigs but which chewed a cud like a cow, wandered about in large herds.

The mesohippus was a herbivorous horse about 20 inches high. It first appeared some 58 million years ago. It had four toes on the front feet, and three on the hind feet. Twenty-five million years later, three toes adorned each foot, the largest in the middle, suggesting the formation of a hoof. The mesohippus died out long before the Spanish reintroduced the horse to this continent in the sixteenth century.

The largest known Badlands fossils are the remains of the titanothere, an early ancestor of the rhinoceros. The titanothere stood about 12 feet high. This animal was the largest of the herbivores, or plant-eaters, in its day.

Other fossils include remains of an ancestor of the camel; the fierce and powerful saber-toothed cat; and the protoceras, a fantastic sheeplike creature that had three pairs of horns sticking out on its face and head at different angles.

Modern Animals

After being almost exterminated by white hunters in the nineteenth century, the buffalo (bison) has returned to Badlands National Park. A

Overleaf: The shy and seldom-seen bighorn sheep, which have hard-edged hooves with spongy centers, can maintain good traction on high, steep slopes.

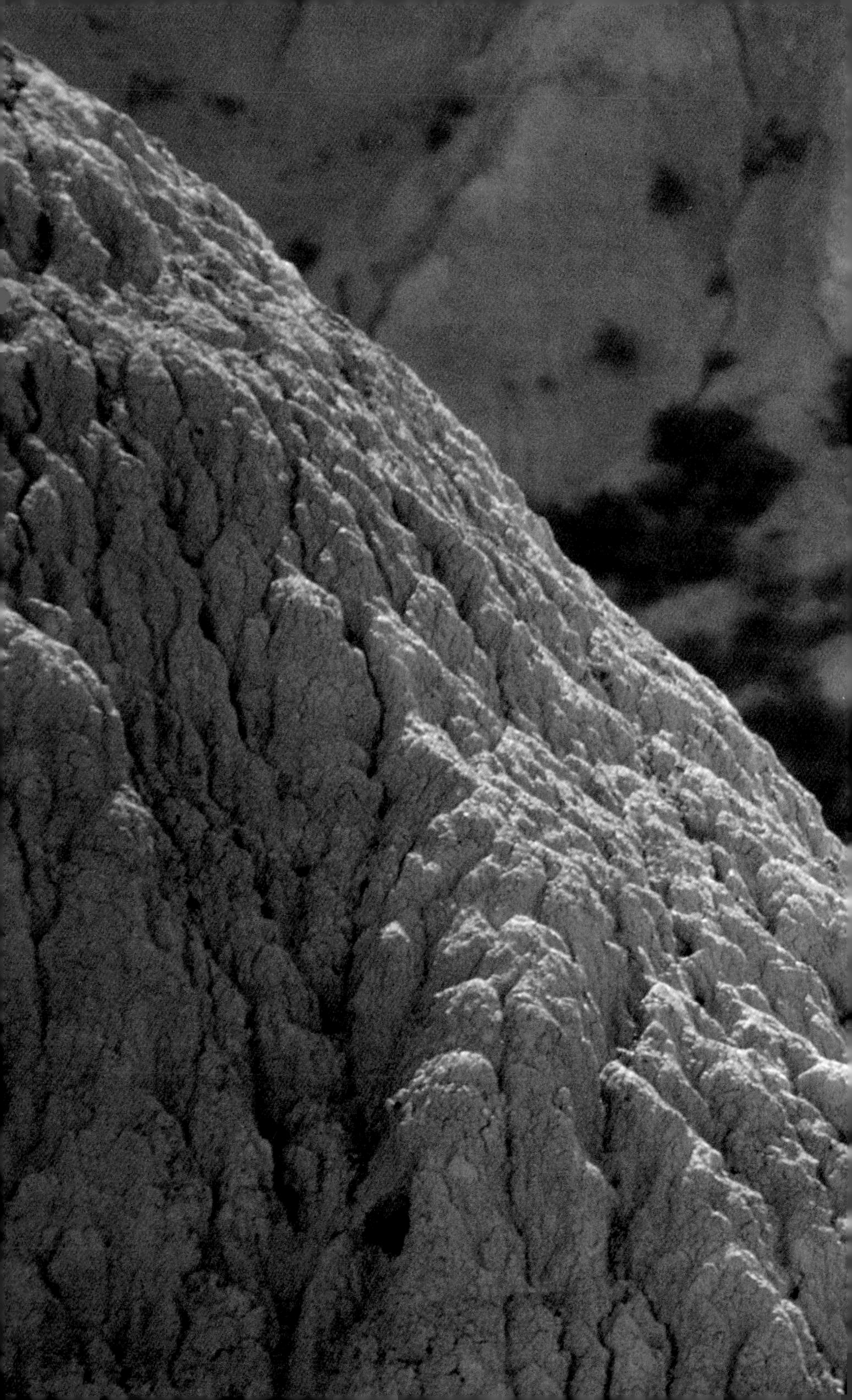

The coyote may travel up to 400 miles in search of food.

small herd was reintroduced in the Sage Creek Basin in 1963; within twenty years it had increased to more than 300 animals.

Other animals have not fared as well. The grizzly bear is gone, the gray wolf also. The American elk disappeared from the Badlands in 1877. The Audubon bighorn sheep has been extinct in the area since the 1920s. A close relative, the Rocky Mountain bighorn, was introduced in 1964. In the mid-1980s, the herd numbered about forty.

The coyote—a hardy survivor in a competitive world—is found everywhere in the park. Its high-pitched yelp, under the beaming face of a full moon, is exhilarating to hear.

Mule deer, distinguished by their large ears, are more numerous than white-tails. Pronghorn antelope can be seen grazing in small bands along the Badlands Loop Road. Smaller than deer, they have simple horns that end in a short hook. With their light bodies and muscular legs, pronghorns are the fastest runners of all North American animals, capable of attaining speeds up to 50 miles an hour.

Several prairie dog towns are located in Badlands National Park. Prairie dogs divide their towns into wards, which are presided over by a male boss. Their burrows are from 10 to 15 feet deep. Voracious grass eaters, they chew the vegetation around their burrows both for nourishment and to keep a clear view for predators.

Other small mammals include the Badlands chipmunk, the eastern cottontail, the white-tailed jackrabbit, and the badger.

The only poisonous snake in the park is the prairie rattlesnake. It is brown, with diamond-shaped markings on its back. Among other snakes is the bullsnake, which resembles the prairie rattlesnake, except that it is longer, has no rattles, and is not poisonous (although it can inflict a painful bite).

Badlands National Park supports a variety of birdlife. Over 120 species have been tabulated; peak time for their activities is from April to the end of July. The black-billed magpie—a bold, saucy bird with a long tail and a black and white body—is observable everywhere. The western meadowlark, whose return to the Great Plains is a sign of spring, pipes out a beautiful song. Around the Cedar Pass Visitor Center can be seen the mountain bluebird.

Predatory birds include the marsh hawk and the golden eagle. The latter is a splendid creature with a 7-foot wingspan. It eats rabbits, prairie dogs, and other rodents.

The turkey vulture, a roving scavenger, is frequently seen in the summer sky. In the tall grass lives the sharp-tailed grouse. Its elaborate courtship displays are believed to have been the prototypes for several Plains Indian dances.

Aware of danger, a prairie rattlesnake extends its tongue to smell the enemy.

Buffalo grass is one of the common plants of the Badlands, where the prairie has been preserved as it was before Europeans settled the continent.

Grasses, Flowers, Shrubs, and Trees

Almost one fourth of the world's vegetation cover consists of grass. Both the tall-grass and short-grass prairies are found in the Badlands area. Elsewhere, Americans have sharply reduced the area covered by grass by adapting the prairies to their own economic uses, but 50 kinds of grass survive in the park today. These grasses provide food for many animals.

The Badlands is not a hospitable environment for vegetation. Moisture is scarce; what rain does fall runs off the steep slopes of the tables and the Badlands Wall instead of soaking into the ground. As in the desert, the surface temperatures are often extreme. And yet the grassy plains above and below the Wall support more than 300 varieties of plants and wildflowers. Hood phlox, prairie golden-pea, and scarlet globemallow are among the most conspicuous of the early blooming plants. Prickly pear is common, as is the soapweed, or yucca. The chokecherry and prairie turnip were two important food sources for the Sioux. A half-dozen kinds of sagebrush dot the landscape; many ailments were treated by the Sioux from remedies boiled down from the stems and roots of this plant.

The few trees of the Badlands are mostly found along watercourses and slumps (a section of a cliff that has slipped down the face of the Wall). Some also grow in protected groves on the north side of ridges and buttes, away from direct sunlight.

The most abundant tree in the region is the Rocky Mountain juniper, often mistakenly called cedar. Except for an occasional ponderosa pine, it is the only evergreen in the Badlands. It attains a height of 20 feet; the scaly bark, mixed with herbs, is known as *kinnikinnick*, the "tobacco" that the Sioux smoke in their ceremonial pipes. Bark of the red willow is also used for this purpose. The juniper's aromatic wood is often utilized in the construction of chests. Its small berrylike cones are bright blue with a whitish coat.

Across the United States, the presence of a cottonwood tree is a clear sign that water, usually flowing water, is nearby. In the Badlands, the plains cottonwood, a western variety of the eastern cottonwood, is found wherever moisture exists in sufficient quantity.

Two other trees, found in sheltered areas of the Sage Creek Wilderness Area, are the green ash and the American elm.

SITES, TRAILS, AND TRIPS

Interstate 90 is the main east–west route through South Dakota. At Cactus Flat, South Dakota 240 turns south off Interstate 90 and then threads its way through Badlands National Park for 30 miles along the Badlands Wall to the Pinnacles Entrance at the west end of the park. Along the route are numerous pullouts and fifteen overlooks that offer superb vistas of the Badlands terrain.

Door Trail. The Door Trail starts between Big Badlands and Windows overlooks. A few steps at the beginning lead through a notch in the Wall and out into the Badlands. The trail is paved with asphalt for the first 200 yards, and then marked by pegs. The path is fairly level, and, except after a rain, it is easy to travel. The trail is .6 mile long, round trip, and gives a good feel for the Badlands topography.

Notch Trail. The head of the Notch Trail is located just beyond the Windows Overlook, at the south end of the parking area. This spectacular trail winds up through the Wall to a wide "window" (a notch eroded out of the top of a cliff) that faces southwest toward Cliff Shelf and Cedar Pass. Marked by red stakes, it is easy to follow; but at times it is difficult to maneuver, with an almost vertical climb at one point (via a wooden ladder) up the face of a clay-stone cliff. Sturdy boots and a sense of adventure are required. The trail is 1.5 miles long, round trip, and takes 1 hour to hike.

Cliff Shelf Nature Trail. The Cliff Shelf Nature Trail is one of the most interesting trails in the park. It winds for .25 mile along the top of a slump. The compaction of the earth led to the formation of pockets, which retain moisture; thus a dense stand of foliage is able to grow within a relatively small area. The trail meanders steeply at times through oases of junipers and prairie grass and cattails watered by sinkholes. Because of the trees, it is a sanctuary for birds. It is also a pleasant place to relax on a hot summer day and enjoy the view of the White River Valley and listen to the sounds. The trail is unsuitable for wheelchairs.

Saddle Pass Trail. South of the Cedar Pass Visitor Center, South Dakota 240 divides, one branch turning toward the village of Interior, 2 miles away, the other continuing along the Badlands Wall. The head of the Saddle Pass Trail is located a couple of miles to the west of this junction. The trail ascends from the parking area off South Dakota 240 through the Wall and onto the upper plain, where it joins the Castle Trail. In some places, Saddle Pass Trail is quite steep, and when wet is virtually unwalkable. The 1.5-mile round-trip hike provides an excellent close-up view of sedimentary banding and the texture of Badlands clay.

Fossil Exhibit Trail. At the top of Norbeck Pass is located the Fossil Exhibit Trail. Along this asphalted, .25-mile trail are casts of fossil deposits that have been displayed where the originals were found. Fossils include remains of the stylemys, the mesohippus, and the oreodont. The trail is the most popular in the park.

Castle Trail. Across the road from the Fossil Trail parking area is the start of the Castle Trail. This 5.25-mile (one way) hike follows an east–west direction, past the Saddle Pass Trail junction (2 miles) to the Windows Overlook parking area. The trail skirts the rim of the Badlands Wall, along the broken edge of the upper plain. The hike is easy, over fairly level terrain. Because there is no tree cover, the hike can be hot in summer. This trail, the longest of the designated hikes in the park, offers an excellent close-up view of grasslands, miniature tables and buttes, and other land formations.

Mule deer often graze near Highway 240, which meanders through the center of the park.

Sage Creek Wilderness Area

An unpaved but maintained road continues westward from the Pinnacles Overlook to the Sage Creek Wilderness Area. Approximately 5 miles from the Badlands Loop Road, on the north side of the gravel extension, is a 700-acre colony of black-tailed prairie dogs. This is a perfect spot to stop and watch them play. Binoculars are helpful, although some of the burrows are so close to the road that the animals are easy to observe. Please do not attempt to feed or pet the prairie dogs; human food is harmful to them, and they are capable of inflicting nasty bites.

The road then swings down through cascading gullies and broken ridges into the Sage Creek Basin. Here is located the Sage Creek Campground. Bordered by natural Badlands walls, this expanse of rolling hills, sheltered groves, and broken prairies serves as a refuge for buffalo, pronghorn, mule deer, and other large animals. The area covers 64,250 acres, and has no designated trails. The adventurous hiker is free to go anywhere. A word of caution, however: buffalo are dangerous and unpredictable; stay at least 100 yards away from them, and have in mind a suitable avenue of escape should they charge.

South Unit and Palmer Creek Area

The South Unit of Badlands National Park—133,000 acres—was added in 1976. This is a ruggedly beautiful section of country, located inside the boundaries of the Pine Ridge Indian Reservation. The White River

Trails of Badlands National Park

Door Trail: Starts and ends at north end of Windows parking area; .6 mile round trip; .5 hour; hard rock trail leads through a natural doorway into Badlands formations.

Notch Trail: Starts and ends at trail head at south end of Windows parking area; 1.5 miles round trip; 1 hour; leads through small canyon, up a ladder onto a narrow canyon rim, and to a large saddle cut into the Badlands Wall; excellent view of White River Valley and the Pine Ridge Indian Reservation.

Castle Trail: Starts at Windows parking area and ends at Fossil Exhibit parking area; 5.25 miles one way; 2 hours; traverses mixture of prairie and badlands topography.

Saddle Pass Trail: Starts at trail head 2 miles northwest of Cedar Pass visitor center on highway 240, Badlands Loop Road, and ends at junction with Castle Trail; 1.5 mile round trip; 1 hour; leads up and through Badlands Wall onto upper prairie.

Visitor Center near Rockyford features Indian cultural exhibits and an audio-visual program on the history of the Oglala Sioux.

To reach the South Unit, continue for 12 miles on the gravel road past the Sage Creek Wilderness Area to the town of Scenic. There, join Bureau of Indian Affairs (BIA) road 27, heading south. Or, bypassing the Badlands Loop Road, drive 32 miles due west of Interior on South Dakota 44 to reach the same turnoff.

From Scenic to the White River Visitor Center is 20 miles. Four miles south of Scenic, on BIA 27, is the turnoff for Sheep Mountain Table. A 7-mile rutted road, impassable during rain, climbs to the top of the table.

Those wishing to camp in the South Unit should consult with the ranger at the White River Visitor Center before doing so.

Interesting trips from the White River Visitor Center include excursions to Cedar Butte and to Stronghold Table, where Sioux warriors in the late 1880s performed the Ghost Dance away from the interfering eyes of the cavalry. Trails at both places are undergoing development. Travel into the Palmer Creek Area is possible only by means of four-wheel-drive vehicles.

The really adventurous traveler—the one who wants to see and explore something different—will take a day or two to visit the South Unit. The scenery is magnificent—wildly eroded Badlands alternating with unbroken stretches of grassy plains. The unit also contains many places of religious and historical significance to the Oglala Sioux.

Opposite: Gray ash deposited by an ancient volcano forms the crest of the Badlands Wall.

JOY

GLACIER NATIONAL PARK

Grinnell Point towers above Swiftcurrent Lake in the eastern section of the park.

GLACIER NATIONAL PARK
WEST GLACIER, MONTANA 59936
TEL.: (406) 888-5441

Highlights: Going-to-the-Sun Road □ Grinnell Glacier □ Saint Mary Lake □ The Narrows □ Avalanche Gorge □ Logan Pass □ Heaven's Peak □ Dawn Mist Falls □ Jackson Glacier □ Bird Woman Falls

Access: Take U.S. 2 and 89. From Canada, take Route 3, 5, or 6. Also Amtrak and air service.

Hours: Open all year, 24 hours daily. Going-to-the-Sun Road open late May to mid-October.

Fees: Entrance, $2/car, 50¢/person in commercial vehicle. Camping, up to $6/unit. Golden Age, Golden Eagle, and Golden Access passports accepted.

Parking: Throughout park; Logan Pass sometimes crowded in summer.

Gas, food, lodging: In park and adjacent areas. Hotels, lodges, chalets, and cabins in park. Reservations needed.

Visitor Centers: Saint Mary, late May to mid-October; Logan Pass, mid-June to mid-September. Information Center at Apgar Village, late May through mid-December, weekends in winter. Slide and interpretive programs.

Museum: Exhibits in all Visitor Centers.

Gift shops: At park hotels.

Pets: Permitted on leashes, except in backcountry, on trails, or in public buildings.

Picnicking: At Apgar Picnic Area, Rising Sun, Sprague Creek, Many Glacier, Two Medicine, Walton Ranger Station.

Hiking: More than 700 miles of trails, some closed during bear scares. Carry water.

Backpacking: Permitted with permit. Carry water. CAMP ONLY AT AUTHORIZED SITES.

Campgrounds: 13 campgrounds; $6/unit, $4/primitive site. First come, first served. Two group sites.

Tours: Many ranger-guided tours during high (summer) season.

Other activities: Cross-country skiing, horseback riding, boating (motor boats restricted on most lakes), fishing with permit, bicycling.

Facilities for disabled: For hearing impaired, printed texts, guided walks, slide shows. For visually impaired, taped park brochure. For mobility impaired, some park areas accessible.

For additional information, see also Sites, Trails, and Trips on pages 57–68 and the map on pages 38–39.

APTLY CALLED THE "CROWN OF THE CONTINENT," Glacier National Park in northwestern Montana is also the southern section of the Waterton-Glacier International Peace Park; the northern area of the international park is Canada's Waterton Lakes National Park, which is just across the border in Alberta. Glacier is adorned with 200 jewel-like lakes, graced with 936 miles of rivers and streams, dominated by 2 majestic ranges of the northern Rocky Mountains, and divided by glorious glacier-carved valleys. The treasures within its 1,013,598 acres include countless cascading waterfalls, fields of flowers, and abundant wildlife, all in a wilderness setting. Dramatic contrasts in elevation, from the surface of Lake McDonald at 3,153 feet to the summit of Mount Cleveland at 10,466 feet, help create an impression of grandeur. Forests festoon almost every slope until forced to recede by the harsh environment of alpine tundra or rocky ridges. The aroma of pine fills the air, and Pacific Northwest breezes bring a refreshing coolness to even the hottest summer day. Fifty small glaciers remain tucked into high mountain cirques.

Cream-colored stalks of bear grass grow near Lunch Creek, below Pollock Mountain.

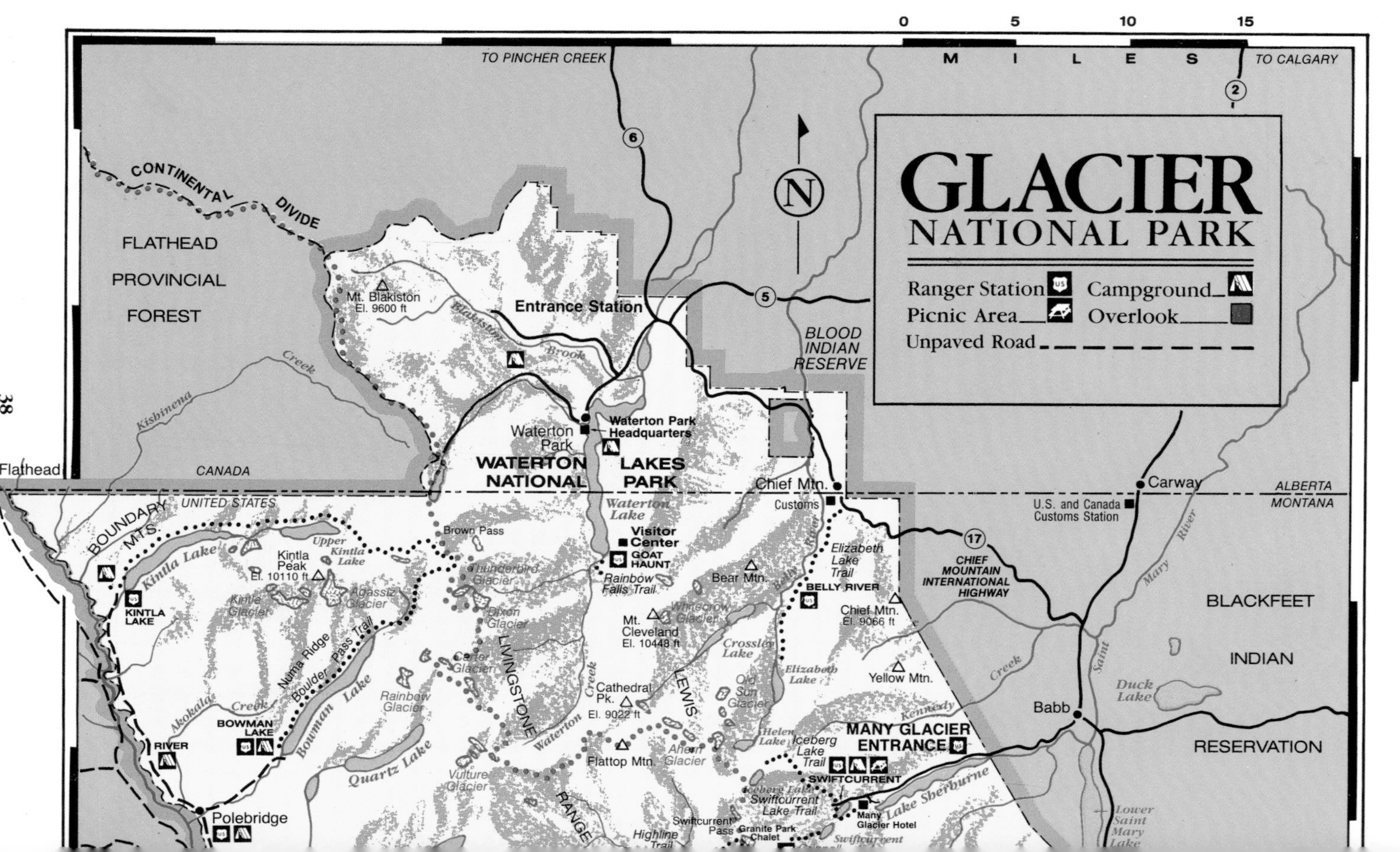

GLACIER
NATIONAL PARK
Ranger Station
Campground
Picnic Area
Overlook
Unpaved Road
0
5
10
15
M I L E S
TO PINCHER CREEK
TO CALGARY
2
6
5
17
CONTINENTAL
DIVIDE
FLATHEAD
PROVINCIAL
FOREST
Mt. Blakiston
El. 9600 ft
Entrance Station
Blakiston
Brook
BLOOD
INDIAN
RESERVE
Creek
Kishinena
Waterton
Park
Waterton Park
Headquarters
WATERTON
NATIONAL
LAKES
PARK
Flathead
CANADA
UNITED STATES
Chief Mtn.
Customs
Carway
ALBERTA
MONTANA
U.S. and Canada
Customs Station
BOUNDARY
MTS.
Kintla Lake
Upper
Kintla
Lake
Kintla
Peak
El. 10110 ft
Brown Pass
Waterton
Lake
Visitor
Center
GOAT
HAUNT
Rainbow
Falls Trail
Bear Mtn.
Elizabeth
Lake
Trail
BELLY RIVER
Belly River
Chief Mtn.
El. 9066 ft
CHIEF
MOUNTAIN
INTERNATIONAL
HIGHWAY
Mary River
BLACKFEET
INDIAN
RESERVATION
KINTLA
LAKE
Kintla
Glacier
Agassiz
Glacier
Thunderbird
Glacier
Dixon
Glacier
Mt.
Cleveland
El. 10448 ft
Whitecrow
Glacier
Crossley
Lake
Numa Ridge
Boulder
Pass Trail
Carter
Glacier
LIVINGSTONE
Cathedral
Pk.
El. 9022 ft
LEWIS
Old
Sun
Glacier
Elizabeth
Lake
Yellow Mtn.
Creek
Saint
Duck
Lake
Babb
Akokala
Creek
Bowman Lake
BOWMAN
LAKE
Rainbow
Glacier
Waterton
Kennedy
Helen
Lake
Iceberg
Lake
Trail
MANY GLACIER
ENTRANCE
RIVER
Quartz Lake
Vulture
Glacier
Flattop Mtn.
Ahern
Glacier
SWIFTCURRENT
Iceberg Lake
Swiftcurrent
Lake Trail
Lake Sherburne
Polebridge
RANGE
Swiftcurrent
Pass
Highline
Trail
Granite Park
Chalet
Many
Glacier Hotel
Swiftcurrent
Lower
Saint
Mary
Lake

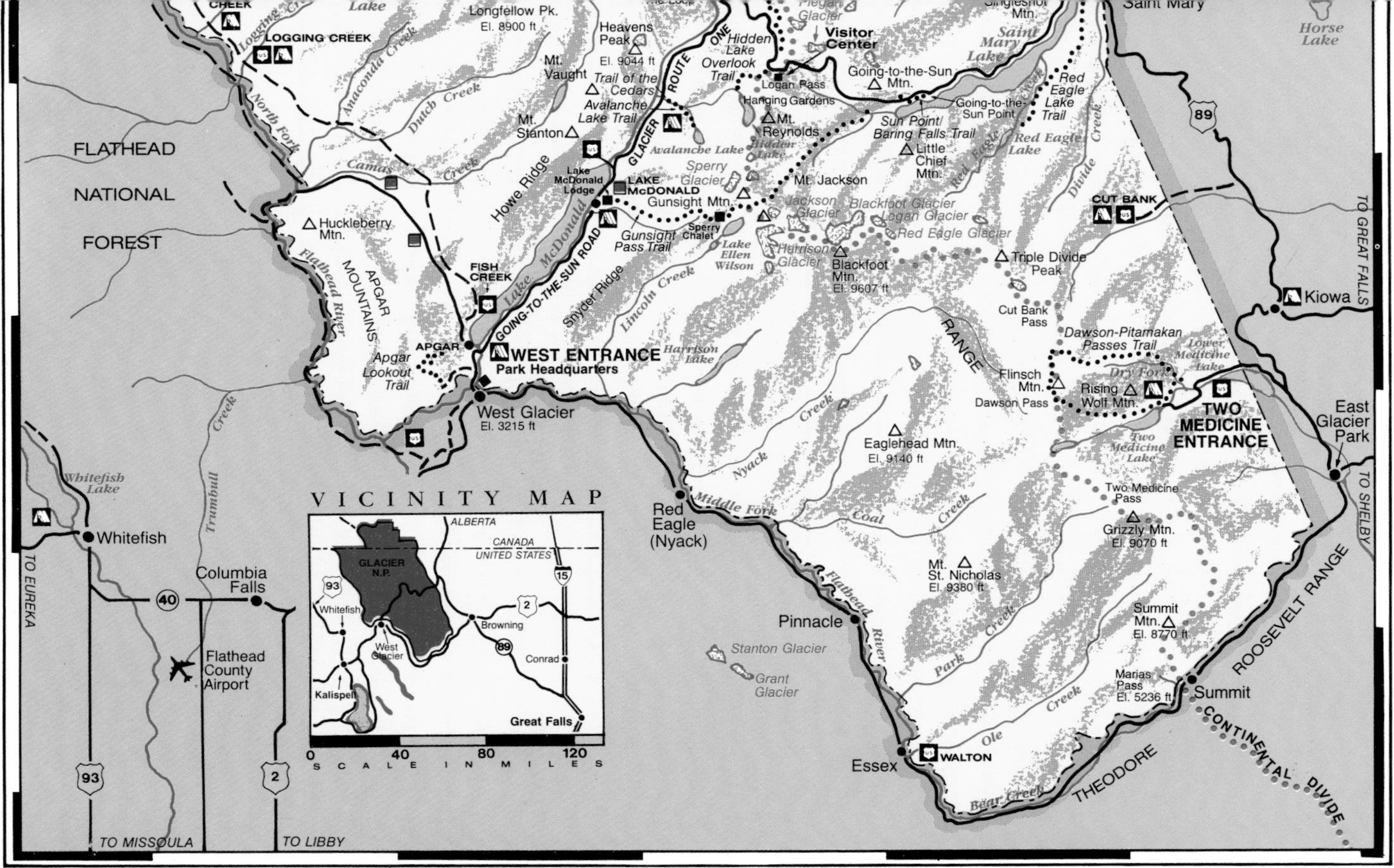
Longfellow Pk.
El. 8900 ft
LOGGING CREEK
Anaconda Creek
Dutch Creek
North Fork
FLATHEAD
NATIONAL
FOREST
Camas Creek
Huckleberry Mtn.
Flathead River
APGAR MOUNTAINS
Apgar Lookout Trail
APGAR
FISH CREEK
Mt. Vaught
Mt. Stanton
Howe Ridge
Lake McDonald
Lake McDonald Lodge
LAKE McDONALD
GOING-TO-THE-SUN ROAD
Snyder Ridge
WEST ENTRANCE
Park Headquarters
West Glacier
El. 3215 ft
Heavens Peak
El. 9044 ft
Trail of the Cedars
Avalanche Lake Trail
GLACIER ROUTE ONE
Avalanche Lake
Hidden Lake Overlook Trail
Logan Pass
Visitor Center
Hanging Gardens
Mt. Reynolds
Sperry Glacier
Gunsight Mtn.
Sperry Chalet
Gunsight Pass Trail
Lake Ellen Wilson
Lincoln Creek
Harrison Lake
Mt. Jackson
Jackson Glacier
Harrison Glacier
Blackfoot Glacier
Logan Glacier
Red Eagle Glacier
Blackfoot Mtn.
El. 9607 ft
Going-to-the-Sun Mtn.
Going-to-the-Sun Point
Sun Point/ Baring Falls Trail
Little Chief Mtn.
Saint Mary Lake
Red Eagle Lake Trail
Red Eagle Lake
Divide Creek
Saint Mary
Horse Lake
89
CUT BANK
Triple Divide Peak
Cut Bank Pass
RANGE
Dawson-Pitamakan Passes Trail
Flinsch Mtn.
Dawson Pass
Rising Wolf Mtn.
Lower Medicine Lake
Two Medicine Lake
TWO MEDICINE ENTRANCE
Kiowa
TO GREAT FALLS
East Glacier Park
TO SHELBY
Eaglehead Mtn.
El. 9140 ft
Nyack Creek
Coal Creek
Two Medicine Pass
Grizzly Mtn.
El. 9070 ft
Mt. St. Nicholas
El. 9380 ft
Summit Mtn.
El. 8770 ft
Marias Pass
El. 5236 ft
Summit
ROOSEVELT RANGE
CONTINENTAL DIVIDE
THEODORE
Park Creek
Ole Creek
Bear Creek
WALTON
Essex
Flathead River
Pinnacle
Stanton Glacier
Grant Glacier
Middle Fork
Red Eagle (Nyack)
Whitefish Lake
Whitefish
TO EUREKA
Trumbull Creek
Columbia Falls
40
Flathead County Airport
93
2
TO MISSOULA
TO LIBBY
VICINITY MAP
ALBERTA
CANADA
UNITED STATES
GLACIER N.P.
93
Whitefish
West Glacier
Kalispell
2
Browning
89
Conrad
15
Great Falls
0 40 80 120
SCALE IN MILES

HISTORY

Glacier's First Visitors

Archeology offers scant evidence regarding any Native American presence in Glacier. Yet it is assumed that various tribes of Indians crossed these mountains for centuries and perhaps hunted mountain sheep, mountain goats, or elk. Certainly the Indians established a few temporary camps and tramped some primitive trails. The first recorded event involving Native Americans in the Glacier region occurred in 1792. In that year, Hudson's Bay Company agent Peter Fidler traveled to the Chief Mountain area accompanied by a band of Piegans, a subdivision of the Blackfoot. During the 1700s, the Blackfoot roamed over most of Montana's plains and mountains, from Alberta southward to the Yellowstone River. Skillful hunters, they relied on the vast herds of bison for subsistence. The European introduction of horses and guns enhanced Blackfoot aggression and extended their dominion.

Other Indian tribes attempting to hunt buffalo on the Great Plains had to evade Blackfoot warriors. Smaller tribes, such as the Flathead, Kutenai, and Kalispel, were gradually prevented from entering the plains at will and were forced to live in the wooded valleys to the west of the Continental Divide. Similarly, the Mountain Stonies, or Assiniboine, lived an impoverished life by subsisting along the eastern foothills. These groups grew more familiar with Glacier's mountains out of necessity, hunting deer, mountain sheep, or other game, and harvesting berries and camas roots. One sketchy tale relates a skirmish between Kutenai and Blackfoot near Glacier's Cut Bank Pass. But other evidence of such violence is rare. Glacier's inhospitable mountains did not serve as a permanent home for any tribe and acted as a barrier between rival groups.

Trappers and traders slowly succeeded in invading Blackfoot country. As they were weakened by war, whiskey, and recurrent smallpox epidemics, the Blackfoot retreated toward the mountains. In the 1850s, they were dominating most of north-central Montana. But within a generation, the rapidly disappearing buffalo herds made hunting precarious, and the Blackfoot suffered acute starvation. Rising pressure from prospectors by the 1880s brought demands that the Indians relinquish their rights to the Rockies, and in 1895, the Blackfoot ceded their mountain land east of the Continental Divide for $1.5 million. That ceded strip of land eventually became the east side of Glacier National Park. Helping to recall that prior ownership, however, are the numerous Indian names that still dot the landscape; Heavy Runner, Almost-A-Dog, Napi, and Red Eagle are typical examples of a long list. And the Blackfeet Indian Reservation, adjacent to Glacier's eastern

Blackfoot Indians, shown here in the park in the 1920s, once dominated most of Montana.

boundary, continues to remind us that Native Americans were really the first visitors to and occupants of the region.

Trappers, Traders, and Other Travelers

With the Blackfoot guarding the Rocky Mountain passes and roaming the Great Plains, fur trappers and traders ventured cautiously as they approached the area. Indeed, most of those early adventurers simply traveled elsewhere, leaving Glacier unexplored and unexploited. Aside from the 1792 visit by Peter Fidler, only a handful of trappers had the courage to seek beaver pelts in this section of the Rockies. In 1810, for example, trader Finian MacDonald attempted to enter Blackfoot country, only to face immediate attack. MacDonald learned to avoid such hostile territory on future trips. During the decades that followed, other trappers and traders may have tried to exploit this region, but they left no trace or tales of their journeys.

Once disease and war had weakened the Blackfoot, traders ascending the Missouri River grew bolder. Posts like Fort McKenzie and Fort Benton were established during the 1840s, bringing commerce and "civilization." Missionaries began to carry their messages to the various tribes, and one Catholic priest even paused to name Saint Mary Lake. Exploration parties sent out by the government started arriving during the 1850s; A. W. Tinkham's journey across Cut Bank Pass in

1853 probably was the earliest historical observation of the region. When the forty-ninth parallel was established as the international boundary around 1860, the surveyors were accompanied by the artist James Madison Alden, who painted the first landscapes of Glacier's peaks. And, somewhat less official, a handful of "whiskey traders" set up posts to ply the Indians with illicit drinks.

The discovery of gold in Montana by the 1860s introduced hundreds of curious prospectors to this frontier. With Blackfoot power weakening, a search for mineral wealth within their territory could not be denied. Although rumors of gold in Glacier's mountains were occasionally heard, very little precious metal was ever found. Some promising veins of quartz and copper, however, sparked both interest and investment in the Many Glacier region during the 1880s and 1890s. A boom town called Altyn and a tiny settlement called Saint Mary appeared as a result. And traces of oil, discovered first in Alberta, then at Kintla Lake and in the Swiftcurrent Valley, added to the promise of prosperity. But dreams of wealth soon diminished. Neither copper nor oil proved to be abundant or profitable. Most prospectors soon deserted their claims and went elsewhere.

Establishment of the Park

The iron horse first "rode" through this stretch of the Rockies early in the 1890s, crossing through Marias Pass. James J. Hill's Great Northern Railway introduced tracks, trains, and travelers along the southern edge of the present-day park. Settlers soon etched out some homesteads, building their log cabins in the forests of the western slope. There they subsisted by trapping, logging, or raising a few cattle. Pioneers around Lake McDonald also began catering to the few venturesome railway passengers who disembarked at Belton (West Glacier). An infant resort industry slowly took shape.

Among the travelers was George Bird Grinnell, editor of *Forest and Stream* magazine, writer, and conservationist. He journeyed to the Glacier area to publicize the plight of the starving Blackfoot. His interest in big-game hunting also attracted him to these mountains and set him to exploring. A few years later, Lyman Sperry, scientist, college professor, and traveling lecturer, visited the region and started hunting for "live glaciers." Both men became active in publicizing the area's natural wonders. They were enchanted with the alpine scenes, the glaciers, the waterfalls, and the wildlife. In the same mood, conservation leaders of the day selected these mountains to be part of the Lewis and Clark Forest Reserve, which was established in 1897. By the early 1900s, people like Grinnell and Sperry began proposing that a national park be designated in the Glacier area, especially once it became evident that prospecting and mining had failed. Grinnell helped to convince Great Northern Railway officials to promote the park idea, a concept that sparked very little controversy. On May 11, 1910, Congress established Glacier National Park.

Although Superintendent William R. Logan soon arrived to take charge, it was the Great Northern Railway that initiated the development of tourist facilities. Large hotels were built at Midvale (East Glacier Park) and at Many Glacier, both completed by 1915. More than a dozen backcountry tent camps and rustic chalets were also constructed throughout Glacier's wilderness. A network of roads and trails was soon added to link the facilities. Riding horses from railway stations to chalets, from hotels to tent camps, became the primary way tourists saw Glacier National Park during the two decades that followed.

Beginning in 1917, however, a year after the National Park Service was formed, plans for a "Transmountain Road" took shape. The Going-to-the-Sun Road was completed in 1933 and is one of the most scenic highways in the West. Tourism to Glacier boomed once that road provided easy access to the park's interior through Logan Pass. Whereas only 20,000 people had visited the area primarily by horseback in 1921, by the mid-1930s over 200,000 people annually entered the park, using automobiles as the primary conveyance. More than 1.5 million people now visit the park every year, with most arriving in June, July, and August. Regardless of the popularity of Going-to-the-Sun Road, much of the park, both north and south of that highway, has retained its wilderness character.

Camping among the pines in 1920.

G E O L O G Y

Glacier National Park gets its name from ancient rivers of ice that plowed through its valleys and helped carve its landscape. Some fifty modern remnants of the last ice age can still be seen clinging to the rock-walled amphitheaters called cirques found high in the park's backcountry. The giant ancestors of today's retreated glaciers gradually etched the U-shaped valleys and sharpened the ridges that dominate much of the park's interior. Yet much more than just glacial action produced the stony crest of the rugged Livingston and Lewis ranges, the two north–south-trending mountain chains that form the backbone of the park.

The Remains of Ancient Seas and the Lewis Overthrust

Mountain slopes consisting of crumbling ledges and stone, colored in shades of tan, red, brown, and buff, offer a geologic tale from an ancient age. The landscape of Glacier is shaped by layers of sedimentary rock undergoing erosion. The same forces of erosion and gravity, of wind and water, that work to wear the rock away today once helped in its formation. Mudstones, sandstones, and limestones constitute Glacier's most common and oldest rocks. Most ancient is the whitish tan Altyn Limestone, evident along the eastern base of the mountains. Sediments that collected in the shallow seas or tidal flats that covered the area at least 1 billion years ago (during the Precambrian era) formed the 2,200-foot layer of limestone. Fossilized algae, observable in the walls along Going-to-the-Sun Road, offer evidence of primitive life in those primordial seas.

Compressed and hardened through time, the Altyn Formation was slowly covered by the 3,000-foot Appekunny Formation. The Appekunny's dark gray and green mudstones also include occasional bands of red mudstones and white sandstones. Mud cracks, ripple marks, and fossil algae, easily spotted today, offer hints of an ancient scene that may have persisted until 70 million years ago (the end of the Cretaceous period). Above the Appekunny lies the younger, remarkably reddish Grinnell Formation, with its 2,500 feet of mudstones colored by oxygen and ferric iron in the mineral hematite. Another 3,000-foot layer, the Siyeh Formation, rests atop the Grinnell. The tan limestone of the Siyeh Formation dominates most of Glacier's highest elevations. The sturdiness of the Siyeh Limestone helped it resist erosion better than other rocks; it forms the pronounced ridges, cliffs, and crags so

Opposite: A crevasse in Grinnell Glacier, a 300-acre frozen relic from the last ice age.

The knife-edged Garden Wall was created when glaciers attacked both sides of the ridge.

attractive to mountain climbers. On some remote summits, additional layers of limestone of the Kintla Formation and the Shepard Formation may also be found. All these sedimentary formations testify that ancient sea bottoms became mountaintops through time.

The vast layers of sedimentary rock show intrusions of magma that once forced its way through fractures from deep within the earth. Once it cooled and hardened, the magma formed dikes of diabase and basalt. A band of this igneous rock called the Purcell Sill is visible near the crest of the Garden Wall, which is the "backbone" of the Continental Divide. About 100 feet wide, the Purcell Sill rests within the Siyeh Limestone.

After the layers of Precambrian sedimentary rock were formed, they became subjected to a gradual uplifting caused by forces within the earth's crust. Around 60 million years ago, tilting, fracturing, and gravity produced a gradual sliding of these old rocks toward the east. Called the Lewis Overthrust, this movement occurred over millions of years and resulted in giant slabs of Precambrian rock moving some 40 miles northeastward. Eventually the Precambrian layers came to rest on younger Cretaceous sandstones and mudstones formed by a more recent shallow sea. The main overthrust slab became Glacier's easternmost Lewis Range. Chief Mountain, at the park's northeast corner, displays the farthest extent of that Precambrian sliding. The Livingston Range on the park's west side is a second slab of Precambrian layers resting on a Cretaceous base.

Sculpture by Erosion and Ice

Still active today, erosion started working its will on these ranges about 50 million years ago, once the mountains had finished their sliding and uplifting movement. Then wind and rain, flash floods and the force of gravity helped wear away the surface of these massive sedimentary slabs. The adjacent high plains to the east and the valleys of the western slope received tons of rocky refuse from the crumbling crags of the Lewis Overthrust.

Beginning about 3 million years ago, toward the end of the Pliocene epoch, the earth's climate became cool and wet. Then came the Age of Ice—the Pleistocene epoch—during which four distinct invasions of grinding ice sheets crept across this region. Each era of ice was followed by a warmer interglacial period. The last ice age ended a mere 10,000 years ago, and the ninety glaciers first found within the park remained from that cool climate. Their size and number continue to diminish, and fewer than fifty true glaciers remain.

During each icy invasion, only the park's highest peaks escaped being covered by gigantic glaciers. Gouging rivers of ice churned slowly forward, moving as little as a few feet each year. Scraping, plowing, and plucking at the rock surfaces, the glaciers broadened the eroded valleys of the Lewis Overthrust. Gradually the distinctive U-shaped valleys gained their final form. Smaller glaciers joining larger ones left high "hanging valleys" that are easily seen throughout the park. Lake beds were scooped, many extending 6 to 12 miles in length. Once the climate warmed, the glaciers stopped growing and started melting. At the sites of their farthest extent, they left huge deposits of gravel and rock called terminal moraines. Some moraines formed natural dams, and lakes with fingerlike shapes filled the glacier-carved furrows. On either side of the glaciers' path were additional heaps of gravel and debris called lateral moraines, which are now forest-covered ridges that may exceed 2,000 feet in height.

Glaciers that remain in the park remind us of an ancient age of icy sculpture. Each about 300 acres in size, Grinnell and Sperry glaciers are among the most accessible to hikers. Both are found in rock-walled amphitheaters, tucked high in shady hanging valleys. They continue to display crevasses of pale-blue ice, recently deposited moraines, and an interaction of water and rock, climate and geology, carving ice and molded mountains.

Overleaf, left: Yellow lichens grow on a jumble of rocks near Grinnell Lake. Right: In McDonald Valley, pools form in rock that has been sculptured by running water.

When the modern topography of peaks, valleys, lakes, and streams finally emerged, a unique drainage pattern resulted. The park's watershed was split between east and west: the glacier-carved Garden Wall is the Continental Divide. Streams that run westward become part of the headwaters of the Columbia River system. Water that moves eastward is parted by a ridge called Hudson Bay Divide. From the apex of the ridge at the Triple Divide Mountain, streams drain northeastward into the Saskatchewan River system and subsequently into Hudson Bay. Water flowing southeastward enters the Missouri River drainage, eventually reaching the Gulf of Mexico. Glacier Park can claim to be the fountainhead of three major river systems.

NATURAL HISTORY

Beneath the craggy Crown of the Continent rests a mantle of green. Gracing every slope except those too vertical, too high, or too rocky are vast virgin forests. Glades and meadows add a profusion of summertime flowers. Two hundred lakes sparkle with crystal-clear water, and hundreds of waterfalls bestow their splash of decoration. In this magnificent setting, from the lowest elevations to the highest crest, nature displays a rich variety of life.

A Land of Forests, Meadows, and Flowers

Pacific Northwest weather, generally cool and wet, dominates Glacier's climate. Abundant rainfall and snow provide plenty of moisture, making the park's forests damp, dense, and lush. As clouds move eastward, the mountains rob them of most of their moisture. Consequently, the park's eastern slope is drier than the western, with 10 inches less rainfall than the western slope's 28-inch average each year.

Water and elevation, summits and slopes combine to form four distinctive life zones in Glacier. At lower elevations, beginning at an altitude of 3,500 feet, is the Transition Zone. Dry grassland and prairie mark this zone along the park's eastern foothills. On the western slope, the North Fork of the Flathead River flows through large sagebrush meadows usually bordered by mature ponderosa pine. A bit higher on the eastern slope, vast groves of aspen are encountered. And when the crisp winds of autumn turn billions of leaves a golden color, the quaking aspen present a beautiful sight. Some stands of aspen and cottonwood are also located along the lower streams of the western slope.

Ringing the mountains on both sides of the park is the most exten-

Opposite: Western red cedar is second in girth to the giant sequoia among U.S. trees.

Mushrooms of the Russula *genus flourish in the moist soil of McDonald Valley.*

sive biological community, the Canadian, or Montane, Zone. Here massive Pacific Northwest forests spread across the landscape. Dense stands of lodgepole pine cover hundreds of square miles, sometimes creating an impenetrable thicket with their abundance. Western larch, western white pine, Douglas fir, and western red cedar become the giants within this forest if they survive disease, forest fire, or an occasional windstorm. Within this crowded forest are Engelmann spruce as well as juniper, birch, Pacific yew, and willow. Chokecherry, hawthorn, Rocky Mountain maple, pin cherry, and acre upon acre of alder seem to fill every vacant nook. Rich soil and plenty of wet weather combine to create this profusion of plant life.

Springtime in the Canadian Zone brings flowers, especially bear grass —easily among the most prominent blossoms of the park. Actually a member of the lily family, this globelike flower stands 3 feet tall when blooming and fills the green forests of June with a layer of white. As the summer progresses, the bear grass simply follows spring to higher elevations, and the alpine meadows of August are finally filled with their picturesque blossoms. In addition, queencups, Indian paintbrush, fireweed, and hundreds of other flowers grace the forest floors and mountain meadows. All together, the flowers punctuate the deep green of the coniferous forest with a panoply of pastel.

The spotted coat of the mule deer fawn camouflages it from predators.

Only at higher elevations does the climate force forests to recede. First the Hudsonian Zone serves as a transitional region, with an alpine environment found higher on the slopes. Enduring the Hudsonian climate are stands of whitebark pine, subalpine fir, and subalpine larch, and a shroud of hardy alder, all able to withstand windier weather and longer winters than can the forests below.

Above timberline lies the Arctic-Alpine Zone, with its noticeable *krummholz* ("crooked wood") forests. The *krummholz* displays clumps of gnarled and dwarfed subalpine fir. Here subjected to blasting winds and icy pellets of winter's snow, the trees develop a stunted and polished appearance. Aside from a few equally dwarfed willow and birch, no other trees can brave such a hostile environment. Much of this land is buried under giant drifts of snow for most of the year. Still, summer permits a profusion of flowering plants to display their beauty in the high-country meadows. Blossoms of lupine, glacier lily, monkey flower, Indian paintbrush, and yellow buttercup join dozens of other species in decorating this tundra landscape.

Towering above the tundra, the rocky slopes and mountain peaks are also part of the Arctic-Alpine Zone. Foreboding, bleak, and barren-looking at first glance, on closer examination the land displays patches of subalpine fir tucked beside protective rocks and ledges, appearing more like a blanket of shrubs. Flowers and grasses may also be found, but have had to shrink in order to survive. Primitive pioneers of plant life, lichens grow on stony faces even at the highest altitudes.

The Wildlife of Glacier's Wilderness

From its lowest streambeds to its tallest peaks, Glacier offers sanctuary to a multitude of wild creatures. Moose, the largest mammals of the park, inhabit the watery low country along streams, marshes, and bog lakes. They are frequently seen feeding on aqueous plants, dipping their heads beneath the glassy surface of a pond. The Pacific Northwest forest also provides plenty of forage for white-tailed and mule deer, quite commonly observed, as well as for abundant but more elusive herds of elk. Quite a variety of smaller mammals—pine squirrels, golden-mantled ground squirrels, chipmunks, pine martens, badgers, rabbits, and coyotes—inhabit the dense woodlands. Beavers are becoming more common. Sometimes spotted are mountain lions, and most rare are northern Rocky Mountain wolves.

Black and grizzly bears also roam these forests. Infrequently seen along roadsides, black bears may also be blond, cinnamon, or brown. Its smaller size and longer, straight snout distinguish the black bear from the grizzly. Grizzly bears, numbering about 200 within the park, are considered an endangered species. Glacier is part of their shrinking domain within the lower forty-eight states. Identified by a noticeable hump on their fore shoulders, a dished-in face, long claws, and a larger size than black bears, grizzlies have developed a reputation for unpredictable and occasionally aggressive behavior. Like black bears, grizzlies feed on roots, berries, squirrels, and carrion as they scavenge through the forests. The grizzlies tend to migrate toward higher elevations as summer progresses, following the snow line, later seeking low-country dens to nap the winter away. Caution is always advised for hikers entering grizzly territory, which includes most of the park's interior.

Haunting the higher elevations are mountain sheep and mountain goats. The Rocky Mountain bighorn sheep, quite easily spotted in the Many Glacier region and seen roaming throughout the Arctic-Alpine slopes, has a tan or brownish coat. Older rams carry a huge set of horns, enlarged and forming a coil with age. And generally ranging at the park's highest altitudes are Rocky Mountain goats, distinguished by their sharp black horns, long narrow heads, and shaggy white coats. Their agility and climbing ability allow them to inhabit the steepest cliffs and ledges. The goats' curious nature and somewhat friendly demeanor help classify them as one of the park's most popular wild creatures.

Also found in the high country are hoary marmots, largest members of the squirrel family. These sometimes begging rodents may reach 2 feet in length. Their fur ranges in color from gray to reddish orange. Much more difficult to glimpse are small alpine rabbits called pika. Living near slopes of scree, they use quick, elusive movements to help keep themselves well hidden.

Within the forests and above the ridges range more than 200 species of birds. Owls and osprey, robins and ravens, hummingbirds and hawks are among thousands of birds to be seen. Canada geese, mallards, harlequin ducks, herons, and loons grace the park's waterways. The dipper, or water ouzel, can be spotted bobbing up and down beside many a creek or gorge. Spruce grouse haunt the forests, while white-tailed ptarmigan are the only permanent feathered residents of the alpine regions.

Perhaps most remarkable are the golden and bald eagles. Even though very few of these giant birds would call Glacier a year-round home, each autumn dozens of these migrants gather along lower McDonald Creek to feed on Kokanee salmon, which die after spawning. At least 350 eagles annually congregate there between October and December, presenting a spectacle of nature rarely seen elsewhere.

Mountain goat.

Juvenile great horned owl.

Life also abounds in the park's 200 lakes and in the 936 miles of rivers and streams. Varieties of trout predominate, with cutthroat, brook, lake, brown, and rainbow common in many lakes and streams. Among others are Arctic grayling, bull trout, whitefish, and Kokanee salmon. Near those waterways, turtles, frogs, and an occasional garter snake may be spotted. Glacier has no poisonous snakes.

It is impossible to note every species of wildlife here. Glacier National Park is truly a wildlife preserve. From its dense lodgepole thickets to its open rocky tundra, many forms of life have found a haven.

SITES, TRAILS, AND TRIPS

Glacier National Park displays superlative Rocky Mountain alpine scenery. A panorama of mountain peaks and forested valleys greets the eye. Of gorges and glaciers, waterfalls and wilderness, there is too much to be seen in only a brief visit. This is land that demands much time. National park patriarch John Muir once suggested that visitors spend at least a month exploring Glacier. But whether travelers have a day, a week, or a year, they will discover highways, trails, and waterways that provide avenues to adventure.

Glacier's main avenue, Going-to-the-Sun Road, courses through the center of the park; paved highways follow the park's eastern and southern perimeter; blacktop and gravel roads permit access to the Cut Bank and North Fork regions. All roads lead to the fringe of wilderness. And within the park wilderness are 800 miles of trails, open for hikers or horseback riders. The solitude of wild country awaits. Rafting the rivers as well as boating, sailing, or canoeing on the waterways may offer additional pleasures.

Going-to-the-Sun Road

Few would argue that Going-to-the-Sun Road, open from June through October, is the best introduction to Glacier National Park. This 50-mile road runs roughly east and west, cutting across the Continental Divide through Logan Pass at an elevation of 6,664 feet above sea level. Scenes along this highway give hints of Glacier's wild interior. This drive demands that frequent stops be made to ponder the many wonders of nature seen along its length. The trail heads along the road should tempt us to saunter into the woods, leaving cars and concrete behind.

Listing a few highlights hints at the treasures in store. Only 3 miles from the park's west entrance, *Lake McDonald* shimmers alongside

Opposite: The white-tailed ptarmigan, mostly brown in summer, is pure white in winter.

the highway. Its 11-mile length and 440-foot depth show the handiwork of an ancient glacier making a vast ice-carved trough. Going-to-the-Sun Road winds along the lakeshore forest for nearly 10 miles. Then, civilization interrupts with the enclave of Lake McDonald Lodge. Here rustic accommodations sit astride the shoreline about 1 mile from the head of the lake. Nearby trails may be followed to Sperry Chalet, a backcountry hostel lying 6 miles southward. Lake McDonald Lodge recalls the style of an earlier era when visitors arrived by lake launch or saddle horse.

Less than 2 miles farther on, Going-to-the-Sun Road begins paralleling McDonald Creek and soon nears the thundering *McDonald Falls*. Time must be taken to stop at the falls and observe the force of water cutting through the walls of Appekunny Argillite. Few of Glacier's waterfalls are as massive as this one, although numerous cascades on upper McDonald Creek and on the cliffs above will catch the traveler's attention. Moose Country, another mile up the road, may sometimes provide glimpses of stodgy-looking moose plodding through a marshy pond. As the roadway winds onward, mountain walls appear to form an ever steeper valley. Mount Brown towers to the south; Mount Cannon lies eastward; Mount Stanton, Mount Vaught, Mount McPartland, and Heavens Peak form a glacier-polished wall to the north. A mature forest of cedar almost engulfs the roadway.

Avalanche Creek is crossed after 16 miles of travel. A campground, picnic area, and the .5-mile *Trail of the Cedars* entice travelers to stay and explore. At the end of the Trail of the Cedars lies Avalanche Gorge, its red rock walls well worth a few minutes of walking. Two miles beyond the gorge is Avalanche Lake, presenting a cool, shady hike on even the hottest summer day.

Going-to-the-Sun Road then winds through upper McDonald Valley. Avalanche chutes, displaying long slopes green with alder but cleared of forest, testify to the power and pathways of sliding snow. Past Red Rock Point, a vista of the Garden Wall appears, with its section of the Continental Divide looming ahead. The roadway to Logan Pass may be seen high on the flanks of Haystack Butte. After passing Logan Creek, the road ascends steadily, climbing 3,000 feet in the next 11 miles. Soon after the West Side Tunnel is passed, a large turnout at The Loop provides dramatic views of Heavens Peak and valleys to the north as well as distant views of Mount Oberlin and Logan Pass.

The 8 miles from The Loop to Logan Pass offer alpine vistas growing ever more dramatic as the tree line is left below. The highway narrows as it hugs walls and cliffs. Waterfalls are always in view, with the Weeping Wall and Bird Woman Falls merely two of many worth seeing. Here,

A 2-mile trail along Avalanche Gorge leads to a lake fed by high waterfalls.

too, slopes filled with the white blossoms of bear grass or slowly melting snowdrifts tempt travelers to pause.

At the summit of this drive is Logan Pass. A modern Visitor Center introduces the Arctic-Alpine environment. Trails attract walkers toward the tundra or 2 miles to Hidden Lake or 7 miles to Granite Park Chalet, another of the high-country hostels. Extensive meadows sporting their summertime array of flowers demand a short stroll and some timely observation. Mountain peaks close by challenge travelers to spot mountain goats roaming the slopes. Skiers may be seen here in July. And mountain climbers practice their sport upon the rocky faces of Mounts Oberlin, Clements, Reynolds, and Pollock.

As the road descends eastward, views encompass the vast U-shape of Saint Mary Valley, revealing more work of ancient glaciers. The highway runs near the base of its namesake, Going-to-the-Sun Mountain. At Jackson Glacier Overlook, it is possible to see a live glacier, although Jackson Glacier rests some 5 miles distant, and binoculars are helpful to look for the opening crevasses of August. Three miles farther on, Baring Creek is crossed. Nearby is *Sunrift Gorge*, only 75 feet from the highway. This unusual gorge should be seen, since its perpendicular walls are unlike those cut by water elsewhere.

Overleaf: Lake McDonald is accessible by auto, boat, or foot.

Trails of Glacier National Park

The following trails are selected as particularly outstanding from the more than forty in the park.

Short Hikes

Swiftcurrent Lake Trail: Starts at trail head in picnic area pullout between Swiftcurrent Lake and Many Glacier Campground, and ends near south end of Many Glacier Hotel; 2.6 miles round trip; 1–2 hours; leads around lake counterclockwise for excellent views of Mount Gould, Grinnell and Salamander glaciers, and Grinnell Point.

Trail of the Cedars: Starts at trail head just north of entrance to Avalanche Campground off Sun Road, and ends at trail head across Avalanche Creek; 1 mile round trip; .75 hour; named for the western red cedars that dominate the area, this trail leads through a climax forest of cedars and western hemlocks that are in the process of eclipsing all other plant life, a part of nature's reforestation; trail crosses Avalanche Creek gorge.

Hidden Lake Overlook Trail: Starts 196 feet up boardwalk behind Logan Pass visitor center, and ends at Hidden Lake Overlook; 3 miles round trip; 1–3 hours; most popular trail in park leads through delicate highcountry vegetation with excellent view of Glacier's peaks; trail crosses Continental Divide.

Running Eagle (Trick Falls) Trail: Starts at trail head on Two Medicine Road just north of where bridge crosses Two Medicine Creek, and ends at Trick Falls; .6 mile round trip; .5 hour; leads through lush forest of Douglas fir and Engelmann spruce to Trick Falls, which, curiously, can at times be either one long fall, two falls, or only part of one.

Sun Point/Baring Falls Trail: Starts at Sun Point parking area, and ends at Baring Falls; 1.6 miles round trip; 1 hour; leads through forest of Douglas fir along the north side of St. Mary Lake for some spectacular scenery; side trail leads off to Going-to-the-Sun Point, from which Glacier's major peaks can be seen; opportunity to see water ouzel.

Rainbow Falls Trail: Starts at trail head located a short distance from dock at southern end of Waterton Lake, and ends at Rainbow Falls; 1.9 miles round trip; 1.5 hours; pleasant, brief hike paralleling Waterton River through lodgepole pine forest to Rainbow Falls; opportunity to see abundant wildlife.

Long Hikes*

Apgar Lookout Trail: Starts at trail head in a clearing approximately 2.5 miles from the Sun Road, .3 mile from the west entrance station, and ends at Apgar Mountain Lookout; 5.6 miles round trip; 4–6 hours; begins as a closed-off road and turns into trail after about 1.3 miles; long, steady climb through area swept by 1929 fire up Apgar Mountain through series of switchbacks; ideal time, mid-June; take water.

Avalanche Lake Trail: Starts at Avalanche Campground, and ends at Avalanche Lake (do not confuse with **Avalanche Trail**); 5.6 miles round trip to head of

*Overnight hikers must obtain backcountry permits and campground reservations in person at the visitor center.

lake; 4–6 hours; pleasant hike through forest, with excellent views of Avalanche Creek along way, to west shore of Avalanche Lake.

Elizabeth Lake Trail: Starts near U.S. Customs station on Chief Mountain International Highway (Montana 17), and ends at Elizabeth Lake; 19.4 miles one way; overnight; winds through aspen groves and open meadows to the lake with its abundance of rainbow trout and Arctic grayling.

Grinnell Glacier Trail: Starts at the picnic area parking lot off Many Glacier Road between Many Glacier Hotel and the Many Glacier Campground, and ends at the Moraine overlook at the foot of Grinnell Glacier; 10.4 miles round trip; 1 day; leads by Swiftcurrent Lake and Lake Josephine to the largest glacier in the park; ideal time, late July; save 3.4 miles by taking excursion boat from Many Glacier Hotel; daily walks conducted by naturalist.

Gunsight Pass Trail: Starts at Jackson Glacier overlook along Sun Road, and ends opposite Lake McDonald Lodge; 18.7 miles one way; overnight; trail follows Piegan Pass Trail to Deadwood Falls, goes by St. Mary River, Mirror Road, and Gunsight Lake to Lake Ellen Wilson, then leads to Lincoln Pass and the Sperry Chalets (advance reservations necessary for chalets); arrangements should be made for transportation back to trail head; prime viewing area for mountain goats; ideal time, mid-July.

Highline Trail: Starts at trail head across Sun Road from Logan Pass visitor center parking area, and ends at "The Loop" on Sun Road; 11.6 miles one way; 4–6 hours; hike parallels Continental Divide for first 7.1 miles, past junction at Chalet, through highcountry landscape, with abundance of wildflowers and wildlife—mountain goats and bighorn sheep; ideal time, mid-July; advance chalet reservations required.

Iceberg Lake Trail: Starts at trail head in a cabin area east of the Swiftcurrent Coffee Shop and Campstore, and ends at Iceberg Lake; 9.5 miles round trip; 1 day; follows Ptarmigan Trail for first 2.5 miles along lower slopes of Mount Henkel to Ptarmigan Falls, then drops down to Iceberg Lake; even in July one may find snow around and ice in the lake; be alert and make noise—this is prime grizzly habitat.

Boulder Pass Trail: Starts at lower Kintla Lake, and ends at Bowman Lake; 36.6 miles one way; 3–4 days; the most rugged and spectacular scenery in the park; abundant wildlife; make noise—prime area for grizzlies.

Dawson-Pitamakan Passes Trail: Starts and ends at Two Medicine Campground; 16.9 miles loop; 2–3 days; hike follows north shore of Two Medicine Lake, ascends through Bighorn Basin to Dawson Pass, then follows narrow trail behind Flinsch Peak and Mount Morgan, and descends Pitamakan Pass, then descends to Oldman Lake and on the base of Rising Wolf Mountain and down Dry Fork Creek to return to campground; ideal time, mid-July.

Red Eagle Lake Trail: Starts at trail head near St. Mary Ranger Station, and ends at Red Eagle Lake; 14 miles round trip; overnight; follows an old, closed road for 3.8 miles before becoming a trail; trail is 4 miles across two suspension bridges over Red Eagle Creek, and then down to Red Eagle Lake, where one might find rainbow and cutthroat trout.

Within 1 mile, Going-to-the-Sun Point brings a side road, a picnic area, and some hiking trails that skirt the shore of *Saint Mary Lake*. A historical marker reminds us of the old Going-to-the-Sun Chalets, which once graced this rocky promontory. The highway continues to wind along the 10-mile length of Saint Mary Lake. The scene of Wild Goose Island, the lake itself, and a backdrop of mountains will charm many photographers.

After passing The Narrows, with its cliffs of Altyn Limestone, the road reaches Rising Sun, which has resort facilities, camping, boating, and picnic areas. A trail leads along Roes Creek into the backcountry valley containing Otokomi Lake. As the final 6 miles are driven, Singleshot Mountain looms to the north and Triple Divide Mountain acts as a sentinel on the south. As the road passes the remainder of Saint Mary Lake, meadows merge into grasslands, soon to become prairie. After 50 miles of scenic roadway, Saint Mary River and Divide Creek are crossed, and the park is left behind.

Other roads penetrate Glacier's valleys at half a dozen locations. At the end of each roadway are small enclaves of resort or campground. But terminating roads simply mark the start for local trails. Each of Glacier's resorts or campgrounds is a hub for the park's 800-mile network of trails.

Two Medicine Valley and Cut Bank

Two Medicine Valley, at the park's southeastern corner, offers one such tangent approachable by paved highway. There, *Running Eagle Falls*

Only a mile from the Continental Divide, Iceberg Lake may contain ice even in summer.

and *Two Medicine Lake* are scenic highlights for travelers who wish only to sample the region. On the shore of Two Medicine Lake, a chalet complex once served horseback riders arriving from the large railway hotel at East Glacier Park. Today, a camp store, lake launch, ranger station, and campground recall that resort of an earlier era. Trails heading into the backcountry skirt the base of Rising Wolf Mountain, leading to Old Man Lake and crossing Cut Bank Pass. To the west and south, Dawson Pass and Two Medicine Pass afford equally attractive outings, with gems like Cobalt Lake, No Name Lake, and Upper Two Medicine Lake seen as splendid examples of high-country beauty.

Farther north, the Cut Bank Valley exhibits a more rustic setting. Its old chalet has been totally destroyed. Only a ranger station and primitive campground remain at the end of a 4-mile gravel road. Trails here follow Cut Bank Creek toward Medicine Grizzly Lake and over Triple Divide Pass, heading northward to the Saint Mary Valley. Hikers may also head southward, passing Morning Star Lake as they climb toward Cut Bank Pass. Many of the wilderness lakes found in this region are especially attractive to fishermen.

Many Glacier

Site of Glacier National Park's largest resort hotel, Many Glacier also contains a campground, a camp store, and other accommodations. This popular eastern slope area is approachable by 12 miles of paved highway. Wildlife seems most abundant here, especially with mountain sheep seen at close range. Grinnell Point towers above Swiftcurrent Lake and serves as a base for numerous trail heads. Pathways lead to *Iceberg Lake*, noteworthy for the icy features that float on its glassy surface, making it well worth the 5-mile hike. The trail to Ptarmigan Lake and through Ptarmigan Tunnel leads the hiker northward into the Belly River region.

Grinnell Glacier is the objective of a 5-mile trail that climbs nearly 2,000 feet. Hikers are rewarded by a close encounter with one of the park's largest glaciers. Other trails lead over Swiftcurrent Pass or Piegan Pass, or to spots like Cracker Lake, where a deserted copper mine may be observed. A variety of trails and sites draw people into the backcountry here. The Many Glacier Valley is a hiker's paradise, to say nothing of all the nearby summits that attract climbers and the panoramas that enchant photographers.

Belly River

At the Chief Mountain customs station, a trail starts southward into the Belly River region, which is accessible only to hikers and horseback riders. Here riders and hikers discover an 8-mile trail leading to Belly River ranger station. And from there, additional paths lead to Elizabeth Lake, toward the Ptarmigan Tunnel (and Many Glacier), or over Redgap Pass. Other trails wind over Gable Pass or meander along Cosley and Glenns lakes, heading up the Mokowanis Valley and across Stoney Indian Pass toward Waterton Lake. Seekers of a wilderness experience should enjoy these miles of trails punctuated with features like Dawn Mist Falls and Gros Ventre Falls.

Waterton Lake and Goat Haunt

The primary access to Glacier's northernmost section is from Alberta's Waterton Lakes National Park. There, a public lake launch provides transportation southward across the 7-mile, 317-foot-deep *Waterton Lake.* As the boat crosses the international boundary line, evident by cleared swaths on the forested forty-ninth parallel, Glacier Park is reentered. Goat Haunt ranger station is poised on the southern shore of the lake. Mount Cleveland towers nearby; its 10,466-foot summit is the highest in the park. From Goat Haunt, trails lead toward Stoney Indian Lake and Stoney Indian Pass, crossing into the Belly River drainage. The main valley trail goes southward past Kootenai lakes, where moose commonly graze. Gradually this trail climbs across Fifty Mountain, hugs the Continental Divide, visits Granite Park and its chalet, and heads toward Logan Pass, some 30 miles from Goat Haunt. Leading southwest, a trail skirts Janet and Francis lakes, crosses Brown Pass, and provides access to the North Fork area of Bowman Lake and—via Hole-in-the-Wall and Boulder Pass—to the Kintla lakes. High-country vistas, remote wilderness, and sterling solitude make all the trails from Goat Haunt especially appealing.

The North Fork

For travelers willing to explore a few miles of gravel road and tramp a few trails, a number of large western-slope lakes may be visited. Starting near Fish Creek Campground on Lake McDonald, the 43-mile, gravel Camas Road heads northward into the valley of the North Fork of the Flathead River. The winding, narrow character of this road stems from its origin as a 1901 avenue for oil exploration. Today it makes a more isolated section of Glacier accessible.

After 7 miles, Camas Creek is crossed. This is a stream popular among fly fishermen. A trail here leads toward a chain of lakes—Rogers, Trout, Arrow, and Camas—all discovered after about 12 miles of hiking. Logging Creek, encountered after 10 more miles of driving, provides a campground and a 4.4-mile trail to Logging Lake. Trimmed with forested ridges, *Logging Lake* displays another 6-mile-long glacier-carved basin. Although the North Fork road parallels the North Fork of the Flathead River, surrounding lodgepole forests permit only rare glimpses of that waterway. Yet occasional meadows and stands of ponderosa pine add variety to the drive.

Polebridge ranger station, 26 miles from Lake McDonald, sits beside the North Fork of the Flathead River. Its adjacent bridge offers an alternative entry to this region through Flathead National Forest. Less than 1 mile north of the ranger station, a 6-mile tangent road heads to Bowman Lake. The 7-mile-long *Bowman Lake*, with Rainbow Peak towering on one side and Numa Ridge rising on the other, presents a scene worthy of contemplation. Where the road terminates, a primitive campground is provided. Trails here lead southward to the Quartz lakes and eastward across Brown Pass.

The North Fork road runs north through Big Prairie and Round Prairie, with their sagebrush flats permitting wider vistas of the region. Fifteen miles from Polebridge, the end of the road grants a view of Kintla Lake. Only part of the 6.5-mile length of *Kintla Lake* can be seen because of the lake's gently curving shape. Another primitive campground is located here. Hikers and canoeists will enjoy exploring this region. A trail leads to Upper Kintla Lake and also climbs toward Boulder Pass. Agassiz Glacier may be observed from the trail, and Kinnerly and Kintla peaks act as rocky sentinels.

The Middle Fork

U.S. 2 follows Glacier's southern boundary, paralleling the Middle Fork of the Flathead River for 32 of its 54 miles as it links the villages of East Glacier Park and West Glacier. For only 4 of those miles, near Walton ranger station, does U.S. 2 actually enter the park. But in that short stretch, there is a unique feature called *The Goat Lick*. There, cliffs of clay carry salt. Those salty cliffs attract mountain goats, and many of those nimble animals are easily spotted at this site.

The valleys of the Middle Fork region are perfect for people seeking longer backcountry trips. Here wilderness predominates. Trails penetrate the valleys of Lincoln Creek, Harrison Creek, Nyack Creek, Coal Creek, Park Creek, and Ole Creek. Each one of those drainages boasts its own special treasures, found in the form of lakes, waterfalls, and wild country.

Two West-Side Trails

The 6-mile trail from Lake McDonald to Sperry Chalet climbs nearly 3,500 feet as it leads to one of Glacier's two remaining backcountry hostels. Sperry Chalet caters to hikers and horseback riders just the way a more extensive network of chalets and tent camps did through the 1930s. *Sperry Glacier*, about 3.5 miles from the chalet, is the highlight of a journey to this region. Lake Ellen Wilson and Gunsight Pass, however, also deserve attention.

The *Highline Trail*, which heads northward from Logan Pass, is one of Glacier's most popular day-hiking routes. Following the Garden Wall toward Granite Park, most of this trail remains high above timberline, affording unrestricted views along the 7-mile walk to Granite Park Chalet. The chalet itself, like its counterpart at Sperry, acts as a hub for trails. There hikers have the option of continuing northward toward Waterton Lake, eastward across Swiftcurrent Pass, and downslope toward The Loop on Going-to-the-Sun Road.

Two East-Side Trails

From Siyeh Bend on Going-to-the-Sun Road, a trail climbs toward *Preston Park*. Superlative high country is entered after only 2.5 miles of hiking. Piegan Pass invites a crossing for those interested in traveling toward Many Glacier. But a saunter into Preston Park presents quite a display of alpine scenery and *krummholz* forest. A climb to Siyeh Pass, crossed at an elevation of 8,150 feet, also introduces some rugged tundra and views of the distant plains. A 1-mile spur trail leads closer to *Sexton Glacier*, an icy flow easily visible from the main trail.

A 7-mile trail to *Gunsight Lake* parallels the Saint Mary River. Making a gradual ascent, the pathway leads toward a magnificent high-country cirque. There Gunsight Lake mirrors the rocky walls of vast sedimentary strata. With Jackson Glacier nearby and a continuing trail leading across Gunsight Pass, this is a journey well worth the time.

A Hiker's Paradise

Too many miles of trail mean too many attractions taking too much time. Glacier will require more than a month to explore. And weather and the will to walk may limit ambition. But there is much to see, and only a spare sample has been suggested in this chapter. With 200 lakes to look for and 205 miles of roadway to drive and 800 miles of trail to travel, Glacier's visitors are ensured variety and promised adventure.

Glacier has been termed a hiker's park. While that is certainly true, it has much more to offer. It is an alpine preserve; it is a wildlife sanctuary; it is a vision of primitive America; it is a place to ponder. Glacier is the Crown of the Continent; surely, it is a royal treat.

Opposite: A trail overlooks Hidden Lake, which occupies a glacier-carved bowl, or cirque.

GRAND TETON

NATIONAL PARK

Grand Teton, at 13,770 feet, is the highest peak in the Teton Range.

GRAND TETON NATIONAL PARK
P.O. DRAWER 170, MOOSE, WYOMING 83012
TEL.: (307) 733-2880

Highlights: Cathedral Group (Teewinot Mountain, Grand Teton, and Mount Owen) □ Jenny Lake □ Jackson Lake □ Oxbow Bend □ Indian Arts Museum □ Signal Mountain □ Inspiration Point □ Cunningham Cabin □ Leigh Lake □ Cascade Canyon

Access: From Jackson, take hwy. 187, 89, 26. Bus and air service available.

Hours: All year, 24 hours daily, some roads closed during winter.

Fees: Entrance, $2/car; Camping, $7/unit during summer.

Parking: Throughout park; Jenny Lake crowded in summer.

Gas: At Flagg Ranch Village, Colter Bay, Jackson Lake Lodge, Signal Mountain, Moose.

Food, lodging: Flagg Ranch Village, Colter Bay, Jackson Lake Lodge, Jenny Lake, Signal Mountain, Moose.

Visitor Centers: At Colter Bay and Moose. Permits; map and publications sales.

Museum: Indian Arts Museum at Colter Bay Visitor Center.

Gift shops: At Colter Bay, Flagg Ranch Village, Jackson Lake Lodge, Moose, and Signal Mountain.

Pets: Permitted on leashes, except in backcountry, on trails, or in public buildings.

Picnicking: At Colter Bay, Jackson Lake, and String Lake.

Hiking: More than 200 miles of trails. Carry or treat water.

Backpacking: Permitted with permit, overnight reservations needed.

Campgrounds: 6 areas. Jenny Lake, tents only. Restrooms available. Group sites at Colter Bay and Gros Ventre, reservations needed.

Tours: A variety of ranger-led tours.

Other activities: Horseback riding, cross-country skiing, float trips, fishing (license required), mountaineering (permit needed).

Facilities for disabled: Contact park for information.

For additional information, see also Sites, Trails, and Trips on pages 96–106 and the map on pages 74–75.

Mules' ears and pink geraniums carpet Jackson Hole, beneath the Teton Range.

THE TETON RANGE IS HYPNOTICALLY ATTRACTIVE. IT is recognizable, perhaps only subliminally but surely, as the backdrop for Westerns and cigarette commercials. It is all a mountain range could want to be, if mountain ranges were able to worry about what people think of them. These are stereotypical, almost archetypal, mountains, the kind that children draw on construction paper.

But they are not cheapened by our commercial applications of their form, any more than they are dignified by our reverent, slack-jawed stares. They are simply there, their character and faces changing with the fade and surge of the light, darkened now by cloud shadow, bathed now in alpenglow.

Grand Teton National Park, 485 square miles in northwestern Wyoming, almost abuts Yellowstone National Park to the north. It is a long, flat river valley, Jackson Hole, bordered on its west side by a long, narrow range of peaks that reach as much as 7,500 feet over the valley floor. Most hiking is done in the canyons between the peaks, and the peaks themselves attract an army of expert climbers every summer. The valley draws millions of tourists, who alternate between gazing at the peaks and wondering at the richness of wildlife along the shores of the rivers and lakes. The Tetons, looking not at all like the breasts for which some lonesome trapper is said to have named them, quite literally overshadow the ecological diversity of Jackson Hole. Therefore, many visitors, no matter how many elk, moose, and eagles they may have seen, remember most vividly the power of this range.

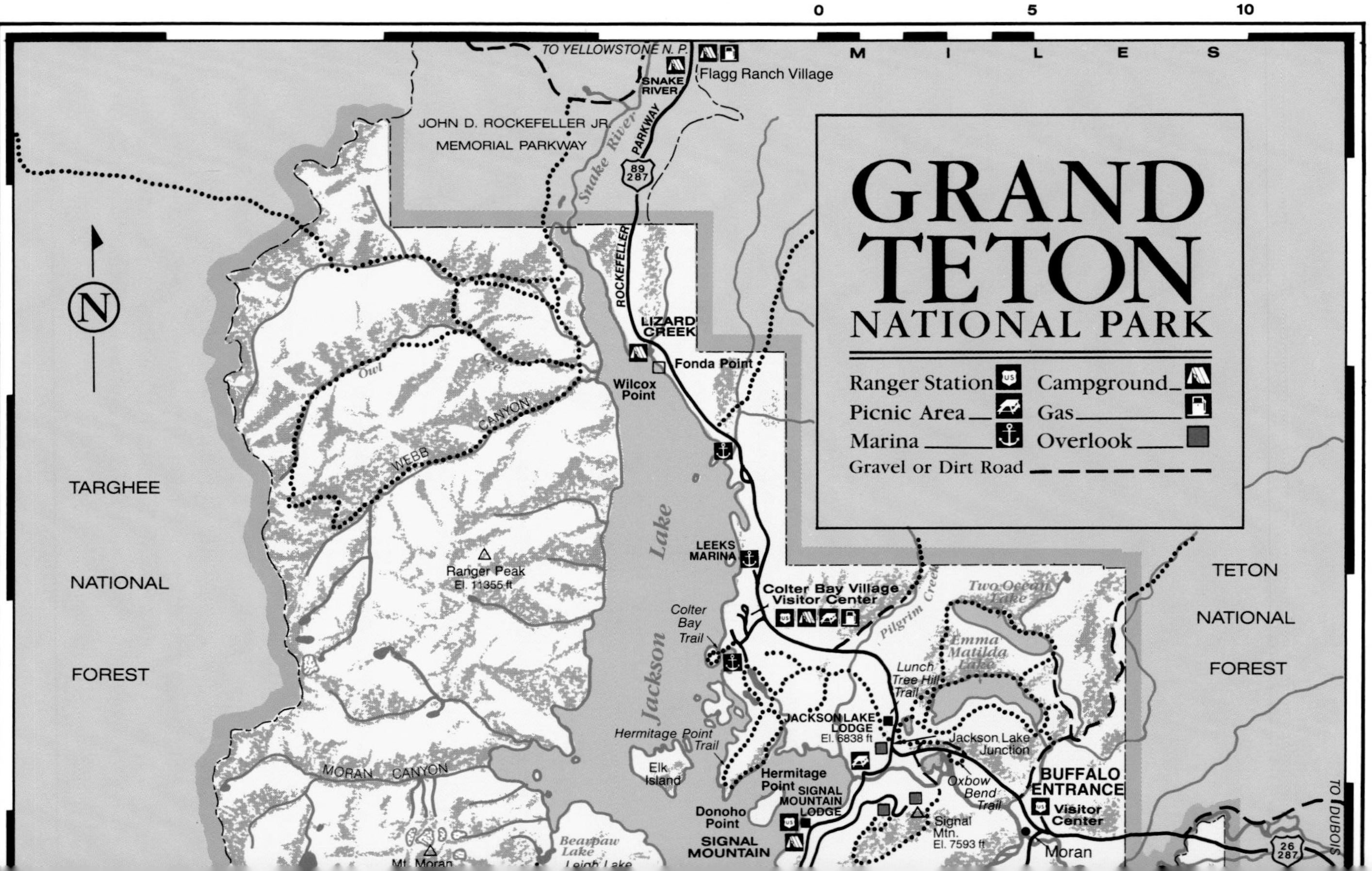

GRAND TETON NATIONAL PARK
Ranger Station
Picnic Area
Marina
Campground
Gas
Overlook
Gravel or Dirt Road
0
5
10
MILES
TO YELLOWSTONE N. P.
Flagg Ranch Village
SNAKE RIVER
JOHN D. ROCKEFELLER JR. MEMORIAL PARKWAY
Snake River
PARKWAY
89 287
ROCKEFELLER
LIZARD CREEK
Fonda Point
Wilcox Point
Owl Creek
WEBB CANYON
TARGHEE NATIONAL FOREST
Ranger Peak El. 11355 ft
Jackson Lake
LEEKS MARINA
Colter Bay Village Visitor Center
Colter Bay Trail
Pilgrim Creek
Two Ocean Lake
Emma Matilda Lake
Lunch Tree Hill Trail
JACKSON LAKE LODGE El. 6838 ft
Jackson Lake Junction
Hermitage Point Trail
Elk Island
Hermitage Point
SIGNAL MOUNTAIN LODGE
Donoho Point
SIGNAL MOUNTAIN
Oxbow Bend Trail
Signal Mtn. El. 7593 ft
BUFFALO ENTRANCE
Visitor Center
Moran
MORAN CANYON
Bearpaw Lake
Mt. Moran
TETON NATIONAL FOREST
TO DUBOIS
26 287
N

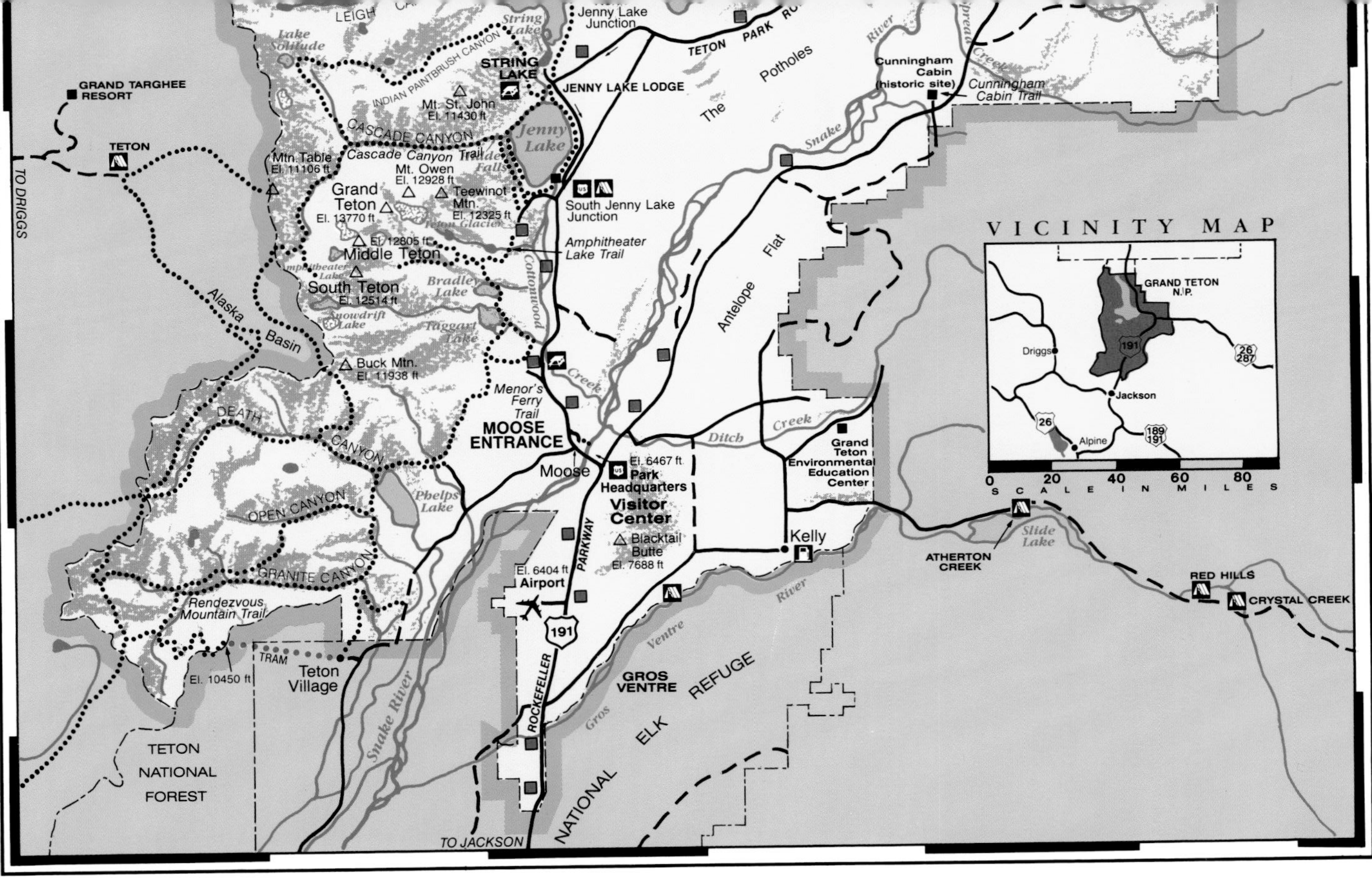
LEIGH
String Lake
Jenny Lake Junction
TETON PARK ROAD
The Potholes
Snake River
Spread Creek
Cunningham Cabin (historic site)
Cunningham Cabin Trail
Lake Solitude
INDIAN PAINTBRUSH CANYON
STRING LAKE
JENNY LAKE LODGE
GRAND TARGHEE RESORT
Mt. St. John El. 11430 ft
CASCADE CANYON
Jenny Lake
TETON
Mtn. Table El. 11106 ft
Cascade Canyon Trail
Hidden Falls
TO DRIGGS
Mt. Owen El. 12928 ft
Grand Teton El. 13770 ft
Teewinot Mtn. El. 12325 ft
South Jenny Lake Junction
Teton Glacier
El. 12805 ft Middle Teton
Amphitheater Lake Trail
Amphitheater Lake
South Teton El. 12514 ft
Bradley Lake
Cottonwood Creek
Antelope Flat
Alaska Basin
Snowdrift Lake
Taggart Lake
Buck Mtn. El. 11938 ft
Menor's Ferry Trail
MOOSE ENTRANCE
DEATH CANYON
Moose
El. 6467 ft. Park Headquarters
Visitor Center
Ditch Creek
Grand Teton Environmental Education Center
OPEN CANYON
Phelps Lake
Blacktail Butte El. 7688 ft
Kelly
PARKWAY
El. 6404 ft Airport
GRANITE CANYON
Rendezvous Mountain Trail
191
TRAM
Teton Village
El. 10450 ft
Snake River
ROCKEFELLER
Gros Ventre River
GROS VENTRE
ELK REFUGE
NATIONAL
TETON NATIONAL FOREST
TO JACKSON
VICINITY MAP
GRAND TETON N.P.
Driggs
191
26
287
Jackson
26
Alpine
189
191
0 20 40 60 80
SCALE IN MILES
ATHERTON CREEK
Slide Lake
RED HILLS
CRYSTAL CREEK

Gatherers in the High Land

Even before the time that geologists now consider the end of the last ice age in Jackson Hole, perhaps 8,500 years ago, hunters and gatherers were wandering the country in summer, searching for food. A simple blade of obsidian (a dark, glasslike volcanic rock) found near Emma Matilda Lake, and campsites and projectile points found elsewhere in northern Grand Teton National Park, suggest a human presence in the valley of at least 8,000 years' duration; it seems probable that some earlier peoples followed the retreating ice up the canyons between the peaks.

Popular legend and tradition in the Jackson Hole area hold that the valley was an Indian paradise, a game-rich country where winter-weary tribes gathered for fat, easy summers. Archeological evidence does not agree. Game was more common in lower country to the east and west, and the valley's offerings were not sufficient to entice roving bands to settle. This pattern is evident in historic times, as the long-resident Athapaskan peoples were driven north by other tribes after about 1600. The new tribes, most notably Shoshonean groups that moved north with Spanish horses, occupied much of the country around Jackson

The pioneer town of Moran, shown here about 1930, was dismantled and moved 5 miles east in 1959 before the Jackson Lake dam was built.

Hole but did not use the Hole as much as the Athapaskans had, apparently because their culture was based on horses and they were unwilling to adopt the food-gathering habits of their predecessors. By 1800, there were Shoshone to the west and south, Bannock to the west, Blackfoot and Gros Ventre (pronounced "grow vaunt") to the north, and Crow to the east; although any of them might leave tracks, artifacts, or names on the landscape, none seem to have considered Jackson Hole their personal territory.

Explorers and Settlers

Other people, of a more territorial bent, were on their way. In 1804, Thomas Jefferson launched the Lewis and Clark Expedition to explore, map, and strengthen American claims to the Louisiana Purchase. John Colter, an adventurous member of the party, was given permission to leave the home-bound expedition as it passed through Montana. In the winter of 1807/08, Colter wandered south into present-day Wyoming prospecting for furs among the Indians; he probably visited both Jackson Hole and the Yellowstone country to the north (he left no written record, but related his experiences to others who did). Historians, unencumbered by any reliable evidence, have traced, retraced, and argued over Colter's probable route through the Hole that winter; but

it matters more historically that, whether or not he traveled through, others soon would.

From 1821 to 1840, Jackson Hole was visited almost annually by at least a few trappers. In the early 1840s, when beaver hats went out of style, most of the trappers either retired or moved on to other wilderness work; but during the previous twenty years, most of the great mountain men—Bill Sublette, Jim Bridger, Kit Carson, Jedediah Smith—walked along the foot of the Tetons at least once. It was Sublette, in fact, who in 1829 named the valley Jackson Hole in honor of fellow trapper David Jackson (high isolated valleys were referred to as "holes" in the mountains).

The 1850s and 1860s were quiet; the only visit of any lasting importance occurred in 1860, when Captain William Raynolds and a small army expedition, led by Jim Bridger, visited Jackson Hole just long enough to improve the still-sketchy maps of the region. The first formal survey of the valley was conducted by Ferdinand Vandiveer Hayden and his government party in 1872. They named many of the features (after themselves), and two of their number, Nathaniel Langford and James Stevenson, claimed—perhaps falsely—the first ascent of Grand Teton. Later parties were still mapping and exploring the valley when the first settlers arrived.

Some came to prospect and settled. Others came to settle and prospected as well. By 1890, the first families (Mormons) had arrived, and in 1892, Bill Menor built his ferry across the Snake River, near the present-day settlement of Moose, to handle the small but steady traffic in the valley. The Jackson town plan was laid out in 1897, but the town grew slowly; early settlers found winters in Jackson Hole just as trying as had the Indians.

Establishment of the Park

Beginning late in the century, visitors to the area came to think that it should be preserved. Most suggested that it simply be added to Yellowstone National Park, which had been established to the north in 1872. Attempts to attach the mountains and Jackson Hole to Yellowstone were unsuccessful, and the area was soon settled enough with ranchers (some cattle, some dude) and others that local opposition to government control of the land was powerful. In 1926, Yellowstone superintendent Horace Albright interested John D. Rockefeller, Jr., in protecting the Tetons; over the next few years, Rockefeller quietly bought more than 33,000 acres of land in the valley, intending to turn it over to the National Park Service when a planned Grand Teton national park was created. When locals learned that "outside interests"

Visitors at Jenny Lake in 1930, one year after the park was established.

were trying to take over their valley, resentment grew and politically powerful factions in the state kept the federal government from accepting Rockefeller's gift for many years. In 1929, Grand Teton National Park was created, but it protected only the mountains and some of the smaller lakes at their base.

The political bickering continued until after World War II. The establishment of the park as it now stands is considered a classic case of special interests versus a more broadly perceived national good. By 1943 the Rockefellers were impatiently threatening to dispose of the land they had held (and paid taxes on) for fifteen years. President Franklin D. Roosevelt declared parts of Jackson Hole a national monument, thus halting further development and opening the way for government receipt of the Rockefeller holdings. Additional bickering followed, but in 1950, Congress added the monument to the park.

As has so often happened, the money-laden tourists who flocked to Grand Teton National Park made believers of the park's worst opponents in only a few years. In the Wyoming–Idaho area, one can hear loving tributes to the beauty and value of Grand Teton National Park from politicians who earlier in their careers had echoed the anti-park cries of their short-sighted constituents.

G E O L O G Y

Pardonable Intrusions

As you stand in the valley of the Snake River, in the heart of Jackson Hole, and look upward to the peaks of the Teton Range, you look from young land to old. In the fashion of so much of the earth's biography, the oldest rocks in sight are the highest. Although these oldest rocks are more than half the age of the earth, the mountains themselves are mere infants geologically. The Tetons are so spectacular, and so grand, because they are so young.

The deepest part of the earth's crust that geologists have any knowledge of is composed of metamorphic rocks: rocks that have been chemically altered (or metamorphosed) by the intense pressure of the rocks above them and by the equally intense temperature of the earth's molten core beneath them. These rocks, known as gneisses and schists, were formed in the Precambrian era, some 2.5 billion years ago. In later times, as the earth's crust shifted and folded, molten rock from below "intruded" into cracks in the Precambrian layer, where it cooled into bands of multicolored and unevenly strong granites and granitelike rocks, or, in later intrusions, into diabase, a dark volcanic rock.

The Precambrian rocks that now stand as the highest peaks of the Teton Range are in places cross-hatched by lighter bands of these intrusive rocks. The east face of Mount Moran, easily visible from Jackson Hole, is the textbook example of intrusive rocks here; narrow, uneven bands of granites crisscross the face, and one dark vertical band, the famous 150-foot-wide "black dike" of diabase, runs from the top of the ridge down to near the shore of Leigh Lake (both Grand Teton and Middle Teton have smaller black dikes).

While the intrusions and dikes were being formed deep in the earth, the landscape at the surface was being altered. At the close of the Precambrian era, about 570 million years ago, portions of the ancestral Pacific Ocean covered this area. Until about 85 million years ago, during what geologists refer to as the late Cretaceous period at the end of the Mesozoic era, seas came and went, and they deposited sediments that are many thousands of feet thick. An easily seen remnant of these deposits is the thin sandstone cap atop Mount Moran, directly above its black dike.

Most of the Rocky Mountains were formed by a geologic event known as the Laramide Orogeny or the Laramide Revolution. Some 60 million years ago there began a stupendous mountain-building era that lasted

Opposite: The Snake River, which drains Jackson Hole, flows south through the park.

The Gros Ventre Slide was created when the side of a mountain collapsed.

about 20 million years; the earth's crust was buckled and twisted, thus establishing the foundation for the modern Rockies. Local volcanic activity occurred during and after the orogeny, covering much of the Jackson Hole area with deep flows of ash and lava. In such vast expanses of time, many other forces were also at work, especially erosive ones—wind and ice—and minor builders and movers—lakes and streams. As soon as some major force, a volcano perhaps, rearranged the land, these smaller forces persistently chewed away at the high places, softening the lines and evening out the highs and lows. Entanglements and mixings of this sort make reading an area's geological record so difficult because they muddle the picture.

Sinking Valleys, Climbing Mountains

Ten million years ago the stage was set for one last mountain-building episode; the park area had its main geological components, but it did not yet have its mountain range.

The earth's crust, resting on the much hotter mantle that makes up most of the mass of the earth, is subject to massive slips and pitches. Where the crust is weakest (it is only 15 to 30 miles thick), there may be faults; faults are points at which sections of the earth's crust break free of one another. Most are minor, revealing their weakness by occasional earthquakes. The Teton Fault is much more. It is a huge block fault, where the two faces of the fault move in opposite directions—one up, one down—for great distances. There are actually two blocks. The obvious one is the rising Teton Range, a 40-mile by 15-mile slab of land that is bordered on the west by the Idaho–Wyoming boundary and on the east by the front row of the Tetons. The other block runs east from the foot of the Tetons into the Gros Ventre Range. The fault itself runs along the foot of the Tetons where they rise from the floor of Jackson Hole. For the past 9 million years, while the eastern edge of the Teton Range block has been rising (an average of 1 foot every three or four centuries), the western edge of the Jackson Hole block has been slowly dropping. The slippage is greatest right along the fault itself; since this action began, there has been a vertical displacement of almost 30,000 feet. It continues today. As you stand in Jackson Hole and look upward to the peaks of the Teton Range, you are seeing rock layers as much as 7,500 feet above your head whose precise equivalents are more than 4 miles beneath your feet.

What Goes Up

As always, nothing gets built up that does not get torn down. In the past 300,000 years, at least three major ice ages have come and gone in Jackson Hole. Glaciers have buried the Tetons almost completely, and erosion has removed all but a few traces of the deep sedimentary deposits that once overlaid the hard rocks on the peaks. Farther west, where the uplift was not so great, many of the deposits can still be seen, slanting up to the east; the west edge of the Teton block has moved relatively little and has been likened to the hinged side of a trap door. The high eastern edge, where the Tetons now stand, was most vulnerable to the forces of erosion, and the tight river-carved canyons between the peaks were broadened and scoured by the passage of glaciers to their present U-shaped profiles.

Glaciers, like rivers and wind, do more than erode; they haul and dump. In the park, glacial moraines (deposits laid down by the moving ice) are common. Moraines form the beds and natural dams of the series of lakes at the foot of the Teton Range. As the geological story comes closer to our own time, the scale of events can more easily be imagined. Although the Teton Range continues to rise, what *we* see is the tearing down: the gradual carving of glacier-fed streams, the bulldozing of the glaciers themselves, the tireless wind-weathering of protruding rocks, and the patient thaw–freeze cycle during which ice expands in cracks to split rock.

Overleaf: Sunrise lights the north face of Grand Teton above Teton Glacier.

There is a story in Jackson Hole that a newcomer to the area happened to pass the house of an old-timer who had lived at the foot of the Tetons for his entire life. The stranger could not resist asking him, "Don't you get tired of looking at those same mountains all the time?" The old-timer looked up at the peaks high above the valley floor and drawled, "Young fella, those mountains are *never* the same."

N A T U R A L H I S T O R Y

The wild inhabitants of Grand Teton National Park are the living legacy of its geological foundations. Offering habitats from near-desert to lush marsh to harsh alpine peak, the park has welcomed a broad assortment of life forms in the relatively short time it has been free of ice. Nearly 700 types of plants (not including lower forms, such as algae) and 300 kinds of animals (including birds, but not insects) have found niches in this diverse area.

Hardy Hangers-On

The glacial outwash plains that dominate the floor of Jackson Hole are poor plant producers, but spring wildflowers flourish amid the sagebrush and a few coarse grasses. Directly in the flood plain of the Snake River and its tributary streams, on richer alluvial soils, are stands of blue spruce and cottonwood with willows, alders, and aspen around them. Many of the small buttes and foothills that dot the valley support communities of bunch grass and rabbitgrass on all but their north-facing slopes. The glacial moraines associated with the streams and lakes at the foot of the Tetons and up into the canyons support a variety of trees, especially lodgepole pine (about 75 percent of the park's trees are lodgepoles, found up to about 7,300 feet), subalpine fir (to timberline, at about 9,200 feet), Engelmann spruce (in the high canyons, up to timberline), whitebark pine (in subalpine areas, between 7,500 feet and timberline), and Douglas fir (up to about 8,000 feet on south-facing slopes, and in large stands on the sedimentary soils of the Gros Ventre Range east of the park). Aspen appears throughout the valley where moisture will permit.

Wildflowers of the valley include scarlet gilia, lupine, harebell, and arrowleaf balsamleaf. Stocky geranium, columbine, silky phacelia, and Engelmann aster occupy the canyons. Moss campion, alpine forget-me-not, sky pilot, and alpine sunflower defy the harsher conditions of the highlands.

Opposite: Indians used the slender trunks of lodgepole pines as supports for tepees.

Fire: The Dynamic Manager

Plant communities in the park are profoundly influenced by wildfire. Aspen, for example, suffered a decline in prevalence after about 1900 because settlers suppressed wildfires that were necessary for the natural regeneration of aspen stands. Practically all the aspen groves in Jackson Hole owe their existence to fires that occurred in the last half of the 1800s; because aspen stands commonly begin to deteriorate after about eighty years, many of the park's aspens are at advanced ages and are not being replaced naturally. Recent National Park Service policies of permitting natural (lightning-caused) fires to burn are aimed in part at restoring a healthy aspen growth.

Lodgepole pine, on the contrary, has benefited from fire suppression. Natural fuels, in the form of dead branches and duff, have been able to build up rather than be burned out by periodic fires. When fires *do* occur in such overfueled stands, lodgepole pine dominance of the area is ensured because lodgepoles can recolonize an area before other types of trees can move in.

The relationships between fire and other species of trees and smaller plants are equally complex, and have serious implications for wildlife that may flourish in one type of forest but perish in another.

Fireweed flourishes in burned-over areas, often in thick colorful patches.

Canada geese are seen frequently in the lakes and marshes of Jackson Hole.

Wildlife in the Park

As usual, life is thickest near water. The south-flowing Snake River, gathering water from both sides of the valley, is the main artery of life; among its fish species is the celebrated Snake River cutthroat trout, a particularly durable strain of the cutthroat. It and its fellow fishes are prey for any number of osprey, bald eagles, and great blue herons, and they keep more peaceful company with Canada geese, trumpeter swans, and the various ducks that ride the currents and eddies. Otters work the trout pools, and beavers den in the riverbanks in peaceful coexistence with the park's largest mammal, the moose.

Songbirds often seen and heard in the park include the mountain bluebird, western tanager, pine grosbeak, common yellowthroat, and white-crowned sparrow.

The variety of mammals is perhaps the biggest surprise to visitors who come expecting only scenery. Besides several hundred summering moose, the park is home to a small herd of bison (a few dozen at most) that wanders the sagebrush country south of Jackson Lake; swift and sharp-eyed pronghorns that frequent the appropriately named Antelope Flat east and north of Moose; bighorn sheep that share the upper slopes of the Teton Range with tiny grass-gathering pikas; black bears that are seen infrequently, at random or near the campgrounds; coy-

Despite their playful antics, black bears are dangerous if approached closely.

otes that are seen anywhere in the valley; mule deer that spend much time near the larger lakes and on the lower canyon trails; and elk—the park's most perplexing wildlife-management challenge.

Compromises for Survival

Elk were seasonal users of Jackson Hole in prehistoric times. As the southern end of the hole was settled and fenced, traditional feeding grounds were usurped by humans and their domestic stock. Elk that summered in surrounding high country to the east and north of the valley could no longer reach their winter food, and by the early 1890s there was a serious problem. Concern expressed both locally and nationally resulted in the establishment, in 1913, of the National Elk Refuge just north of the town of Jackson where elk could be fed during the winter. From the beginning, sport hunting was used as a way to keep the herd's numbers at a manageable size. As part of the elaborate political maneuvering that resulted in the establishment of Grand Teton National Park, sport hunting is still allowed in some parts of the park. Hunting is rare in national parks, and the philosophical truce between those who favor it here and those who oppose it is an uneasy one. For the foreseeable future, Grand Teton National Park will be viewed by many people as a flawed reservation because of this practical and political expedient.

And there are other expedients. Because the park was established so long after the valley was developed and settled, its boundaries are not a solid line of protection for the wilderness within. Many small parcels of private land, known as inholdings, dot the southern park landscape. Other expedients trouble purists even more. Jackson Lake is much larger than it originally was because it was dammed, many years ago, to provide irrigation water for ranches to the south and west. A dam is hardly in keeping with the National Park Service's goal of naturalness, but, again, necessity had to be faced if the area was to be preserved at all. A hotter source of controversy has been the Jackson Hole Airport, along the southern boundary. Local business interests have waged a long battle with conservationists over the expansion of this small airfield, which would further develop park lands.

But no national park is a perfect reservation; no park is complete ecologically. For all its philosophical limitations, Grand Teton's natural world operates for the most part without human interference. The wild setting here is in surprisingly good shape considering all that has been done to restrict it.

Overleaf: Elk receive supplemental feed each winter at a refuge southeast of the park.

SITES, TRAILS, AND TRIPS

Visitors make unconscious decisions when they come to the Tetons. Many people, without realizing it, limit their activities to places from which they can see the range. For them, a good part of the joy of the place is having the Tetons as a background for whatever they do. Leaving Jackson Hole and going up into the mountains would cost them that background, even though it would get them closer to it.

Rarely is the stratification of use so distinct in a natural area. There are valley visitors, there are backcountry hikers, and there are mountain climbers. And, fortunately for all, the Tetons serve them well. Most of the 3 million annual visitors stay in the valley, where they find what they want: lovely natural settings with a spectacular backdrop. Hikers are a small fraction of the total, and they discover that the trails between the peaks, where practically all overnight hiking occurs, are breathtaking in more ways than one. Climbers are a small fraction of the hikers, although in summer a dozen climbers reach the summit of the Grand Teton almost every day. The climbers are the rare and fortunate ones who reverse the experience of the valley visitors; they enjoy the heights with thousands of square miles of low country as background.

Scenic Drives

All the drives in Grand Teton National Park are scenic. Wherever you go, you will be hard-pressed to stop looking toward the west. The jagged upward sweep of the Teton Range is a constant presence, always tantalizing your consciousness. When the peaks go out of sight behind a nearby ridge, or get lost in a roadside forest, you become anxious for their reappearance. They form a physical and mental boundary that occupies one whole edge of your thoughts.

Jackson Hole: The Flats. Going north from the town of Jackson, U.S. 26/89/187 skirts the east foot of East Gros Ventre Butte, an ancient outcropping of igneous rock that the glaciers were unable to cut down; the butte will block the view of the Tetons for a few miles, so watch the flats to your right. They are part of the National Elk Refuge, and a few elk may be there even in summer, though most will have retreated to their summer range in the mountains.

One enters the park four miles north of Jackson, after which the highway is identified as the John D. Rockefeller, Jr., Memorial Parkway.

Preceding overleaf: A beaver pond catches a reflection of the Cathedral Group of peaks.

After eight miles the parkway meets the Teton Park Road. A left turn here leads to the village of Moose, the Moose Visitor Center and Park Headquarters, and the south entrance station to the park.

From Moose, the Rockefeller Parkway continues up the east side of the Snake River, with frequent pullouts for viewing the mountains and the river, for 18 miles to Moran and the Buffalo Entrance Station (which serves visitors entering from the east on U.S. 26/287). Antelope Flat, north and east of Moose, is home to pronghorn, coyotes, and numerous smaller animals. Strangers think they are seeing prairie dogs here; the small grayish animals that scurry from the sage along the road are actually Uinta ground squirrels. Beyond the north end of the flats, about 6 miles south of Moran, is the partly restored Cunningham Cabin, where in 1893 a local posse shot and killed two men suspected of horse thievery.

At first glance, the old saying "sage is monotonous, unless you're a botanist" may seem true, but these wild unwalked flats are a great place for a short stroll. Even if you see no wildlife, just moving far enough from the road so that its sounds are replaced by the gentlest rustle of the wind in the big sage is justification for the trip.

Jackson Hole: Up the Gros Ventre. Two roads, one just north of where the Rockefeller Parkway crosses the Gros Ventre River and one just north of Moose, lead to the southeast corner of the park. The road from Gros Ventre junction follows the Gros Ventre River upstream along the park boundary to Kelly, a small town that was nearly wiped out in 1927 when Slide Lake, outside the park to the east, tore through its dam and flooded the valley below. The road north from Kelly has spurs up the Gros Ventre to Slide Lake and up Ditch Creek to the Grand Teton Environmental Education Center, but the main-traveled route turns west, back across Antelope Flat to the Rockefeller Parkway just north of Moose.

There are numerous inholdings in this part of the park; be careful not to wander inadvertently onto someone's private property.

Jackson Hole: At the Foot of the Range. The road that goes west from Moose to skirt the foothills and lakes along the main Teton Range is called the Teton Park Road. About 2 miles from Moose, after the road crosses Beaver Creek, a geological peculiarity becomes apparent: the streams that come out of the Tetons do not flow directly east to the Snake River. Because the fault line is right at the base of the mountains, these streams come out of their canyons and almost immediately turn south as part of Cottonwood Creek, which joins the Snake River far-

Trails of Grand Teton National Park

The following trails are representative of the more than 200 miles of trails in the park.

Menor's Ferry Trail: Starts and ends at parking area for Chapel of the Transfiguration in Moose; 1.5 mile round trip; 1 hour; trail circles through historic district beside Snake River.

Cascade Canyon Trail: Starts at Jenny Lake boat dock (for a fee a concession-operated boat can shorten hike nearly 2.5 miles), and ends at Lake Solitude; 8.5 miles one way; all day; leads along a stream and by a large waterfall; watch for moose.

Oxbow Bend Trail: Starts and ends at trail head down a short spur road 3 miles east of Jackson Lake Junction; 1 mile round trip; 1 hour; circles through trees and meadows along Snake River for glimpses of eagles, waterfowl, and moose.

Colter Bay Trail: Starts and ends at end of .5 mile walk from Colter Bay Visitor Center; .5 mile round trip; 1.5 hours; loops one mile on a wooded isthmus in Jackson Lake for panoramic view of Teton Range.

Cunningham Cabin Trail: Starts and ends at trail head 6 miles south of Moran Junction; .5 mile round trip; 1 hour; loops through an old homesite in valley.

Lunch Tree Hill Trail: Starts and ends at Jackson Lake Lodge parking area; .5 mile loop;.75 hour; slight elevation gain on this magnificent trail, which John D. Rockefeller, Jr., used so often and which inspired him to form the now famous Snake River Land Co., the land-buying company responsible for so much of the park.

Hermitage Point Trail: Starts and ends at the Colter Bay parking area; 8.5 miles loop; 4 hours; flat trail leading along Jackson Lake through lodgepoles and marshes where moose, elk, trumpeter swans, and various waterfowl are common.

Leigh Lake Trail: Starts at the String Lake picnic area parking lot, and ends at Bear Paw Lake; 7 miles round trip; 5 hours; leads along Leigh Lake with views of the lake and Indian Paintbrush Canyon.

Rendezvous Mountain Trail: Start by taking tram at Teton Village (outside park boundary) to top of Rendezvous Mountain; follow trail to park boundary and down through Granite Canyon to tram parking area; 12.3 miles one way, not including tram trip; 8 hours to all day; trail leads to magnificent views of forests and glacial canyons; abundant wildflowers in mid to late summer.

Amphitheater Lake Trail: Starts at Lupine Meadow parking area and ends at Amphitheater Lake; 9.6 miles round trip; 6–8 hours; steep but manageable trail that climbs to 9,700 feet for a sweeping view of Jackson Hole.

Opposite: Snowfall in the park averages 16 feet during the six months of winter.

The immense Jackson Hole has room for both parkland and private enterprise.

ther downstream. The water flows this way because the fault, at the very base of the peaks, is the lowest part of the valley, lower than the Snake River (as the valley continues to sink, the Snake River is gradually moving its channel westward, toward the fault).

At South Jenny Lake junction, the Teton Park Road turns straight northeast for almost 4 miles to North Jenny Lake junction, from which a one-way road heads west to String Lake, Jenny Lake Lodge, and a glorious drive along the east side of Jenny Lake itself, before returning to South Jenny Lake junction. The Cathedral Group Turnout, one of the most popular of all roadside vistas of the Tetons, is on this one-way road less than 1 mile east of Jenny Lake Lodge. The Cathedral Group, composed of Teewinot Mountain, Grand Teton, and Mount Owen, is probably the park's most photographed group of peaks. Grand Teton, at 13,770 feet, is the tallest in the Teton Range. Mount Owen (12,928 feet) was named for a claimant to the title of first to climb the Grand Teton. W. O. Owen was a prominent and influential Wyoming resident who campaigned for many years on behalf of his own claim, which was officially recognized by the state of Wyoming. Many historians believe that one or two parties reached the summit before Owen did in 1898, and the controversy will probably never be settled.

Jenny Lake, the park's second largest lake, is named for the wife of

Christian Creek is one of many streams that wind through the valley near Jackson Lake.

an early settler, Dick Leigh, for whom Leigh Lake to the north is named. It is fed primarily by Cascade Creek as it comes out of Cascade Canyon to the west, and rests in a moraine deposited by a glacier that carved its way down Cascade Canyon.

Jackson Hole: Along Jackson Lake. From North Jenny Lake junction, the Teton Park Road runs east, then north, for 8 miles to Jackson Lake junction. At first it passes to the north of a large irregular and dusty plain called The Potholes. Here, glaciers left huge chunks of ice mixed with the land they deposited, and as the ice melted, many depressions and deep pits remained. Bison are frequently seen at The Potholes.

About 4 miles from North Jenny Lake junction, the Signal Mountain Road branches to the right. It is a 5-mile spur that climbs 1,000 feet to the top of Signal Mountain for one of the best all-encompassing views of the lakes, mountains, and river valley.

Beyond the Signal Mountain Road, the Teton Park Road passes through a large field of boulders deposited here by prehistoric rivers that flowed from the north. Shortly after the road crosses the Snake River (over Jackson Lake Dam), you get a good look at one of the many marshes along the shoreline; there are many ponds and lodges that are used by beavers in this area.

Jackson Lake and North. From Jackson Lake junction, a road follows the Snake River for 5 miles east to Moran. To the south of this road is the famous Oxbow Bend of the Snake River, one of the best wildlife areas in the park; great blue herons nest here, and moose, deer, sandhill cranes, and osprey are seen frequently.

At Jackson Lake Lodge, the Teton Park Road meets the Rockefeller Parkway. The lodge at Jackson Lake is the source of another philosophical debate, this one over how comfortable lodgings in a natural area need be. The lodge is worth a visit just for its grand architecture and its superb views of Jackson Lake and the Teton Range. The Rockefeller Parkway continues north from the lodge, then west to the village of Colter Bay on Jackson Lake. The village's main attraction is the Indian Arts Museum, which exhibits artifacts of the Plains Indians.

From Colter Bay it is a fairly quick drive to the north boundary, and the Rockefeller Parkway continues into Yellowstone National Park. Jackson Lake is frequently in view as far along as Fonda Point, only about 3 miles from the north gate. By now you are well north of the main Teton Range, but it still dominates the view across the lake even as it is lost to sight behind you in the dense lodgepole forest.

Trails

A Word for the Flats. Most hikers in the Tetons head for the lakes or the mountains, where well-established, and sometimes crowded, trails are found. Some other places that you might expect to be good for hiking, such as the shoreline of the Snake River, are not always easy; the tangles of willows can be impenetrable, and the shifting currents can cut off progress. But there *are* places to strike out on your own. The sagebrush country already has been mentioned but should be recommended again. Other unusual but rewarding hikes include the climb up *Blacktail Butte*, a high limestone hill just east of Moose. There are other possibilities, all opportunities to vary your visit from the ordinary routine. Ask a ranger, or try to find them on your own.

The Lakes. Grand Teton National Park offers more miles of fantasy-quality, idyllic woodland settings than one would believe possible in one universe. Within 1 or 2 miles of the road there are places so picturesque, so flawless, that they seem almost unnatural.

There is a 6.5-mile loop trail around *Jenny Lake* that can be picked up anywhere along the east side of the lake. Many people start near

---

Opposite: Sunrise lights Grand Teton and adjacent peaks above Schwabacher Landing on the Snake River.

Blacktail Butte, a low limestone hill, is a short hike from park headquarters.

Jenny Lake Lodge and make the loop from there. On the west side of the lake, at the mouth of Cascade Canyon, Hidden Falls (250 feet) can be seen from near the trail, and a steep climb of about .5 mile goes up Cascade Creek to Inspiration Point, from which you can look out across the lake and Jackson Hole (many people stop here, pooped by the short, steep climb and not realizing that the next several miles of Cascade Canyon are an easy walk). To the north of Jenny Lake, a trail along the east shore of narrow little *String Lake* connects Jenny and Leigh lakes, and the trail continues up the east shore of *Leigh Lake*.

About 2 miles north of Moose is the trail head to *Taggart* and *Bradley lakes*, two sizable lakes that are not visible from the road. Both can be visited in a 5-mile walk, which passes through open sagebrush country, grassy meadows, and lodgepole forests.

Jackson Lake provides numerous hiking opportunities. An old service road heads north from North Jenny Lake junction about 1.5 miles to *Spalding Bay*. There is a network of trails around and to the south of the village of Colter Bay. These lead to *Heron Pond* and *Swan Lake*, hikes good for part of a morning or more (depending on your pace), or farther down the lake shore to the tip of *Hermitage Point* (about a 9-mile loop from Colter Bay) or across *Willow Flats* all the way to Jackson Lake Lodge.

Jackson Lake Lodge is the starting point for trails east, away from the lake. *Christian Pond*, only a few hundred yards from the lodge, is home to trumpeter swans and an assortment of smaller waterfowl, as well as an occasional moose. Watch for yellow-headed blackbirds that nest in

Aspens usually reach their peak color during the first week of October.

the reeds by the pond. Two larger lakes sit farther back from the lodge; *Emma Matilda Lake* and *Two Ocean Lake* can be reached by a variety of loops for a trip of 9 to 12 miles. Both are excellent for wildlife watching.

The shoreline of Jackson Lake is good for walking almost anywhere you can reach it. The Rockefeller Parkway follows it closely for some miles north of Colter Bay.

The Canyons. Hiking in the Teton Range itself, unless you are going to climb the peaks, is mostly a matter of working your way up the canyons that run east and west between the mountains. A surprising number of the canyons do not have maintained trails. The Teton Range north of Leigh Lake and all along the west side of Jackson Lake contains few trails; the most-used trails are in the southern half of the park.

Although most access is up the canyons from the valley floor, the *Teton Crest Trail* enters the park near its southwest corner and meanders along near the west boundary, loosely connecting many of the canyon trails. Several trails continue into Targhee National Forest to the west of the park, but many hikers prefer a trip that keeps them in the park.

In the extreme southern portion of the park, trails climb up *Granite*, *Open*, and *Death canyons* and then join the Teton Crest Trail near the west boundary. The mountains are lower here than they are at the heart of the range, but the country is as rugged as could be asked for, and there are fine views of Phelps Lake from points on the Death Canyon Trail. A trail leaves the Death Canyon Trail and heads north to the *Alaska Basin*, just west of the park boundary, where geologists have identified many sedimentary deposits related to those that have been mostly eroded away from the higher peaks in the Teton Range.

Farther north, just off the Teton Park Road, there is a trail west from Bradley Lake that climbs quickly to *Surprise* and *Amphitheater lakes*, at over 9,600 feet. Amphitheater Lake sits below Disappointment Peak, under a large glacial cirque (an amphitheater-shaped basin that has been carved by ice from a mountainside). In all directions are vivid examples of glacial action at work: the moraine of Teton Glacier is close at hand to the west; Delta Lake, with its opaque glacial tints, is below to the east; and the cirque itself is directly above.

West of Jenny Lake, the *Cascade Canyon Trail* climbs gradually for about 9 miles to Lake Solitude, then for another 10 miles over Paintbrush Divide (at 10,720 feet) and down Paintbrush Canyon to String Lake. This loop is one of the most popular overnight hikes in the park, again providing graphic lessons in the local geography and glorious scenic vistas. Hikers may have trouble obtaining a camping permit for this route because of its popularity.

The northern part of the park does offer some hiking, but the trails are not well maintained. This has the advantage of less company on the trails, and the disadvantage of frequent surprises in the forms of detours and tricky fords. From the Berry Creek patrol cabin on the west shore of Jackson Lake (reachable by boat or by a long hike down the west shore), trails go up *Webb Canyon*, *Owl Creek*, and *Berry Creek* (the latter leaving the park at the marvelously named Jackass Pass).

National Park Service publications about hiking in the Tetons are heavy on the warnings and cautions; these grow more serious when discussing technical climbing in this mountaineers' mecca. One of the reasons that permits are required for overnight trips is to ensure that hikers hear the minimum necessary cautionary advice. The Teton high country has its own special hazards, and even in midsummer, hikers should be aware of the possibility of avalanches and treacherous ice and snow. The Tetons are young mountains; their youth makes them extraordinarily instructive and enriching, but it also makes them unstable. Although hiking is rarely dangerous, climbing often can be. The Tetons are changing fast, and are being worn down even faster than they can rise into the restless air above their sinking valley. As the old-timer said, these mountains are *never* the same.

Opposite: A climber on Exum Ridge on Grand Teton, which is by far the most popular climb in the park.

ROCKY MOUNTAIN NATIONAL PARK

A summer storm passes over Longs Peak while the sun warms Trail Ridge.

ROCKY MOUNTAIN NATIONAL PARK
ESTES PARK, COLORADO 80517
TEL.: (303) 586-2371

Highlights: Trail Ridge Road □ Longs Peak □ Moraine Park □ Bierstadt Lake □ Goblin's Forest □ Bear Lake □ MacGregor Ranch □ Lava Cliffs □ Glacier Gorge □ Hallett Peak □ Wild Basin □ Alberta Falls □ Bridal Veil Falls □ Nymph Lake □ Flattop Mountain □ The Keyhole □ Lulu City

Access: From Estes Park, 3 miles; from Boulder, 36 miles; from Denver, 65 miles on hwy. 36.

Hours: All year, 24 hours daily.

Fees: Entrance, $2/car when Trail Ridge is open; $1/car otherwise.

Parking: At public-use areas throughout park.

Gas, food, lodging: At Estes Park. Snack bar on top of Trail Ridge Road.

Visitor Centers: At Headquarters, Moraine Park, Alpine (Trail Ridge Road), West Unit (Grand Lake). Orientation displays and publications sales.

Museum: At Moraine Park.

Gift shop: At Fall River Store adjacent to Alpine Visitor Center.

Pets: Permitted on leashes, except in backcountry, on trails, or in public buildings.

Picnicking: Throughout park along major roads.

Hiking: Permitted.

Backpacking: Permitted with permit. Treat water.

Campgrounds: First come, first served. Winter camping, primitive. Tents only at Longs Peak, no hookups. Reservations needed during summer for Glacier Bay and Moraine Park areas.

Tours: By private lines. Daytime ranger-led nature walks.

Other activities: Horseback riding, skiing, fishing with permit and license.

Facilities for disabled: Special backcountry Handicamp area.

For additional information, see also Sites, Trails, and Trips on pages 130–148 and the maps on pages 112–113 and 133.

WHEN PIONEER NATURALIST ENOS MILLS FOUGHT to preserve Rocky Mountain National Park at the turn of the century, Longs Peak was his talisman. Dozens of summits rise along the Front Range in the park, and more than 100 of them are over 12,000 feet high. Longs Peak stands highest, at 14,255 feet a major landmark of the southern Rockies.

Here the Continental Divide makes its easternmost swing. Ice age glaciers left unmistakable marks: sheer walls, narrow ridges, deep U-shaped valleys, and conspicuous moraines in the lowland parks. Bear Lake Road dead-ends in the middle of this glacial landscape at 9,475 feet, below gorges filled with strings of lakes, flowery meadows, and fragrant woods.

Much of the park lies above timberline. Trail Ridge Road runs from 8,930 feet at Deer Ridge Junction, up to 12,183 feet and over the Divide, then back down to the headwaters of the Colorado River and Grand Lake. It passes from ponderosa pine–Douglas fir forest to spruce and subalpine fir, then curves across the tundra for 11 miles.

Some 355 miles of trails spiderweb Rocky Mountain's 266,957 acres. Only two hours from Denver, the park is visited by 3 million people annually, and 600,000 day hikers. Traffic on Trail Ridge Road peaks at 700 cars per hour. With fragile resources like tundra, bighorn sheep, and subalpine meadows, the park's ruggedness saves it. A maze of gorges and streams, impassable headwalls and dense woods, off-trail Rocky Mountain National Park remains a wilderness.

Hallet Peak reflected in Sprague Lake at sunrise, in the eastern section of the park.

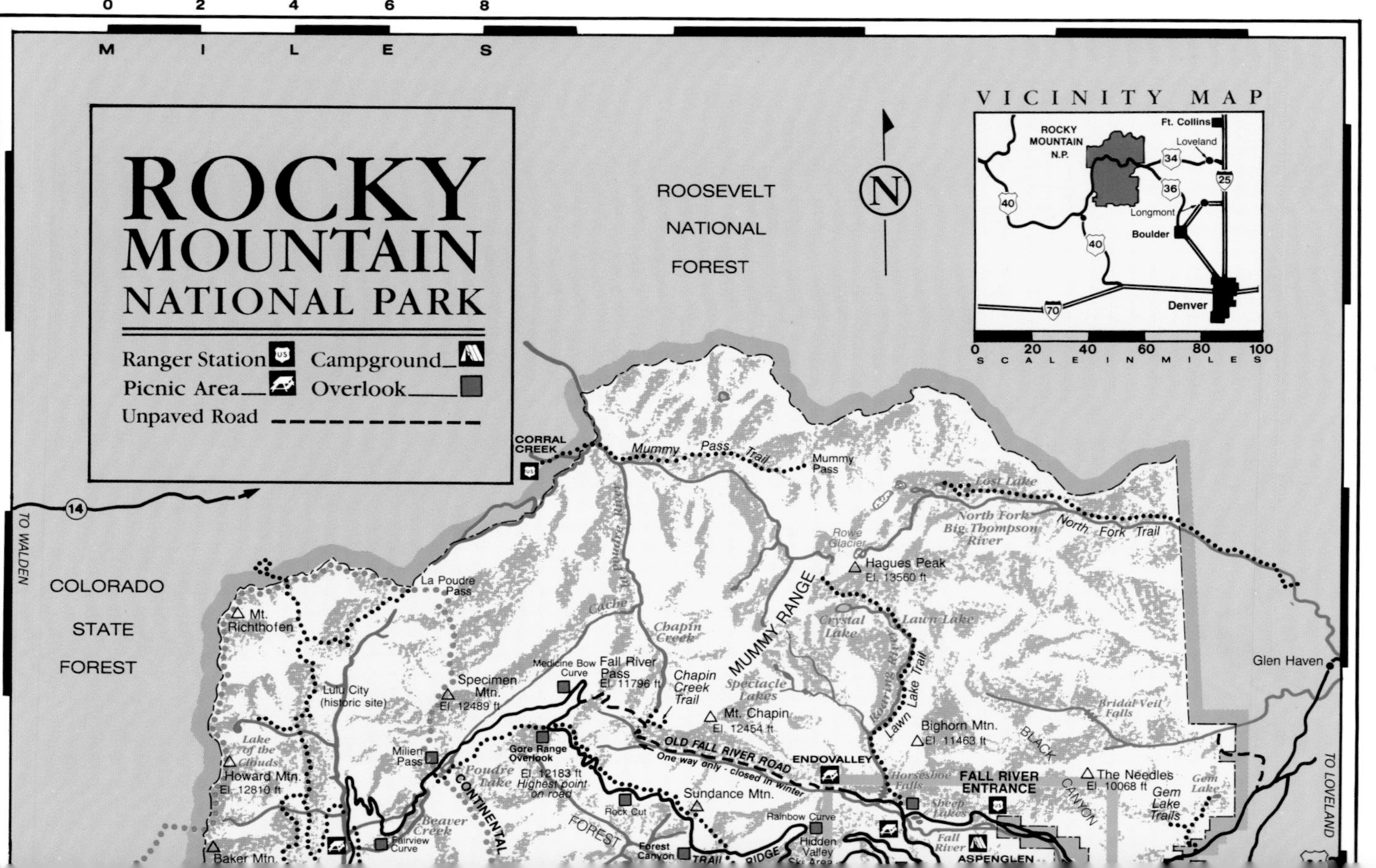

MILES
0
2
4
6
8
ROCKY MOUNTAIN NATIONAL PARK
Ranger Station
Campground
Picnic Area
Overlook
Unpaved Road
ROOSEVELT NATIONAL FOREST
VICINITY MAP
ROCKY MOUNTAIN N.P.
Ft. Collins
Loveland
Longmont
Boulder
Denver
0
20
40
60
80
100
SCALE IN MILES
TO WALDEN
COLORADO STATE FOREST
CORRAL CREEK
Mummy Pass Trail
Mummy Pass
Lost Lake
North Fork Big Thompson River
North Fork Trail
Rowe Glacier
Hagues Peak El. 13560 ft
La Poudre Pass
Cache la Poudre River
Chapin Creek
MUMMY RANGE
Crystal Lake
Lawn Lake
Roaring River
Lawn Lake Trail
Mt. Richthofen
Lulu City (historic site)
Specimen Mtn. El. 12489 ft
Medicine Bow Curve
Fall River Pass El. 11796 ft
Chapin Creek Trail
Spectacle Lakes
Mt. Chapin El. 12454 ft
Bighorn Mtn. El. 11463 ft
BLACK CANYON
Bridal Veil Falls
Glen Haven
Lake of the Clouds
Howard Mtn. El. 12810 ft
Milner Pass
Gore Range Overlook
El. 12183 ft Highest point on road
Poudre Lake
OLD FALL RIVER ROAD
One way only - closed in winter
ENDOVALLEY
Horseshoe Falls
FALL RIVER ENTRANCE
The Needles El. 10068 ft
Gem Lake
Gem Lake Trails
TO LOVELAND
Sundance Mtn.
Rock Cut
CONTINENTAL
Beaver Creek
FOREST
Rainbow Curve
Sheep Lakes
Fairview Curve
Forest Canyon
TRAIL RIDGE
Hidden Valley
Fall River
ASPENGLEN
Baker Mtn.

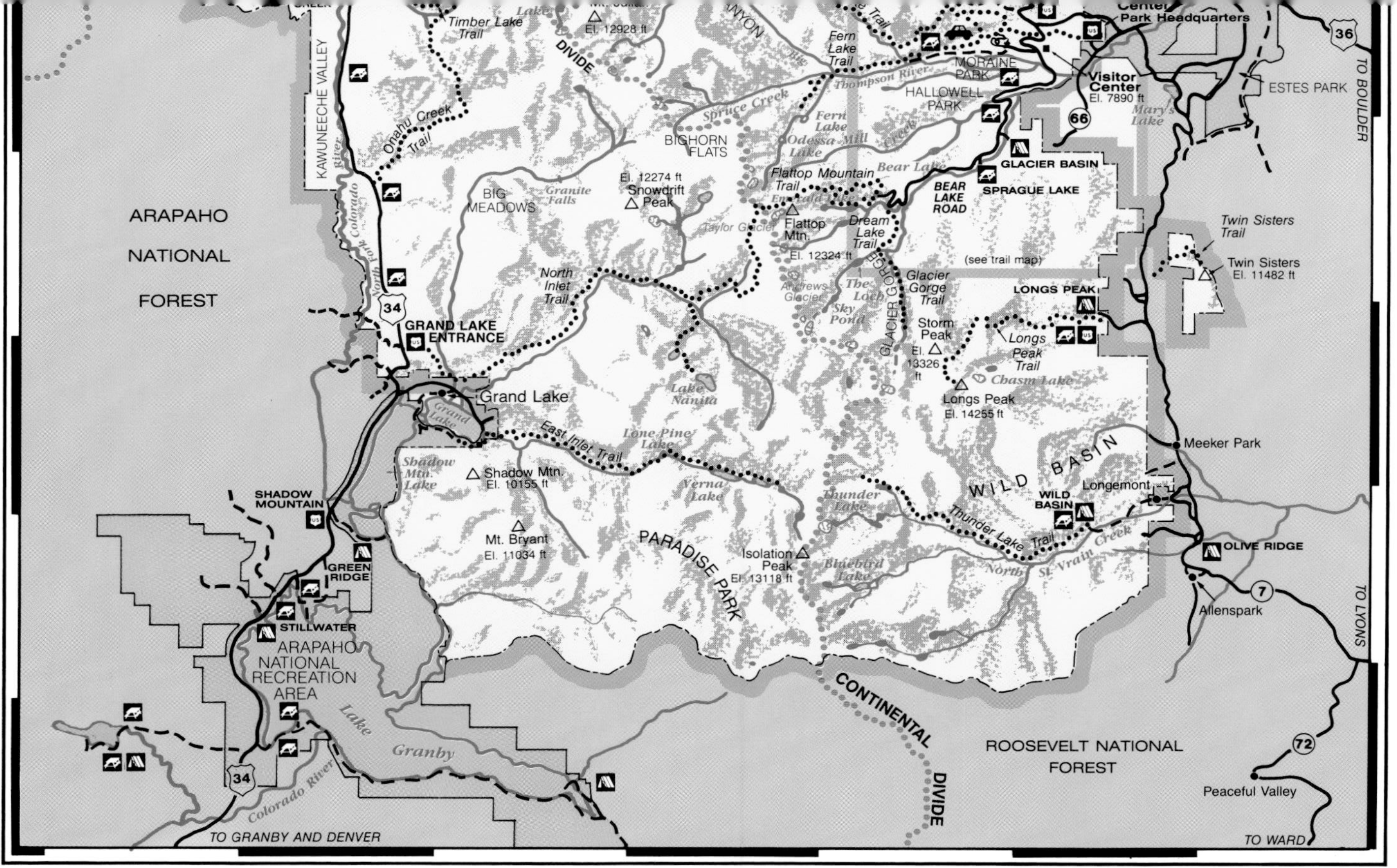

Timber Lake Trail
El. 12928 ft
DIVIDE
Fern Lake Trail
Park Headquarters
36
TO BOULDER
KAWUNEECHE VALLEY
Onahu Creek Trail
Thompson River
MORAINE PARK
Visitor Center
El. 7890 ft
ESTES PARK
HALLOWELL PARK
66
Mary's Lake
Spruce Creek
Fern Lake
Odessa Lake
Mill Creek
BIGHORN FLATS
GLACIER BASIN
Bear Lake
Flattop Mountain Trail
El. 12274 ft
Snowdrift Peak
BEAR LAKE ROAD
SPRAGUE LAKE
BIG MEADOWS
Granite Falls
ARAPAHO NATIONAL FOREST
North Fork Colorado River
Taylor Glacier
Flattop Mtn.
El. 12324 ft
Dream Lake Trail
Twin Sisters Trail
Twin Sisters
El. 11482 ft
(see trail map)
North Inlet Trail
Andrews Glacier
The Loch
Glacier Gorge Trail
GLACIER GORGE
LONGS PEAK
34
Sky Pond
GRAND LAKE ENTRANCE
Storm Peak
El. 13326 ft
Longs Peak Trail
Chasm Lake
Longs Peak
El. 14255 ft
Lake Nanita
Grand Lake
Grand Lake
East Inlet Trail
Lone Pine Lake
Meeker Park
Shadow Mtn. Lake
Shadow Mtn.
El. 10155 ft
WILD BASIN
Longemont
Verna Lake
SHADOW MOUNTAIN
Thunder Lake
WILD BASIN
Mt. Bryant
El. 11034 ft
PARADISE PARK
Thunder Lake Trail
OLIVE RIDGE
Isolation Peak
El. 13118 ft
Bluebird Lake
North St. Vrain Creek
GREEN RIDGE
7
Allenspark
STILLWATER
TO LYONS
ARAPAHO NATIONAL RECREATION AREA
CONTINENTAL DIVIDE
Lake Granby
ROOSEVELT NATIONAL FOREST
72
Peaceful Valley
Colorado River
TO GRANBY AND DENVER
TO WARD

H I S T O R Y

History in Rocky Mountain National Park reflects the great Continental Divide dominating the landscape. Here western and eastern slope peoples met; the high, smooth buttress of Trail Ridge connected them.

Bison Hunters on the Tundra

Humans wandered south into Colorado some 15,000 years ago. Soon afterward, they began to use the high country along the Continental Divide as summer hunting grounds: Trail Ridge has yielded one of their elegant fluted Clovis spearpoints.

Without horses, these early peoples moved over the land slowly, using dogs to help carry belongings. They foraged for plants and small game. When they could catch them, they roasted mammoth and giant bison. Between 7,000 and 6,500, and again, between 6,000 and 5,500 years ago, drought on the plains sent people to the mountains.

Even then, the tundra provided fine summer hunting: bison ranged that high, although mammoths were extinct. Low rock walls remain on Trail Ridge—used by game drivers to funnel bighorn sheep, wapiti (elk), and deer upward through a low pass where hunters could ambush them. Crouch at the apex of these walls, and you can almost hear the cries signaling that the herd is on its way.

Mounted Warriors

Modern Indian nations gradually moved into the mountains within the last thousand years. Utes and Shoshones came in from the west. On the eastern plains, waves of peoples moved south—the Apache in late prehistoric times, next the Comanche. Last came Arapaho and Cheyenne, who arrived in Colorado after 1800 from Great Lakes woodlands. Along the base of the Front Range, Longs Peak and Mount Meeker marked their passage: the Arapaho called these neighboring summits the "Two Guides."

Horses introduced by the Spanish transformed native North America, turning farmers into buffalo hunters, and enabling once weak tribes to raid traditional enemies. Utes were mounted by 1675. Plains buffalo-hunting cultures like the Arapaho—the classic image of North American Indians—developed with the horse and the mobility it granted.

Rocky Mountain National Park lies on the Arapaho–Ute frontier. Both

Opposite, top: Enos Mills (hatless at left), who led the fight to create the park, attends the dedication in 1915. F. O. Stanley, co-inventor of the Stanley Steamer, waves a flag. Bottom: Two Arapaho participated in the 1914 Fall River-Grand Lake pack trip.

peoples came to the tundra to hunt, crossing the Continental Divide between Estes Park and Grand Lake on ancient trails over Flattop Mountain and Trail Ridge and up Fall River. They fought here, too, at Grand Lake, in Kawuneeche Valley, and around Estes Park, paying little heed to the Arapaho belief that their god Man-Above had created the Rockies as a barrier to separate the Arapaho from their enemies, the Ute and Shoshone.

Stephen Long's Peak and Joel Estes's Park

Colorado had long been known to French trappers from the north and Spanish traders from the south when American explorer Zebulon Pike traversed southern Colorado during 1806 and 1807. After the United States won the War of 1812, Congress decided to promote American interests in the West by sending additional exploring parties into the still largely unknown Louisiana Purchase.

One such expedition penetrated Colorado in 1820. From far out on the Great Plains, Major Stephen Long's men spotted the peak that dominates the northern Front Range. Like any westbound tourists, first they had to decide "whether what we saw were mountains, or banks of cumulous clouds skirting the horizon." The mountains proved real, and by 1825 the highest peak had acquired the name of their leader.

In 1876, the prospector Joe Shipler built a cabin (left) on the North Fork of the Colorado River.

In the 1830s came the great rivalries in the fur trade, with beaver-filled streams below the park prominent in the story. From 1842 to 1844, explorer John Charles Frémont saw the park from a distance from both the east and the west. And in 1843, trapper and tourist Rufus Sage wrote of Wild Basin, Mary's Lake, and Moraine Park—our first close-up view.

Gold-rusher Joel Estes, hunting the Big Thompson River in 1859, reached what came to be called Estes Park and singlehandedly moved park history into its settlement era. He and his son Milton returned in 1860 to build a home and raise cattle.

Irish Lords and Stanley Steamers

The Estes family tired of long mountain winters and sold out in 1866. Within the next ten years, Estes Park—easily accessible to tourists arriving from the east—became a lodestone for vacationers and the raconteurs needed to entertain them.

One such character, hunter and trapper Rocky Mountain Jim Nugent —half his face torn away by a bear—was guide and unlikely lover of Isabella Bird, stout-hearted English travel writer. Jim hauled his admirer to the top of Longs Peak only five years after John Wesley Powell had led the first ascent in 1868.

Lord Windham Thomas Wyndham-Quin, the Irish earl of Dunraven, first hunted in the area in 1872, and was so delighted that he tried to preempt Estes Park as his private hunting preserve. He laid claim to 15,000 acres before the courts and his angry neighbors made further gains difficult. When F. O. Stanley drove up from Denver in 1903 in the Stanley Steamer he had helped to invent, he was able to buy out the remains of Dunraven's holdings. By 1909, he had completed the Stanley Hotel, still a stately local landmark.

The isolated west slope of the Continental Divide grew more slowly. In the 1880s, mining above Grand Lake lasted a surprising six years, considering the low-grade ore and the lack of transportation and smelters. Squeaky Bob Wheeler came to Grand Lake in 1885, when the village was still a mining and ranching center. When in 1907 Wheeler opened his tourist camp, the Hotel de Hardscrabble, Grand Lake had become a quiet resort complete with yacht club.

Establishment of the Park

Enos Mills invented Rocky Mountain National Park. With the help of many people, he saw his idea reach fruition in 1915.

Mills arrived in Estes Park in 1884, a fourteen-year-old Kansan with "weak digestion" in search of health. He went to work guiding tourists on Longs Peak, and in 1887 he climbed Longs solo. The experience galvanized him; two years later, on a trip to San Francisco when he was nineteen, Mills met John Muir. The elder naturalist became Mills's inspiration and encouraging correspondent for the next twenty-five years.

Seven months in Yellowstone in 1890 planted the seed. Mills dreamed of a national park along the Front Range from Longs Peak to Pikes Peak. The fight began in 1909. Although Mills narrowed his sights to the Estes Park region, proposed park boundaries remained vague until James Grafton Rogers of the newly formed Colorado Mountain Club drafted a bill to submit to Congress in 1913.

Summertimes saw Enos Mills guiding on Longs; his lifetime total of climbs to its summit reached 296. Each winter he preached his message throughout the East. In his zeal, Mills made enemies, lost friends, and invented conspiracies.

But his absolute dedication combined effectively with the political savvy of Rogers, J. Horace McFarland of the American Civic Association, and the Colorado congressional delegation. After two years of political wheeling and dealing, Congress created a 358-square-mile Rocky Mountain National Park. Subsequent additions have enlarged it to 417 square miles.

G E O L O G Y

From Alaska to Patagonia, a 10,000-mile mountain chain—backbone of the Americas—divides Atlantic from Pacific drainage. The Rocky Mountains form this divide in Canada and the United States. The park preserves almost 40 miles of the Continental Divide in the southern Rockies, which stretch from southern Wyoming to New Mexico. This is not merely a random sample of mountains; as Enos Mills put it, "The Rockies are not a type, but an individuality. . . . "

The Mountains Rise

This "unstable area" through the center of North America keeps producing mountains. First came the Ancestral Rockies, uplifted here 300 million years ago and then worn away to plains. More mountain building began about 40 to 60 million years ago, eventually giving rise to the modern Rocky Mountain ranges.

The oldest uplifted rocks are ancient. Dark, banded Precambrian schist and gneiss date to more than 1,700 million years, as old as layers exposed at the bottom of Grand Canyon. Molten rock that invaded it deep beneath the earth's surface several hundred million years later cooled and crystallized into pink and gray granite.

These two kinds of rocks—metamorphic gneiss and schist and igneous granite—make up the core of the Front Range. Even from a distance they are distinct: the gneiss and schist erode to jagged crags; the granite, to domes and rounded knobs.

As ancient as they are, these Precambrian rocks formed after two-thirds of geologic history was over. When the rocks were uplifted in the modern Rockies, mammals were just taking over the land from dinosaurs. Just short of 99 percent of earth time had passed.

Mushroom rocks were formed when a softer rock eroded faster than the resistant caprock.

The Pulsing Uplands

Every millennium since has been a race between uplift and erosion. Both work slowly: 2 feet of uplift along an earthquake-generating fault, 1 inch eroded from a canyon floor. The mountains rose in pulses over millions of years. They bowed up sedimentary layers that once covered them; today only steeply tilted rocks survive, dramatized by the sandstone hogbacks along the mountain front.

Uplift accelerated over the entire Rocky Mountain region between 7 and 5 million years ago. While some blocks of land moved up along faults, others dropped, as has the Estes Park valley. The rolling upland of today's Trail Ridge and other summits preserves an old erosional surface left intact through millions of years. Over the last 60 million years, uplift has totaled about 20,000 feet; judging from recent faulting, it continues today.

A Revolution in Ice

Uplift created the mountains, but streams and glaciers carved them into the airy ranges we see. For about the past 2 million years, the earth's climate has cycled between cold and warm periods. With each cold period came an ice age, although continental glaciers moving south from the Arctic never reached Colorado.

High in the Rockies, snow carried by the dominant westerly winds drifted in the heads of valleys on the lee side of the Continental Divide, where it piled much deeper than annual precipitation could accomplish on its own. In cold periods, snow accumulated faster than it melted.

Recrystallizing in masses of ice granules called névé, and deepening year by year, the snow compacted into solid ice. On an incline, the lower layers of ice, when heavy enough, began to flow. Geographers have called the ice age the most recent significant event on the planet, for the glaciers revolutionized land forms and drainage patterns: they *created* the modern landscape.

The earliest glaciation whose work remains visible in the park occurred about 160,000 years ago. Between about 127,000 and 70,000 years ago, two advances known as the early and middle Bull Lake left behind telltale lines of debris called moraines—conspicuous still, although deeply weathered.

The last major ice age glaciation—the Pinedale—reached its maximum extent about 15,000 years ago. Early glaciers roughed out the mountains, but the Pinedale glaciers scoured and polished until the faceted peaks looked modern. When the ice retreated, it left piles of morainal debris, mountains in themselves.

The New Land

Streams cut V-shaped valleys; until the time of the glaciers, the park's valleys were as narrow as Big Thompson Canyon, which leads from Estes Park to Loveland. But ice flowing down these valleys from the Divide gouged V's to U's, quarried cirques along headwalls, and polished bedrock underneath. Each glacier left along its edge the rock eroded during all this grinding: lateral moraines After retreat, a terminal moraine at the glacier's snout marked the farthest advance of ice.

The full force of what Enos Mills called "the Ice King" scoured basins and "giant staircases" from valley floors. But the spectacle of Glacier Gorge and the sheer east face of Longs Peak owe their ruggedness to constant quarrying by water at ice margins. Even the largest glaciers melted a bit in summer, and trickles of water at their heads and edges seeped into fractures. With nightfall, the water froze and expanded, prying off blocks and steepening cliffs.

A memorial to a climber killed on Longs Peak blends with rocks broken by expanding ice.

When the climate began to warm about 13,000 years ago, Pinedale glaciers started to advance and retreat in pulses, until glaciers several miles long and 1,500 feet thick swept back to their headwalls in less than 1,000 years. They left behind huge moraines, some of which dammed lakes (Grand Lake survives from this time).

Remnant glaciers disappeared from even the high cirques about 7,500 years ago. The five tiny glaciers that survive in the park first formed 3,800 years ago. They are wasting away, but even in this century have shown cycles of thickening and retreat.

Snow still swirls over the Divide to collect in the leeward basins. All it would take is a few cold centuries, and glaciers would advance once more. We will not see them in our lifetimes. But it makes more dramatic our picture of the past—when rivers of ice filled the park—knowing we also may be imagining the future.

NATURAL HISTORY

Nine thousand vertical feet separate the plains from the crest of the Front Range; in these 15 miles, climate varies from temperate to arctic. Living things vary as well in concert with these climates.

Chinook Winds and Alpine Deserts

At 7,522 feet, the town of Estes Park lies more than 2,000 feet above the Great Plains, but its 16-inch annual rainfall scarcely exceeds that of the plains. Storms drop most of their moisture on the west slope—about 20 inches annually.

Winter westerlies roar across the tundra until subalpine forest catches the snow in drifts. Spring storms bring more effective moisture—in maritime Gulf air from the southeast—just in time for the growing season. In summer, warm thermals generate afternoon thundershowers.

The Front Range is one of the world's windiest places. Gales recorded on top of Longs Peak have gusted to 201 miles per hour. Wind so dries out the tundra that it qualifies as desert—an alpine desert. Downslope, chinook winds blow warm and dry enough to raise temperatures 30° F in three minutes, scorching away east-slope spring snows overnight.

Moving up the steep mountain front during the day, temperatures drop about 3° to 5° F with each 1,000-foot rise. But at night, cold air pools in valleys and in grassy mountain "parks," so that high alpine ridgetops may be much warmer than the basins below them.

Ponderosa Parklands

At the edge of the plains, ponderosa pines stand as vanguards of the green mountain wall of the Rockies. On south-facing slopes up to about 9,000 feet, unmistakable orange-barked pines spread wide their roots to find crucial water, and thus stand apart, savanna-like.

Occasional Rocky Mountain junipers give this foothill forest a southwestern flavor. Bitterbrush, the ultimate deer browse, grows in meadows grassy enough to support wintering wapiti. Berries from shrubs like wax currant and wild rose feed chipmunks, robins, and bluebirds. Tassel-eared squirrels make their living completely from ponderosas, eating seeds and the fresh cambium in twigs.

In winter, great flocks of chickadees, nuthatches, juncos, kinglets, sparrows, and woodpeckers range through the ponderosas. Bark-beetle–infested pines draw huge numbers of woodpeckers, which in

Opposite: Rocky Mountain columbine — the state flower of Colorado.

turn help control the spread of the voracious beetles.

On north-facing slopes in ponderosa country, soil temperatures average 10° lower than on south-facing slopes. A dark forest takes advantage of this shade and longer-lasting moisture. Here, Douglas firs grow in somber stands, a miniature patch of the Northwest.

Spruce, Fir, and Fire Trees

These dark glens of Douglas fir presage the true mountain forest, the band of subalpine fir and Engelmann spruce that cloaks peaks up to treeline. This is the wettest area in the park, where—even undrifted—winter snows pile 5 feet and more.

Climbing into the park's subalpine (boreal) forest mimics traveling 1,000 miles north to Canadian boreal forest. Lichen-draped spruce and fir have the elegant spires of Christmas trees. Chickarees, Clark's nutcrackers, and gray jays scold hikers. Martens and snowshoe hares leave tracks in the snow. Blueberry and other members of the heath clan form the leather-leaved understory.

On the windiest, rockiest, nastiest ridges, only limber pine survives, gnarled and twisted, growing more weathered by the year. Spruce and fir hug the ground in the treeline elfin woodland, pruned by the wind. This *krummholz* ("crooked wood") lines the mountains between 10,000 and 11,500 feet, last trees before the dwarf plant world of the tundra.

Here and there, the subalpine forest gives way to dense rows of olive-green lodgepole pines. These are "fire trees" whose cones open only in response to very hot days or forest fires. They reseed fresh burns. They thrive for centuries, and then give way to spruce and Douglas fir that sprout in their shade.

Aspen, too, colonizes fresh burns, reproducing after fire from suckering roots. Aspen trees may grow to good size or may form low thickets on rocky slopes above streams. Wapiti sometimes feed so heavily on aspen bark that whole stands of trees suffer. Above 10,000 feet—too high for the two fire pioneers—forests recover slowly from burns.

Meadows, Creeks, and Too Many Wapiti

These paragraphs suggest forests as neatly banded as the tail of a goshawk. They are not quite that regular. Grassland meadows break up the groves, from parks fringed by ponderosas to avalanche tracks at the top of the spruce and fir forest; lush wildflower displays fill these clearings in summer.

Opposite: Blue spruce grows in bottomlands along mountain streams.

Riverbank forests cut through all other communities: willow and water birch, thin-leaf alder and Rocky Mountain maple. Narrow-leaf cottonwoods rise along streams below 8,500 feet. Colorado blue spruce line creeks at middle elevations.

In streams live threatened native greenback cutthroat trout (on the east slope) and Colorado River cutthroat (on the west), competing with rainbows, browns, and brookies introduced years ago for fishing. The park's 156 large lakes range from the highest glacier-scoured tarns—almost sterile they are so cold—to lower pools rich in insects, muskrats, waterfowl, and frogs. Beavers dam streams and create new meadows, turning morainal parks back into marshes.

The park's wapiti herds rely on grassland—especially in Estes Valley—for winter range. Native wapiti disappeared by the early 1890s. Reintroduction came in 1913, but the controlling predators were gone. Neither past reduction of herds by the National Park Service nor current public hunting outside the park keeps the wapiti under control. In 1982, the park had twice as many wapiti as the range could handle without deteriorating.

One plan may help keep wapiti in balance with their range: the National Park Service is considering the reintroduction of gray wolves. The park and adjacent national forest could support about twenty wolves; even then, wapiti will need additional management.

Above the Trees

Alpine tundra covers fully one-third of Rocky Mountain National Park; no park south of Alaska offers such extensive and accessible alpine country.

Alpine openness exhilarates after the dark, close subalpine forest: in *Land Above the Trees*, Ann Zwinger calls tundra "the landscape of ultimate freedom." But the slow growth of tundra plants imposes a restraint on our freedom. A 3-inch-high dwarf clover may be 200 years old. Damaged tundra near parking areas will take 400 to 1,000 years to recover—if the parking areas remain completely closed to use.

Lack of water limits the upward advance of trees on the mountains. Low-growing alpine plants that do survive have mastered the extreme environment. Nearly all are perennials: with a growing season as short as six weeks, they need more than one year's chance to reproduce successfully. They carefully protect half-formed flower buds through the winter, so flowering can occur quickly after snowmelt the next season.

Lichens and mosses work on boulders that have been split by frost. They add debris to windblown dust, making traces of soil where cush-

A beaver, less at ease on land than in water, sniffs the air for a sign of danger.

ion plants (like alpine forget-me-not and moss campion) can gain a foothold. Other plants push through the cushions. With enough time, a wind-scoured field of rock (fellfield) eventually may become a grass- and sedge-dominated alpine meadow or turf. Where snow lingers late, or along streams, grow marsh marigolds, snowlover, and king's and queen's crown.

Pocket gophers churn soil into temporary "gopher gardens." In the crevices of talus, sharp-eyed weasels hunt, as sinuously graceful as snakes. Pikas store winter hay piles in boulderfield dens. Yellow-bellied marmots live in alpine rockpiles, too, but also dwell in rocky country down to the ponderosa parklands. Ptarmigan are the only year-round tundra birds; rosy finches, water pipits, and horned larks come in summer.

One-third of the park wapiti herds live in tundra year-round. Bighorn and wapiti—both grazers—minimize competition by favoring different landscapes. Sheep never stray far from steep, rocky areas —escape routes from danger. Wapiti prefer alpine meadows and turf.

Originally, the local mountain sheep numbered 4,000. Market hunting, shrinking winter range, and scabies reduced them to 1,000 by 1915. Competition with cattle and chronic diseases like lungworm and pneumonia dropped the total to about 200 by the 1930s, and the population remains at that number.

Overleaf: The trunk of a limber pine that has been weathered by the elements.

Two herds roam the park, one in the Mummy Range and a larger one in the Never Summer Mountains. Even seemingly healthy sheep react to stress by failing to reproduce or by succumbing to parasites. Symbol of the park, bighorn sheep also symbolize its fragility; they are one of the most sensitive of wilderness indicators.

Rocky Mountain National Park rises as an island above a sea of urban sprawl. Subdivisions in meadows along the east boundary encroach on wapiti and sheep range. Three million people seek refuge here each year. We clamor for more water, more wilderness, more development, more roads, more timber, more game, more freedom. We clearly cannot have them all.

SITES, TRAILS, AND TRIPS

Colorado is the watershed of the nation. From high along the Continental Divide, great rivers lead off in every direction. The park has the same radial drainage in miniature; basins and divides are its natural order. Organizing the trail system is more difficult: with 355 miles of interconnected trails, possible trips are infinite.

The East Side

Moraine Park. "Of all the large and rugged mountain ranges in the world," Enos Mills wrote, the Rockies are "the most friendly, the most hospitable." The range's unique mountain parks—from huge grasslands like Middle Park to smaller sheltering valleys like Estes and Moraine parks—contribute much to that feeling.

Soon after passing park headquarters, the Bear Lake Road turns left, and within its first mile crosses into Moraine Park over the north lateral moraine left by the last Big Thompson glacier. Moraine Park always has been a favored homesite; Abner Sprague homesteaded here in 1875, eventually building a resort. On your left, watch for a cabin with rock columns on its porch: journalist William Allen White summered here from 1912 to 1943.

Two trails on the west edge of Moraine Park lead to *Cub Lake* (2.3 miles) and to *Fern Lake* (3.8 miles). These trails start in lowlands, with pleasant walking in meadows, along streams and pools, and in ponderosa pine–Douglas fir forest. Possible loops return to Moraine Park or join trails from Bear and Bierstadt lakes.

Bear Lake Road. About 5 miles from the beginning of Bear Lake Road

Opposite: Bear Lake, a starting point for several trails leading into the backcountry.

Trails of Rocky Mountain National Park

The following trails are representative of the more than 300 miles of trails in the park. Hiking times are contingent on hikers' condition and trail elevations.

Gem Lake Trails: Two trails lead to Gem Lake; one starts at Twin Owls, a large rock formation on Lumpy Ridge on the MacGregor Ranch; the other starts at a parking area on Devils Gulch Road, 1.8 mile from center of Estes Park; both end at Gem Lake; first is 1.8 mile one way; second is 2 miles one way; elevation gain of 910 feet from Twin Owls, 1,090 feet from Devils Gulch Road; altitude 8,830 feet; trail leads through ponderosa pine woods and open meadows to the natural amphitheater of Gem Lake.

Chapin Creek Trail: Starts near a parking area about 6.5 miles from beginning of Old Fall River Road at the western end of Horseshoe Park, and ends at Chapin Pass; 1.5 mile one way; elevation gain of 1,814 feet; altitude 12,454 feet; steep trail that provides a magnificent view of the rugged, glacier-carved east face of Mount Chapin.

Fern Lake Trail: Starts at parking area 1 mile up valley from Cub Lake trail head, near Moraine Park Campground, and ends at Fern Lake; 3.8 miles one way; elevation gain of 1,375 feet; altitude 9,530 feet; winds beneath Arch Rocks, crosses Big Thompson River, runs beside Fern Falls, and then crosses Fern Creek to lake.

Dream Lake Trail: Starts at Bear Lake parking area, and ends at Dream Lake; 1.1 mile one way; elevation gain of 425 feet; altitude 9,900 feet; passes Nymph Lake to Dream Lake, the park's most photographed lake, inaccessible by car; magnificent views of Longs and Hallett peaks and Flattop Mountain; Emerald Lake is 1 mile farther on this trail.

Twin Sisters Trail: Starts at trail head 1 mile off Route 7 in Tahosa Valley, and ends at the saddle between Twin Sisters Peaks; 3.7 miles one way; elevation gain of 2,300 feet; altitude 11,413 feet; recommended for cool, clear, nighttime hiking, or early morning hours, for the magnificent sunrise and incredible view of Longs Peak to the west.

Mummy Pass Trail: Starts at Corral Creek, and ends at Mummy Pass; 6.3 miles one way; elevation gain of 1,120 feet; altitude 11,120 feet; passes through what once was the most remote part of park; outstanding area to view tundra wildflowers.

Flattop Mountain Trail: Starts at Bear Lake, and ends at Flattop Mountain; 4.4 miles one way; elevation gain of 2,849 feet; altitude 12,324 feet; ancient flat land surface among jagged peaks.

Longs Peak Trail: Starts at Longs Peak Ranger Station, and ends in a boulder field below Longs Peak; route continues across boulders; 8 miles one way; elevation gain of 4,855 feet; altitude 14,255 feet.

Ute Trail: Starts at Beaver Meadows, and ends near Beaver Creek area in Kawuneeche Valley; 15 miles one way; elevation gain of 4,000 feet; altitude 12,000 feet; trail drops down to 9,200 feet in the valley.

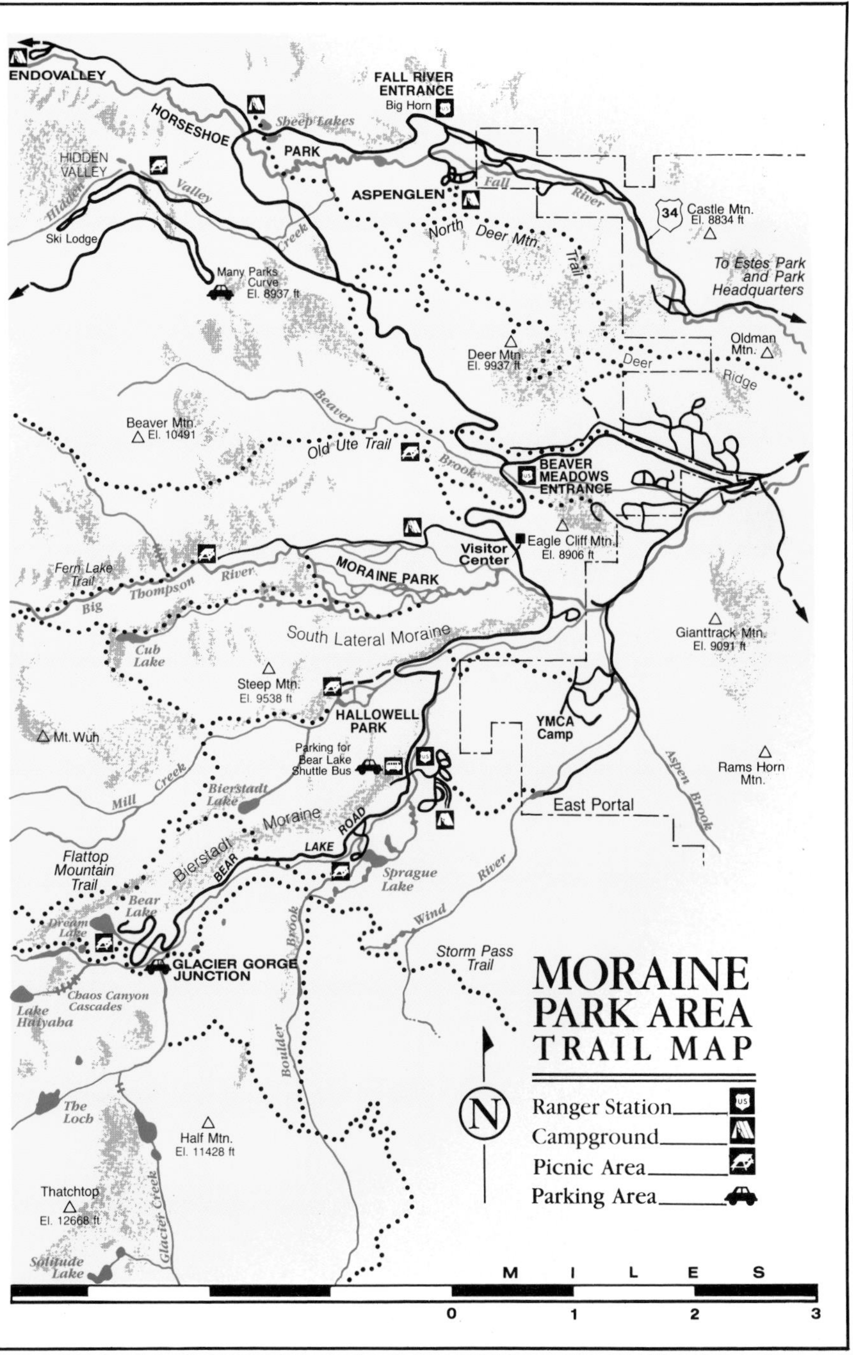
MORAINE
PARK AREA
TRAIL MAP
Ranger Station
Campground
Picnic Area
Parking Area
N
MILES
0
1
2
3
ENDOVALLEY
HORSESHOE
PARK
Sheep Lakes
FALL RIVER
ENTRANCE
Big Horn
HIDDEN
VALLEY
Hidden
Valley
Creek
ASPENGLEN
Fall
River
34
Castle Mtn.
El. 8834 ft
Ski Lodge
Many Parks
Curve
El. 8937 ft
North
Deer Mtn.
Trail
To Estes Park
and Park
Headquarters
Deer Mtn.
El. 9937 ft
Oldman
Mtn.
Deer
Ridge
Beaver
Beaver Mtn.
El. 10491
Old Ute Trail
Brook
BEAVER
MEADOWS
ENTRANCE
Visitor
Center
Eagle Cliff Mtn.
El. 8906 ft
Fern Lake
Trail
Big
Thompson
River
MORAINE PARK
South Lateral Moraine
Giantttrack Mtn.
El. 9091 ft
Cub
Lake
Steep Mtn.
El. 9538 ft
HALLOWELL
PARK
YMCA
Camp
Mt. Wuh
Parking for
Bear Lake
Shuttle Bus
Rams Horn
Mtn.
Aspen
Brook
Mill
Creek
Bierstadt
Lake
Bierstadt
Moraine
East Portal
BEAR
LAKE
ROAD
Flattop
Mountain
Trail
Sprague
Lake
River
Wind
Bear
Lake
Dream
Lake
Brook
GLACIER GORGE
JUNCTION
Storm Pass
Trail
Chaos Canyon
Cascades
Lake
Haiyaha
Boulder
The
Loch
Half Mtn.
El. 11428 ft
Thatchtop
El. 12668 ft
Glacier Creek
Solitude
Lake

lies Glacier Basin Campground, and here begins a summer shuttle-bus service. In the 4 miles up to the lake lie trail heads that lead to some of the park's most spectacular scenery—and most crowded trails (try to hike here on a weekday or off-season).

First comes the *Bierstadt Lake Trail*, which goes 1.4 miles up enormous Bierstadt Moraine to the lake perched in forest on top. On a $15,000 commission from the Earl of Dunraven in the 1870s, painter Albert Bierstadt based one of his lush images of the romantic West on the fine view of Longs Peak from here. A trail from Bear Lake also reaches Bierstadt Lake.

Three-quarters of a mile below Bear Lake lies Glacier Gorge Junction, trail head for the *North Longs Peak Trail* and for trails to both *Glacier Gorge* and *Loch Vale*. These two valleys offer remarkable glacial landscapes, from ice-scoured knobs to chains of lakes: Mills, Jewel, Black, and Frozen lakes in Glacier Gorge; The Loch, Lake of Glass, and Sky Pond in Loch Vale. Taylor Glacier heads Loch Vale, and Andrews Glacier lies up a tributary canyon.

How far you penetrate the gorges past lovely Alberta Falls depends on taste as well as on energy. Subalpine forest fringes Mills Lake (at 2.5 miles) and The Loch (at 2.7 miles); they feel lush and comfortable. The highest tarns, such as Sky Pond (at 4.6 miles) or Black Lake (at 4.7 miles), lie above treeline. Their bare rock bowls, softened only by tundra gardens of bistort and alpine avens, can seem austere. Lakes between them may be the ideal compromise, their shores garnished with a few picturesque, wind-blasted limber pines.

Another trail system radiates from Bear Lake itself, leading into two more glacial gorges with lakes and polished cliffs. A nature trail encircles Bear Lake, a good walk for seeing traces of the 1900 fire in this valley. The park's classic hike leads from Bear Lake up to *Nymph*, *Dream*, and *Emerald* lakes under the great face of Hallett Peak. Dream Lake lies only 1.1 miles up the trail—the busiest mile in the park. A branch trail goes south to *Lake Haiyaha* in Chaos Canyon and on to Loch Vale.

Heading north from Bear Lake, trails lead to *Odessa Lake* (near Fern Lake—along a good 8.5-mile route from Bear Lake down to Moraine Park) and over *Flattop Mountain* on the Continental Divide. The latter trail climbs to precipitous viewpoints and connects to west-side trails to make the grand traverse of the park to *Grand Lake* in 16.5 miles (via North Inlet Trail) or 18.5 miles (via Tonahutu Creek Trail).

Longs Peak. At 14,255 feet, Longs Peak dominates the north-central

Preceding overleaf: One of many small lakes in the park.

Backpackers can hike for many miles along the Cache la Poudre River (in valley below).

Colorado skyline for 100 miles—one of the landmark mountains of the Rockies. Major Stephen Long may have described it first, but it really is Enos Mills's mountain.

Longs Peak can be challenged by several hikable or climbable routes, but by far the most popular is the *East Longs Peak Trail*, which accommodates most of the 10,000 people who climb the peak each year. The trail begins at Longs Peak ranger station, 10 miles south of Estes Park on Colorado 7. A predawn start—no matter how painful—will get you off the mountain before the onset of possible afternoon lightning storms.

The trail climbs just under 5,000 feet in 8 miles; its named features ring out a magic rhythm: the Goblin's Forest of windblown limber pines; Alpine Brook; Jims Grove, where in 1873 Rocky Mountain Jim serenaded Isabella Bird as she lay in her bower of pines "under twelve degrees of frost, hearing sounds of wolves, with shivering stars looking through the fragrant canopy, with arrowy pines for bed-posts, and for a night lamp the red flames of a camp-fire." Above treeline the names get rockier: Granite Pass, Boulder Field, The Keyhole. Finally a steep granite slab—the Homestretch—leads to the summit.

Longs Peak has a flat top—a surprising 5 acres of ancient unglaciated upland. Views seem endless. The summit receives 25 percent more

The Mummy Range, in the northern third of the park, after an autumn snowstorm.

light and twice as much ultraviolet radiation as does land at sea level. High-altitude sun cuts through the thin, cool air to warm, but a passing cloud has the same exaggerated effect, its shade sharply chilling.

Near timberline, a .5-mile spur trail leads to Chasm Lake. Directly under the 2,500-foot East Face, the lake at dawn seems to reflect more than sunlit granite; mountain essences saturate this place—beauty and power and spirit. Perhaps this helps explain the remarkable feats of rock climbers on the wall above. The Diamond—the sheer center of the East Face—was not conquered until 1960. Since then, climbers have inched up it in winter, alone, and alone without ropes.

Two other summits along the park's east boundary provide fine views: 11,428-foot Twin Sisters, directly across Tahosa Valley from Longs Peak (a pleasing moonlight climb); and graceful, granitic Estes Cone.

Wild Basin. To reach Wild Basin ranger station, drive south from Estes Park a bit over 14 miles and turn right. Walled in by the Continental Divide to the west and by Longs Peak and other peaks to the north, Wild Basin lives up to its name. Not only are its lakes scenic, but who could resist such tantalizing place names as Chickadee Pond, Ouzel Falls, and Calypso Cascades?

In 1917, an early superintendent who felt that the park needed better publicity took advantage of Wild Basin's aura of romance. He hired a young woman to scamper through the area in a leopard skin, living off the land in between her "weekends" at a local hotel. He had no trouble getting the publicity he sought, but soon "Eve" evidently had to be rescued from the pursuit of a self-proclaimed "Adam" clad in a bearskin.

Trails lead toward the headwalls of Wild Basin, tracing the five major tributaries of North St. Vrain Creek like the fingers of an outstretched hand. The northernmost leads 4.2 miles to *Sandbeach Lake*, southern approach for climbs of Longs Peak, Mount Meeker, and Chiefs Head; indeed, the 1868 party led by John Wesley Powell tackled Longs from Wild Basin, along a route scouted by L. W. Keplinger.

The *Ouzel Falls Trail* splits to form the central three fingers of the hand—leading to Lion Lakes, Thunder Lake, and Bluebird Lake, from north to south. Each is about 6 or 7 miles up its respective valley and each is only one of a chain of lakes starting at cirque headwalls. The southernmost trail leads to *Finch* and *Pear lakes*, in the first valley north of the south park boundary.

Numerous possible loops link these trails with summits and passes along the Divide. A major fire in 1978 has left some scars. But Wild Basin still offers dense unburned forests and the possibility of seeing the namesakes of its places: calypso orchids, ouzels along the streams, and maybe even the mountain lion of Lion Lakes.

The Mummy Range. A northeast spur off the main Front Range, the Mummy Range dominates the northern third of the park. Fall River slices neatly across its southern base, and the Cache la Poudre River isolates it on the west. The North Fork of the Big Thompson River drains the range to the east. The range is named for its rough resemblance to a reclining Egyptian mummy.

Bighorns survive here. Rams stay on the tundra from the fall rut through spring; ewes move lower in springtime lambing season, seeking green grass on south-facing slopes. The Mummy Range herd comes lowest at Horseshoe Park, to reach salt licks at Sheep Lakes.

Lord Dunraven built his hunting lodge up the North Fork of the Big Thompson and made his last hunt around Estes Park in 1880. The lodge is gone, but the trail up the North Fork from Glen Haven north of Estes Park still bears his name. Lost Lake, 9.7 miles up, introduces a fine alpine area at the north end of the Mummy Range that includes several lakes and Rowe Glacier, tucked under the cirque between Hagues and Rowe peaks.

Northernmost trail in the park, the *Mummy Pass Trail* meanders through isolated subalpine forest and rolling tundra for 13 miles be-

Overleaf: Alpine sunflowers on Trail Ridge, with the Never Summer Range beyond.

tween Long Draw Reservoir and the Colorado State University field station at Pingree Park, both just outside the park boundary and both reachable from Poudre Canyon Highway west of Fort Collins. *Stormy Peaks Trail* and *Mirror Lake Trail* enter the park from nearby northern trail heads; Mirror Lake is a classic jewel of a tarn set below rugged unnamed peaks.

Unlikely as it seems, along the east park boundary runs the *North Boundary Trail.* Mostly in dense woods, this walk passes near rushing West Creek Falls. It ends at the Indian Head Ranch trail head on the north side of Lumpy Ridge. From here, *Black Canyon Trail* leads to another fine waterfall, Bridal Veil. Lumpy Ridge itself is a rock climber's paradise whose whimsical granite "lumps" rise on the north side of Estes Park.

Gem Lake Trail is the park's easternmost trail, best approached as a 2-mile walk from MacGregor Ranch on the south side of Lumpy Ridge. Gem Lake is not an alpine tarn, but a shallow, stagnant pool dissolved in granite bedrock by rain water and snowmelt—alive with tiny aquatic life. A fine introduction to ponderosa forest and granitic landscape, Gem Lake Trail makes a good winter hike.

The southern Mummy Range faces down Fall River toward Estes Park. The best route for climbing these southern peaks—Mount Chapin, Mount Chiquita, Ypsilon Mountain, and Fairchild Mountain—eases up their gentle backs from Chapin Pass in upper Fall River. From Horseshoe Park, *Lawn Lake Trail* leads up to their headwalls, with branches to Ypsilon Lake (at 4.5 miles, with Spectacle Lakes perched above it) and to Lawn Lake itself (6.2 miles), lowest in a tier of pools that includes Crystal Lake.

Dammed between 1902 and 1907, Lawn Lake feeds the Roaring River, and on July 15, 1982, the river acted out its name. The old dam gave way, and the flood that roared down to Horseshoe Park, into Fall River, and on through Estes Park did $30 million worth of damage and killed three people. Roaring River cut a new gorge and built up an alluvial fan that dammed a new lake. The road over the fan runs 40 feet higher than it did. The Lawn Lake flood left us with an enigmatic question: Which is more "natural," the new landscape or the old?

Trail Ridge Road

Statistics and superlatives fail to describe Trail Ridge Road. It is the nation's highest paved through-highway; it runs above 12,000 feet for 4

Opposite, top: A climber enters the glacier-carved cirque containing Mirror Lake. Bottom: Horseshoe Park from Trail Ridge Road.

miles, and above 11,000 feet for 11 miles. Sixty square miles of tundra are visible from its viewpoints. But numbers say nothing of the bite of icy winds roaring out of Forest Canyon, the energy of a rain squall moving across the top of Longs Peak, the dazzling snowfields on the Never Summer Mountains.

Relief maps show Trail Ridge's usefulness to travelers. Its great ramp slopes eastward toward the foothills, the obvious route through barrier cliffs along the Divide. Isolated between the long gorges of the Big Thompson River (Forest Canyon) and Fall River, Trail Ridge remained unglaciated—above and between the ice rivers. Indian bands used it for millennia, headed for Milner and Forest Canyon passes and the easy descent to the Colorado River Valley.

Fall River Road came first, built in part with convict labor and opened in 1920. But 16 percent grades and a sidehill course subject to landslides and snowdrifts made it a struggle to keep open. Replaced by Trail Ridge Road in 1932, today it offers a lively dirt-road drive one-way from Horseshoe Park past Chasm Falls to Fall River Pass.

Trail Ridge Road (open in summer) officially begins at Deer Ridge Junction, where roads from Fall River and Beaver Meadows meet. From here a 3-mile hike leads to the top of *Deer Mountain*, with fine views over the moraines and parks below. Trail Ridge Road heads up into Hidden Valley, blocked from view by the great lateral moraine built by the Fall River glacier above Horseshoe Park. Beaver ponds dot Hidden Valley, and at its head lies a small ski area.

Above Hidden Valley come two remarkable viewpoints: Many Parks Curve and Rainbow Curve. Nowhere do the remains of the glaciers feel so immediate: parks outlined by moraines leading upward to cirque headwalls. Above Rainbow Curve, the road passes through wind-sculpted limber pines at treeline and onto the tundra. From here to Milner Pass, large-scale glacial landscapes and small-scale tundra details compete for attention. Views sweep out past Longs Peak and the Never Summer Mountains to the distant peaks of the Gore Range and the Medicine Bows.

Paved pathways at Forest Canyon Overlook and Rock Cut preserve the tundra from trampling. The road reaches its high point—12,183 feet—between Lava Cliffs and Gore Range overlooks, but two passes remain. Fall River Pass, where Fall River Road joins Trail Ridge, divides the Fall River and the Cache la Poudre River drainages. Here, too, are a Visitor Center and store. Finally comes Milner Pass and the Continental Divide, back down in the trees at 10,758 feet.

From Poudre Lake at Milner Pass, a trail leads up *Specimen Mountain*—so important to west-side park bighorn sheep that hiking

The many points of interest along Trail Ridge include the Mushroom Rocks.

on the mountain is prohibited during lambing season from May 1 to July 1. The summit remains off-limits all year to protect the site of the herd's favorite mineral lick. Great volcanic ashflows 28 million years ago capped Specimen Mountain and filled the valley at Lava Cliffs above Iceberg Lake.

Three other trails begin at Poudre Lake. The *Ute Trail* crisscrosses Trail Ridge Road along its entire length. Two sections isolated from traffic run from Milner Pass to Gore Range Overlook and from near Forest Canyon Overlook down to Beaver Meadows. A spur leads off Ute Trail to the top of *Mount Ida*, 4.5 miles from Milner Pass. Finally, the *Poudre River Trail* runs north along the Cache la Poudre River for 9 miles to join the Mummy Pass Trail.

Trail Ridge Road switchbacks westward past Farview Overlook and soon drops to the Colorado River headwaters in Kawuneeche Valley.

The West Side

Kawuneeche Valley. The park's largest glacier filled Kawuneeche Valley, flowing for 20 miles from cirques on the Never Summer Mountains and on Specimen Mountain to Grand Lake. Trail Ridge Road reaches the valley a little more than 5 miles below its headwall—once the glacier's beginning and today the headwaters of the Colorado River.

Here, the Colorado begins as a creek almost narrow enough to jump across; beavers dam it regularly. The *Grand* River used to begin here, hence names like Grand Lake. The Grand joined the Green River in Utah, together forming the Colorado River.

In 1921, Colorado boosters persuaded Congress to abolish the Grand, officially extending the Colorado northward in its place, and thereby making Rocky Mountain National Park the headwaters for the great river. By whatever name, Kawuneeche Valley water has a long way to go to reach the Gulf of California—or a diversion leading to a San Diego swimming pool.

From the beginning of the *Colorado River Trail* (about 10 miles north of Grand Lake entrance), the Divide at La Poudre Pass lies 7.3 miles due north. Placer gold was discovered here in 1879, and low-grade silver ore strikes followed. At 2.1 miles on the trail to the pass, Joe Shipler's mine and house stand in ruins. At 3.6 miles lie the ruins of the hottest of the mining camps, Lulu City.

Lulu City blossomed in 1880, with hundreds of miners working the hills surrounding a town plotted for 100 blocks. The town was named after the daughter of Benjamin Franklin Burnett, a prime backer of the area. Squeaky Bob Wheeler swore that Lulu Burnett was "the most beautiful girl I ever saw." In 1883, reality caught up with most of the boys in the hills. By 1885, attention around Grand Lake had turned to ranching. Ruined cabins are all that remains of the mining camps.

The trail up to La Poudre Pass traverses a canyon that was christened Little Yellowstone for its yellow rocks (28-million-year-old eruptive deposits from the Lulu Mountain volcano just above). At the pass, the trail intersects the end of the Grand Ditch, dug by hand with only black powder for help by Chinese and Swedish laborers at the turn of the century. The ditch carries water from streams along the Never Summers over the Divide and on to the Cache la Poudre River, watering farms on the plains 75 miles away.

Three trails leave Kawuneeche Valley and climb eastward. Northernmost is the *Timber Lake Trail*; 4.8 miles up is the lake itself, a good base for a Mount Ida climb. South along Timber Creek is a swampy connection through Long Meadows to the *Onahu Creek Trail*. Onahu Creek Trail and *Green Mountain Trail* make a pleasant 6.5-mile circle hike through Big Meadows.

On the valley floor 7.2 miles north of Grand Lake, for many years Johnny Holzwarth ran a guest ranch on the homestead pioneered by his father in 1917. Today the National Park Service operates Johnny's Never Summer Ranch as a historic demonstration of dude ranching in the 1920s.

The Never Summer Mountains. Added to the park in 1929, the eastern slope of the Never Summer Mountains—with considerable volcanic rock—looks and feels different from other local ranges. These mountains run boldly north to south along the Continental Divide, with their eastern slope draining *westward* into the Colorado River and their western slope draining *eastward!*

Slashing across their foothills is the *Grand Ditch*. Its service road makes a useful trail, contouring from one end of the range to the other; all but 3 miles of the ditch lie in the park. Bridges span it infrequently, however, and it is a cold wade. Three trail systems cross the ditch from Kawuneeche Valley, making numerous loops possible.

Northernmost, the *Thunder Pass Trail* branches off near Lulu City to cross the Divide between Static Peak and Lulu Mountain. The pass lies 6.8 miles from the start of the Colorado River Trail, and also provides climbing access to impressive Mount Richthofen and to Mount Neota and Thunder Mountain. The *Red Mountain Trail* also begins here, best access to lovely Lake of the Clouds (at 6.25 miles), which perches below Mount Cirrus, and not far from Mounts Cumulus, Nimbus, and Stratus. The last two are best reached from Never Summer Ranch.

Grand Lake. The three major trails of the west side all begin at Grand Lake. Two—North Inlet and Tonahutu Creek—connect with the trail

The Colorado, the river of the "Shining Mountains," begins here in Kawuneeche Valley.

from Bear Lake at Flattop Mountain to make the climactic foot traverse of the park.

North Inlet Trail starts just north of Grand Lake village. For more than 6 miles it swings through meadows and lodgepoles, then begins to climb into dense subalpine woods. Switchbacks up Hallett Creek lead to the rolling tundra of Flattop Mountain—gaudy when blossoming—and to back-door routes up peaks from Hallett to Powell along the Divide. At 7.5 miles up, a spur leads to Lake Nanita (11 miles from the trail head)—backed by craggy Ptarmigan Mountain and Andrews Peak, one of the park's classic views.

Tonahutu Creek Trail starts at the same trail head, but leads due north, making a sharp right turn 6 miles in, at Big Meadows, heading west to treeline. In subalpine meadow country before the last climb to Bighorn Flats, a side trail reaches Haynach Lakes. Up on the tundra, Gabletop, Knobtop, and Knotchtop mountains rim Bighorn Flats on the east—all climbable. The trail reaches Flattop Mountain across Ptarmigan Pass.

East Inlet enters the southeast corner of Grand Lake, and the *East Inlet Trail* up the creek from the west portal of the Adams Tunnel runs 7.75 miles to Spirit Lake. From the head of the valley at Boulder-Grand Pass, Fourth, Spirit, and Verna lakes along East Inlet gleam like the melted pools of blue glacial ice that they are.

Finally, a walk along *Shadow Mountain Lake* winds 5 miles in dense lodgepole forest up to Shadow Mountain Lookout. From here the remarkable scope of the Colorado–Big Thompson water diversion comes clear. Grand Lake is natural—the second largest such lake in Colorado. Shadow Mountain Lake and enormous Lake Granby to the south are reservoirs. A complicated system of pumps moves western-slope water through the three lakes and into the Adams Tunnel. This 9.75-foot-diameter pipe, completed in 1947, passes deep under the park for more than 13 miles, and feeds water down the Big Thompson River, watering farmland along the Platte River as far as the Nebraska state line.

Westerners have a complicated relationship with water; Rocky Mountain National Park's current complications include widespread pollution of streams by hikers and acid rain that threatens to acidify lakes. Old dams exist, potential disasters on the scale of Lawn Lake. Resolving such problems will be delicate—as careful a compromise as the one evolved by wolf and wapiti, eagle and rabbit, limber pine and winter wind.

Unfortunately, we have less time than they did.

Opposite: Frost has forced boulders to the surface in tundra meadows along Trail Ridge Road.

THEODORE ROOSEVELT NATIONAL PARK

A geological mosaic: cannonball concretion, fluted slopes, vertical joints, and caprock.

THEODORE ROOSEVELT NATIONAL PARK
BOX 7, MEDORA, NORTH DAKOTA 58645
TEL.: (701) 623-4466

Highlights: Medora □ Painted Canyon □ Maltese Cross Cabin □ Badlands □ Peaceful Valley Ranch □ Wind Canyon □ Buck Hill □ Petrified Forest □ Little Missouri River □ Oxbow Overlook □ Achenbach Hills □ Prairie Dog Towns □ Bison Herd

Access: For South Unit, from Medora and Belfield on I–94. For North Unit, from Watford City on U.S. 85.

Hours: Daily year-round; portions of park roads closed in winter.

Fees: Entrance, $1/car. Golden Age, Golden Eagle, and Golden Access passports accepted. Camping $6/unit.

Gas, food, lodging: In summer in Medora. Year-round at Watford City (for North Unit) or Belfield (for South Unit).

Visitor Centers: South Unit, Medora; open 8 A.M.–4:30 P.M., longer in summer. Painted Canyon Rest Area, open from May 1 to September 30. North Unit, open from June to August. Exhibits and programs are available.

Museum: At Medora Visitor Center.

Gift shops: Books and map sales outlets at all Visitor Centers.

Pets: Permitted on leashes, except in backcountry, on trails, or in public buildings.

Picnicking: At Peaceful Valley (South Unit). At Squaw Creek Picnic Area (North Unit).

Hiking: Permitted throughout park. Carry water.

Backpacking: Permitted with permit. No open fires. Carry water.

Campgrounds: South Unit, 50 sites at Cottonwood Campground. Fires permitted, no showers. North Unit, 25 tent sites at Squaw Creek Campground. RV sites, 50 at Cottonwood, 25 at Squaw Creek.

Tours: During summer, tours of Roosevelt's ranch cabin and guided nature walks.

Other activities: Horseback riding, cross-country skiing, some canoeing, fishing with license.

Facilities for disabled: Visitor Center restrooms. Accessibility guide to be available soon.

For additional information, see also Sites, Trails, and Trips on pages 167–176 and the map on pages 154–155.

Moonrise as seen from Wind Canyon in the South Unit of the park.

THE WEST BEGINS IN NORTH DAKOTA; THEODORE Roosevelt National Park testifies to this truth. This surprising park stretches along the Little Missouri River in southwestern North Dakota where Theodore Roosevelt participated in the passing of the western frontier in the 1880s. Its 70,416 acres contain the best of the Little Missouri badlands, prairie life in abundance, and a large portion of T.R.'s ranch lands.

Entered from the historic village of Medora, the South Unit contains two-thirds of the park's area. Here, lightly vegetated badlands fill the breaks between upland prairie and the Little Missouri. Forty-five miles north, the North Unit preserves the newest river channel, cut along the margin of continental ice age glaciers.

T.R. arrived in Dakota Territory just a few years after the culmination of the fighting between the U.S. Army and the Dakota, or Sioux as they are popularly known. He hunted buffalo (bison) and participated in the last years of the open-range cattle industry. Almost immediately, he saw the buffalo come close to extinction. The severe winter of 1886/87 ended the cattle boom. Roosevelt emerged from the West a conservationist.

Today the park protects more than grassland; it preserves the experience that transformed T.R. Its bustling prairie-dog towns, skies graced with soaring eagles, and great herds of grazers give it the feel of the African plains, where humans share the landscape with many creatures —their equals. This land gives to us what it gave to Roosevelt, an exhilaration: "the beat of hardy life in our veins." And a responsibility: "to preserve... all the living creatures of prairie, and woodland, and seashore... from wanton destruction."

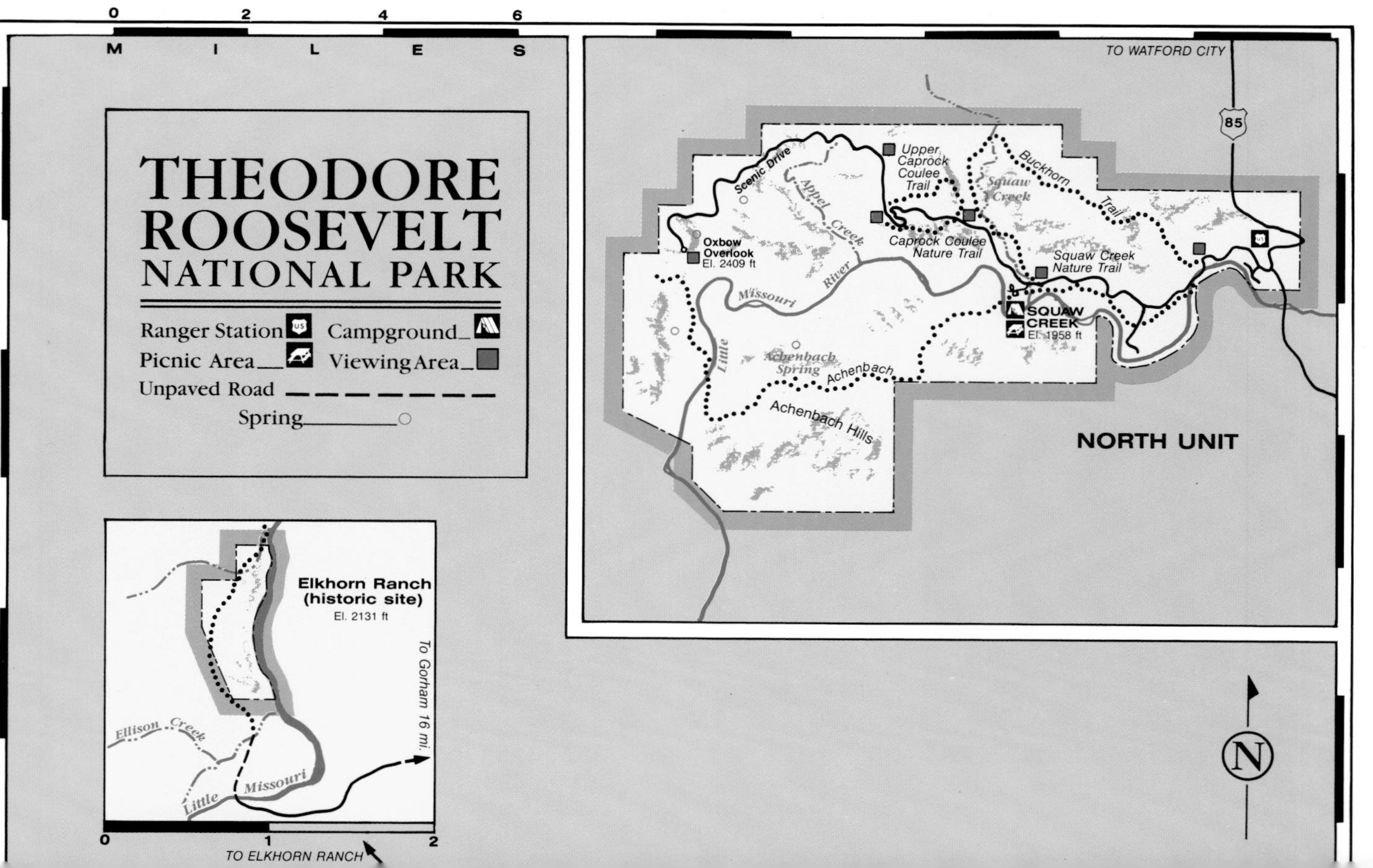

0
2
4
6
MILES
THEODORE ROOSEVELT NATIONAL PARK
Ranger Station
Campground
Picnic Area
Viewing Area
Unpaved Road
Spring
TO WATFORD CITY
85
Scenic Drive
Upper Caprock Coulee Trail
Squaw Creek
Buckhorn Trail
Appel Creek
Caprock Coulee Nature Trail
Squaw Creek Nature Trail
Oxbow Overlook
El. 2409 ft
Missouri River
SQUAW CREEK
El. 1958 ft
Little
Achenbach Spring
Achenbach
Achenbach Hills
NORTH UNIT
Elkhorn Ranch (historic site)
El. 2131 ft
To Gorham 16 mi.
Ellison Creek
Little Missouri
0
1
2
TO ELKHORN RANCH
N

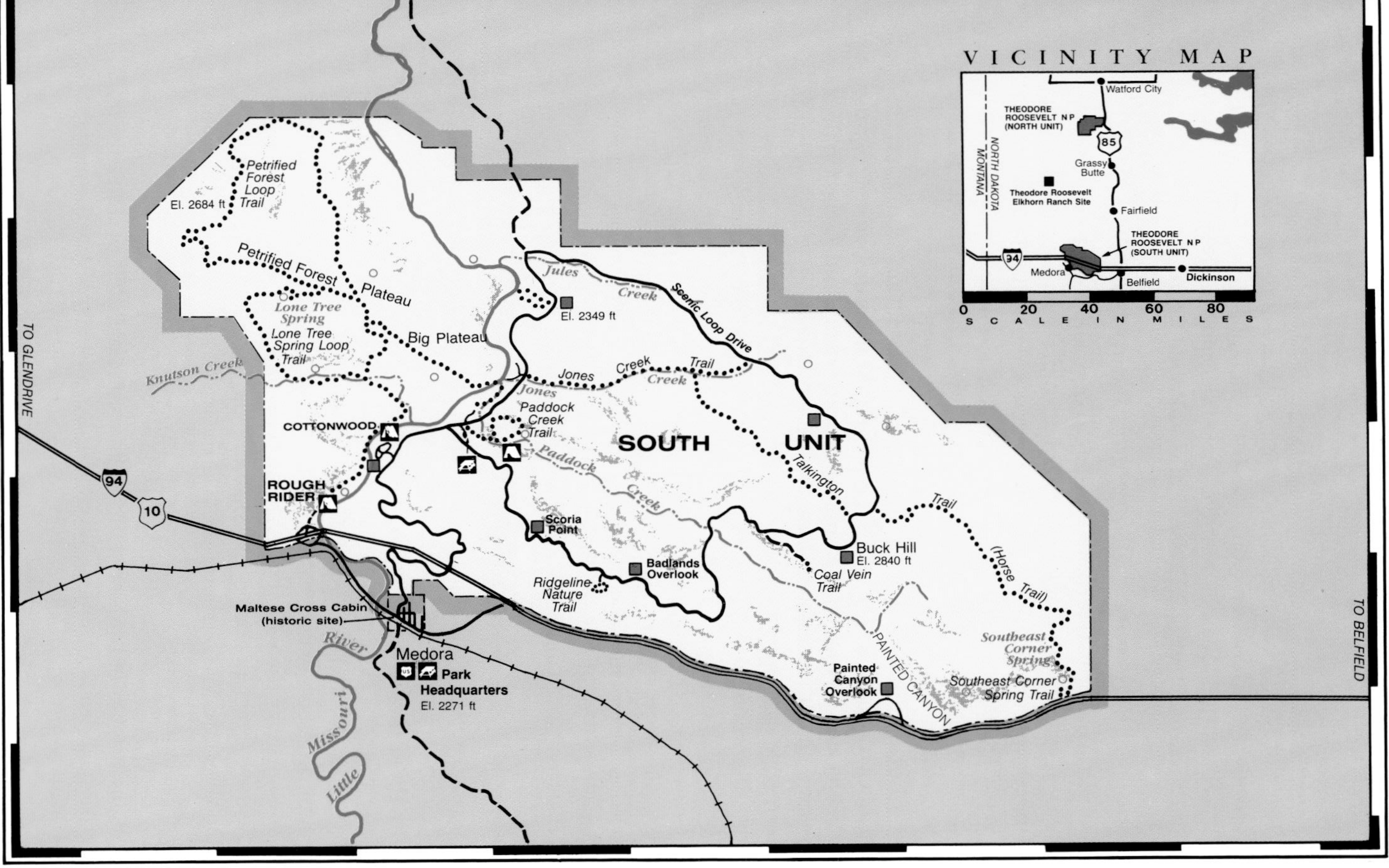
VICINITY MAP
Watford City
THEODORE ROOSEVELT N P (NORTH UNIT)
85
Grassy Butte
NORTH DAKOTA
MONTANA
Theodore Roosevelt Elkhorn Ranch Site
Fairfield
THEODORE ROOSEVELT N P (SOUTH UNIT)
94
Medora
Belfield
Dickinson
0 20 40 60 80
SCALE IN MILES
TO GLENDRIVE
TO BELFIELD
Petrified Forest Loop Trail
El. 2684 ft
Petrified Forest Plateau
Lone Tree Spring
Lone Tree Spring Loop Trail
Big Plateau
Knutson Creek
Jules Creek
El. 2349 ft
Scenic Loop Drive
Jones Creek Trail
Jones Creek
Paddock Creek Trail
SOUTH UNIT
Talkington Trail
(Horse Trail)
Paddock Creek
COTTONWOOD
ROUGH RIDER
94
10
Scoria Point
Badlands Overlook
Ridgeline Nature Trail
Buck Hill
El. 2840 ft
Coal Vein Trail
Southeast Corner Springs
Southeast Corner Spring Trail
PAINTED CANYON
Painted Canyon Overlook
Maltese Cross Cabin (historic site)
Medora
Park Headquarters
El. 2271 ft
Little Missouri River

H I S T O R Y

Theodore Roosevelt National Park is a monument to our twenty-sixth president's adventures along the Little Missouri River. But badlands history started long before the crisp fall morning in 1883 when Theodore Roosevelt stepped off a Northern Pacific Railroad car.

Earthwork Villages and Plains Warriors

As the first North Americans wandered south along melting ice sheets, they reached what is now North Dakota more than 10,000 years ago. In recent centuries, many peoples hunted in the badlands. The Hidatsa, in particular, frequently came to the Little Missouri to trap eagles. They journeyed here from their Missouri River homes, where Mandan, Hidatsa, and Arikara farmers lived in earthwork villages.

Nomadic buffalo hunters traveled to these villages from great distances to trade for corn. The Crow rode in from the west. From the north came Assiniboine; from the south, Cheyenne and Sioux. On their way through the badlands, they established trails that archeologists can still trace on ridge crests.

Once Minnesota woodland Indians, the Sioux took to horses like no other native people. By the mid-1800s, they dominated the northern Great Plains. The Sioux who hunted in the badlands were Lakota people, specifically the Hunkpapa, Sans-Arc, and Blackfoot divisions of the Sioux Nation. Meanwhile, the three sedentary tribes—already decimated by smallpox brought by the new settlers—banded together into a single village of surviving Mandan, Hidatsa, and Arikara.

Across the Wide Missouri

Adventurous French-Canadians reached the Mandan villages by 1738. The first *voyageur* in the badlands may have been Jean-Baptiste LePage. In 1804, he passed down the Little Missouri to the Missouri to join Meriwether Lewis and William Clark—the two American explorers who inaugurated the era of the mountain men.

During the next two decades, fur trappers opened the West. The Missouri was their highway. Through the mid-1800s, a succession of historic travelers floated the Missouri, and some must have explored up the Little Missouri into the badlands.

End of the Frontier

As the frontier moved west, the mighty Sioux did their best to slow its passage. Brigadier General Alfred Sully skirmished his way through the badlands just south of Medora in 1864. General George Armstrong

Custer passed a few miles farther south in 1876 en route to his fateful encounter with the Sioux at the Little Bighorn River. By 1879, the army had broken Sioux resistance.

The next year, Northern Pacific Railroad crews pushed westward across the Little Missouri River. The army then established a small post there, and newspapers began to advertise the country as a paradise for hunters.

The frontier began fading fast in 1883. At the Little Missouri crossing, a French nobleman, the Marquis de Mores, founded the town of Medora (named after his wife). He planned to ship beef from his huge slaughterhouse to the East on refrigerated railroad cars. Texas cattlemen were just to the south—and edging closer. The army abandoned its post as unnecessary. And Theodore Roosevelt arrived to hunt buffalo and had a difficult time finding one.

Boom Days in Medora

In the next two years, Roosevelt bought in to the Maltese Cross Ranch near town and built the Elkhorn Ranch, running up to 4,500 head of cattle. De Mores constructed his château on a bluff overlooking Medora. Cattle replaced buffalo on the range. But the boom was a short one.

When the disastrous winter of 1886/87 almost wiped out his investment, Roosevelt was just twenty-eight years old. He continued to travel to Dakota from New York for short periods in most years up to 1896, reveling in his ranch life—and trying to recoup his losses. When he finally sold out in 1898, as he headed for Cuba with the Rough Riders, Roosevelt had lost about $50,000 to his ranches. By then, Medora was nearly a ghost town.

Establishment of the Park

As early as 1919, the year of Roosevelt's death, local people tried to establish a Roosevelt national park in the Little Missouri badlands. But suitable public lands did not exist.

In Roosevelt's time, ranchers grazed their herds wherever they pleased. After the late 1890s, western North Dakota was surveyed, and homesteaders prospered. Then came the droughts and crop failures of the 1920s and 1930s.

Starting in 1934, the government bought out ruined farmers. Some of the reclaimed grazing lands eventually became a recreational demonstration area, then a wildlife refuge, and, finally, in 1947, Theodore Roosevelt National Memorial Park. In 1978, Congress acknowledged park values in addition to historic ties to Roosevelt by redesignating the area Theodore Roosevelt National Park.

Opposite and right: When he first came west, Teddy Roosevelt was dismissed by Dakotans as just another eastern dude who had led a sheltered life; but Roosevelt, who ranched on land that would become the national park, quickly earned his spurs and became popular among the other ranchers.
Below: Medora (shown here in the 1890s), just south of the park, was founded by a French nobleman, the Marquis de Mores, who attempted to establish a beef-shipping center here.

G E O L O G Y

Theodore Roosevelt called the Little Missouri badlands "a chaos of peaks, plateaus, and ridges." To create this chaos took time—time enough for water to turn a monotonous flat into a maze.

Dakota Crocodiles

As the Rocky Mountains rose over the Great Plains, starting some 70 million years ago, streams eroded the peaks and carried their sediments eastward. For 60 million years, mountain debris spread over the plains. The layer exposed in the park is the Fort Union Formation, made from sediments washed from the Rockies when they were young, in the Paleocene epoch (65 to 55 million years ago).

This was a crucial time in the history of life. Mammals had just taken over from dinosaurs, and fossils found near the park show this transition in all its drama. Palms and ancestral sequoias towered over swamps dominated by crocodiles. In this "early Everglades" lived a wide variety of reptiles, amphibians, birds, and small mammals.

Some plants decayed and later were transformed into coal. Others petrified, for volcanoes in the Rockies poured forth ash that buried the great trees as they died. Volcanic ash weathers to clay rich in silica, which is crucial for fossilization. It is in these silica-rich layers that we find petrified logs in the present-day park.

The Missouri Plateau: Beginnings

The Great Plains sweep from Mexico to the Arctic along the base of the Rockies. They form the dry western half of the continent's central lowland. In the United States, the Missouri River and its huge system of tributaries have eroded the northern end of the plains. This is the Missouri Plateau.

Between 5 and 10 million years ago, the entire West was uplifted, and the Little Missouri River began to carve its badlands—cutting into the soft rocks while dozens of side streams kept pace. Valley walls receded as every rainstorm sent rivulets trickling (and gouging) through the clays and siltstones of the Fort Union layers.

The Great Glaciers

Modern times began for the Little Missouri River just 2 milion years ago. It flowed northward then, joining the old Yellowstone and Missouri rivers to drain northeastward into Hudson Bay. But when continental glaciers moved down from the Arctic, they eventually covered all but the southwestern corner of North Dakota.

The Missouri itself was forced into a new channel along the ice margin from present-day Great Falls, Montana, to Kansas City, Missouri. Unable to flow northward in its old course, the Little Missouri took a sharp turn eastward to meet the Missouri. The park's North Unit lies squarely in this new river pathway; the sheer walls of the canyon through which the river runs testify to its modernity.

Earth On Fire and On the Move

Two layers of the Fort Union Formation make up the park's badlands, the Bullion Creek Member below and the Sentinel Butte Member above. Grays and browns softly color the two beds.

Both members occur in the South Unit. The Bullion Creek Member forms the river valleys and lower slopes. It includes many lignite coal seams, some of which have burned—sparked by spontaneous combustion, lightning, or range fires. Burning lignite bakes the surrounding layers, leaving behind clinker fired like bricks in a kiln. This resistant red clinker (locally called scoria) caps many hills. When a coal seam burns out, the land above it collapses. Such collapsing hillsides encourage gullying and speed up badlands formation.

Mounds of clay remain from debris washed down from the Rockies 60 million years ago.

The Sentinel Butte Member has fewer lignite beds, and thus less clinker than the Bullion Creek Member. But bentonite clay is more common in the former. Upper levels of the South Unit are carved from Sentinel Butte. In the North Unit, the river has cut its new, steep-sided channel exclusively in Sentinel Butte beds. The South Unit is characterized by rolling badlands, but in the North Unit the Little Missouri Valley erodes in landslides and in slumps of great intact blocks.

Today, these forces continue to work on the badlands. Burning coal veins create new clinker. Rains erode drainage channels deeper. Frost pries apart cliff-capping sandstone ledges. Streams undercut banks and tumble away debris.

The Little Missouri slices into the plateau. The Great Plains wash away toward the sea.

NATURAL HISTORY

For millennia, the badlands have teemed with prairie life. More recently, their water and shelter made possible the early cattle industry. Theodore Roosevelt National Park commemorates both ranching frontier and native grassland.

Coping with the Center of the Continent

The park receives about 14 inches of precipitation yearly; it is inevitably a grassland. Hot summers keep evaporation rates high. The intricate topography of the badlands maps a mosaic of plant communities by controlling subtle shifts in water availability.

Far from the moderating influences of ocean air, North Dakota is famous for long winters. Temperatures drop below zero as early as October and as late as April. Summers are equally harsh, with temperatures over 100° F predictable from July to September. June is the wettest month, a key fact for plants: 75 percent of the year's moisture falls during the growing season.

Nowhere do storms seem to move faster than on the Great Plains. Towering over the grasslands, huge cumulonimbuses come from nowhere and sweep over the park. They leave behind grass beaded with moisture, rainbows brilliant against a black sky, and crystalline air.

The Prairie Mosaic

The mixed prairie is a world of grass. Needle-and-thread and blue grama cover the gentle upland plateaus. Long, sloping hillsides nourish west-

Opposite: Junipers, which often grow in rocky soils, are common in the park.

Two young residents of one of the park's several prairie dog towns.

ern wheatgrass. Little bluestem favors steeper, gravelly slopes and the glaciated upland of the North Unit.

On wetter sites, shrubs take over. Silver sage covers large flats that periodically flood. Big sagebrush grows on the drier terraces. Creeping juniper makes some higher slopes look landscaped. And in steep ravines and on north-facing hillsides grows the badlands forest.

Green ash, chokecherry, wild rose, and American elm fill ravines. Aspen grows in the heads of draws with ideal moisture balance, particularly in the North Unit. Stands of Rocky Mountain juniper form the only coniferous woods, although ponderosa pines grow not far south of the South Unit.

Along the Little Missouri River itself, the constant moisture allows ecological succession: willow gradually is replaced with cottonwood and, in its turn, cottonwood with green ash, box elder, juniper, and elm. Snowberry thickets dominate the understory.

Meadowlark Music

Burrowing black-tailed prairie dogs form the center of an underground world that includes desert cottontails, burrowing owls, prairie rattlers, badgers, and, maybe—just maybe—black-footed ferrets.

Aboveground, the open plains offer few places to hide. Animals seek refuge in numbers, like the sociable prairie dogs, and most are tan, to blend with the tawny grass.

The burrowing owl hunts by day in the open prairie.

The grass feeds herbivores from bison to sparrows. Prairie voles build networks of miniature highways in its tangled blades. Sharp-tailed grouse trample permanent open arenas in their springtime dancing rites.

The prairie's theme song is the unmistakable call of the western meadowlark. Sometimes, one sings even at night, a bright flute in soft darkness. For Roosevelt, meadowlark music came "laden with a hundred memories and associations; with the sight of dim hills reddening in the dawn, with the breath of cool morning winds blowing across lowly plains, with the scent of flowers on the sunlit prairie."

View from the Elkhorn

In summertime, Theodore Roosevelt loved to sit in a rocker on the Elkhorn Ranch veranda. He could hear cooing mourning doves and the "shimmering, tremulous leaves" of cottonwoods, and watch spectacular black-and-white magpies coming to the river to drink.

The broken badlands sheltered mule deer and Audubon bighorn sheep. Elk and white-tailed deer ranged the river bottoms. Bison had moved through in numberless herds, but now they were scarce. In 1800, throughout North America, they had numbered 60 million; by the late 1880s, only a few hundred survived. Beyond, on the open plateau, ran pronghorn. Wolf, cougar, and grizzly were the big predators. Coyote, bobcat, weasel, and skunk hunted smaller prey.

The river woodland was alive with bird song at dusk and at dawn (of fifty-four breeding species in the area, thirty-nine nest only in the woodland): overlapping melodies from towhees, yellowthroats, house wrens, song sparrows, yellow-breasted chats. Beaver slapped tail to water; river otter slid zanily down mud slopes. Bats flitted through the trees, come evening. Roosevelt found every one of these creatures fascinating. He would become one of the foremost naturalists of his day.

The Delicate Balance

Today, the Audubon bighorn sheep is extinct—victim of overhunting by 1905. Elk, wolf, and grizzly have retreated far from the badlands. Cougars range through only occasionally. Swift fox and black-footed ferret *may* still exist here. Peregrine falcons have not nested on the river cliffs for years.

Bison had to be reintroduced, and now are thriving. Pronghorn almost disappeared; but augmented by reintroduction, these antelope-like deer range through the park seasonally. California bighorn sheep were introduced to replace the lost native subspecies, but they have not flourished.

Although overgrazing in pioneer days degraded the range, plants have recovered since grazing was controlled and then eliminated in the park. But new problems turn up: in the South Unit to the west of the river, leafy spurge—an exotic—is crowding out native plants.

The National Park Service manages about sixty wild horses (in the South Unit) and about twenty Texas longhorn steers (in the North Unit). These animals exemplify the historic badlands seen by Roosevelt. But their effect on the range remains unknown. To preserve the badlands as a natural prairie and, at the same time, as the place that forged T.R., is our challenge.

The land faces a completely different fire regime—controlled now, frequently burned then. Acid rain exists in the park: impacts unknown. With big predators extinct, herds must be managed in careful balance with their food plants. Meanwhile, in 1983, 1,000 producing oil and gas wells existed within the two counties encompassing the park. A proposed half-dozen energy-producing and -processing plants lie within the regional airshed. Air quality has become the park's most pressing problem.

What will we do about such threats? Roosevelt gave us our guideline: "Wild beasts and birds are by right not the property merely of the people alive to-day, but the property of the unborn generations, whose belongings we have no right to squander. . . . "

SITES, TRAILS, AND TRIPS

Most people do not picture North Dakota as the Old West. But it was the site of more crucial events in frontier history than were many "western" places. And the badlands have ruggedness and wildness aplenty. For Theodore Roosevelt, this land *was* the West.

The park protects three areas in T.R.'s badlands. The South Unit adjoins the historic town of Medora. The North Unit was the terminus for the Long-X cattle trail. Isolated Elkhorn Ranch was T.R.'s home.

The South Unit

Most park visitors see the 72-square-mile South Unit first, for it adjoins Interstate 94, a major route across the United States. From the west, Theodore Roosevelt National Park protects the last rugged country before the smooth descent across the Great Plains to the Missouri River—and the Midwest. From the east, the Little Missouri badlands foreshadow, in a small way, the wild terrain further west.

Painted Canyon Overlook. A fine view over the badlands opens out from Interstate 94 just 7 miles east of Medora. Watch for wild horses on the plateau just to the east. From the overlook, colors of scoria,

Wild horses in the South Unit are descended from horses that escaped from nearby ranches.

Trails of Theodore Roosevelt National Park

North Unit

Squaw Creek Nature Trail: Starts and ends at the Squaw Creek Group Campground; .5 mile round trip; .5 hour; interprets river woodlands, plants and plant uses, and badlands geology.

Caprock Coulee Nature Trail: Starts and ends 1.5 miles west of the Squaw Creek Campground; 1.75 miles round trip; 1.5 hours; leads through dry water gulches, juniper-covered slopes, and breaks in the grassy plains.

Upper Caprock Coulee Trail: Starts where the Caprock Coulee Nature Trail stops, and ends at the Caprock Coulee trail head parking lot; 4 miles round trip; 3 hours; leads to overlook shelter

Buckhorn Trail: Starts and ends at the Cannonball Concretions Wayside pullout; 11.3 mile round trip; 8 hours; leads through plateaus, creek valleys, sage flats, and two prairie dog towns; virtually impossible when muddy.

Achenbach Trail: Starts and ends at Squaw Creek Campground; 19.5 miles round trip; 2.5 to 3 days; leads twice across the river (no bridges), through grass uplands, river bottom, and ash and aspen forests; virtually impossible when wet.

South Unit

Ridgeline Nature Trail: Starts and ends at trail head on Scenic Loop Drive; .6 mile round trip; .75 hour; a brief look at the ridges and valleys of the North Dakota badlands.

Petrified Forest Loop Trail: Starts and ends at Peaceful Valley Horse Ranch; 16 miles loop; 18 hours; wilderness trail through one of the three most significant petrified forests in the United States; 2–3 day hike across vast plateaus and broken badlands topography.

Jones/Paddock Creeks Loop Trail: Starts and ends at Jones Creek trail head (west) or Halliday Wells Group Camp or Paddock Creek Trail/Loop Road junction; 14 miles loop; 15 hours; a 2-day look at one of the roughest areas in the park.

Lone Tree Spring Loop Trail: Starts and ends at either Peaceful Valley Horse Ranch or Cottonwood Campground; 10.2 miles round trip; 12 hours; an overnight hike across a plateau and along Knutson Creek.

Paddock Creek Trail: Starts at Halliday Wells Group Camp, and ends at Southeast Corner Spring; 10.8 miles one way; 13 hours; a scenic trail traversing the Painted Canyon, one of the most spectacular sights in the park.

Talkington Trail: Starts at east end of Jones Creek trail head, and ends at east boundary fence; 10.1 miles one way; 12 hours; a 2-day hike along an abandoned trail, which once served early ranches and homesteads.

Opposite: The erosion of clay sediments has exposed the petrified stump of a tree.

clay, juniper, and grass paint the land. Perched on the rim of upland prairie, Roosevelt's grassland "stretches out in the sunlight like a sea." Below, "the Bad Lands seem to be stranger and wilder than ever."

Medora and the Maltese Cross Cabin. Park headquarters lies in the little village of Medora. The Marquis de Mores's twenty-six-room château (open for tours) presides over the town from its bluff above the river. The brick chimney of his ruined meat-packing plant—remnant of a broken dream—is Medora's single skyscraper.

The Maltese Cross cabin—once headquarters for T.R.'s ranching operations—has been moved from its original site, 7 miles south of Medora, to the Visitor Center grounds. Named for the brand of the cattle operation in which Roosevelt bought an interest on his first trip to Dakota Territory, this cabin was his home in 1884/85.

The cabin has been restored, with a new roof and historically accurate furnishings, many of which were used by T.R. It is easy to picture Roosevelt here, living a dual life unique in the badlands. He rode as hard as anyone on round-ups and hunting trips. But on his return to the cabin, he read works ranging from Greek histories to Uncle Remus and penned letters back East or a new chapter of a book.

Along the River. A paved road loops through the park for about 36 miles. After leaving the Visitor Center and crossing over Interstate 94, the road soon reaches the Little Missouri River and follows its east bank for about 6 miles.

Huge cottonwoods and ash shade bottom lands and shelter white-tailed deer. Here lie Cottonwood Campground and Peaceful Valley Ranch, the latter dating to 1885 and now offering guided horseback rides. Watch for the buoyant flight of marsh hawks, lignite beds in the bluffs, bison crossing the river, and bighorn escaping into the badlands.

One-half mile south of Wind Canyon, the river road passes a fine display of pedestal rocks—pillars of sediment temporarily prevented from crumbling by caps of tougher sandstone. In the barren "gumbo clay" grow delicate evening primrose: "gumbo lilies."

At Wind Canyon itself, the loop road turns east along the north park boundary. Here, a short trail leads past a classic view of the river and into a small side canyon aligned with the dominant northwesterly winds. With the double action of water and wind to whisk away loose silt and sand, the canyon erodes very quickly.

East of the River. Four westward-flowing creeks have carved the scoria-streaked badlands to the east of the river. Interstate 94 follows the

Roosevelt used the Maltese Cross Cabin, named for his cattle-brand design, in the 1880s.

valley of Sheep Creek, the southernmost. The park loop road follows Jules Creek, the northernmost. In between lie Jones Creek and Paddock Creek, both with trails in their valleys.

The 10.8-mile *Paddock Creek Trail* and the 3.7-mile *Jones Creek Trail* bisect the loop road; both follow creek bottoms through rough-and-tumble badlands. The *Talkington Trail* runs 10.1 miles from the park's southeast corner through open country in the headwaters of Paddock Creek, to cross the divide into Jones Creek. Additional short connecting segments make loops possible. Horses can travel all trails.

Along the road are short walks at *Ridgeline Nature Trail* (.6 mile in high badlands) and at *Coal Vein* (a lignite vein that burned from 1951 to 1977, causing the surface above to subside). Buck Hill, at 2,855 feet, offers a 360° view over land that truly feels like Roosevelt's badland "chaos." Boicourt and Badlands overlooks and Scoria Point also have wide views.

West of the River. The west bank of the Little Missouri is the South Unit's wilderness. Lush with grass, two relict upland surfaces, Petrified Forest Plateau and Big Plateau, dominate the area. The density of fossil logs on the eroded flanks of the former gives it its name. These logs lack the bright colors of those at Arizona's Petrified Forest National Park, but many stumps here have fossilized upright.

Overleaf: The Little Missouri River in the North Unit, most of which is wilderness.

Mule deer are ubiquitous throughout the western parks, including Roosevelt.

Two trails leave Peaceful Valley, ford the river, and pass through the Petrified Forest. The *Petrified Forest Loop Trail* runs for 16 miles round trip. A 10-mile alternative that overlaps part of the longer trail reaches *Lone Tree Spring* and returns down Knutson Creek. The Petrified Forest also can be reached from back roads that end at the west edge of the park. These isolated ranch routes still make adventurous traveling where energy exploration has not improved and civilized them.

Elkhorn Ranch

Theodore Roosevelt first went to the badlands in the fall of 1883. Before he left, he handed local cattlemen Sylvane Ferris and Bill Merrifield a check for $14,000 to purchase cows to run for him on the Maltese Cross Ranch. When T.R.'s mother and first wife died within twenty-four hours of each other a few months later, he was twenty-five years old. His grief sent him west with plans to make ranching his primary occupation.

In the summer of 1884, he bought the rights to a second ranch, about 25 miles north of Medora, and convinced two old friends—Bill Sewall and Will Dow, woodsmen from Maine—to go west and manage it for him. Roosevelt named it the Elkhorn, and a year later it was completed. He always called it his "home ranch," a personal retreat, while the Maltese Cross Ranch remained the center of cattle operations.

T.R.'s ranching operations peaked in 1885 and 1886. But the severity of the next winter changed everything: Roosevelt lost 60 percent of his cattle, and beginning in 1887, Medora went into decline. Once again married and passionately involved in family and politics, Roosevelt gradually withdrew from ranching. The Elkhorn Ranch was abandoned between 1890 and 1893. T.R. sold out for good in 1898.

It took only ten years of disuse for the Elkhorn's buildings to disappear. Recent excavations have yielded bits and pieces of its former vitality: cans of Maine oysters, wine bottles, and "Dr. Pierce's Favorite Prescription." But no reconstruction took place.

A visit to the Elkhorn site requires driving on dirt roads for 20 miles north from the South Unit, a river ford, and careful searching for markers showing where the house stood. For a sense of Theodore Roosevelt the ranchman, no place surpasses it.

Near the end of his life, T.R. said: "Do you know what chapter . . . in all my life I would choose to remember? . . . the ranch with its experience close to Nature and among the men who lived nearest her."

The North Unit

Smaller than the South Unit, and more distantly connected with Theodore Roosevelt, the 38-square-mile North Unit may be the scenic climax of the park. It certainly is the wilderness climax, for fewer people visit it, yet the North Unit contains most of the park's designated wilderness. With the extra 45 miles north, spring comes later by a few days. Summer days are long—up to eighteen hours of daylight—and winter days are short.

North of the River. The 13-mile paved park road dead-ends at Oxbow Overlook, one of the finest views over the Little Missouri Valley. Here the river makes a great eastward bend where it changed course in the ice age to carve through the North Unit. At Sperati Point, 1 mile by trail from Oxbow parking area, the Little Missouri passes through the narrowest gateway in the badlands.

In this steep, new canyon—with greater elevational relief than the South Unit—a remarkable complex of landslides and slump blocks has developed. A sign marks one of the most dramatic, 3 miles from the park entrance. Less lignite makes less scoria to cap hills. With more bentonite—incredibly slippery when wet—the land here literally flows.

The park herd of longhorn steers often grazes sagebrush flats in the first few miles of the drive. These steers commemorate the Long-X Trail, up which many thousands of longhorns were driven from Texas, ending their long trip at the Long-X Ranch just north of the park. Along the rest of the drive, watch for bison.

The 11.3-mile *Buckhorn Trail*, rich in variety, circles the first few miles of the park road. It climbs high above the badlands onto smooth prairie on the uneroded plateau. The western leg follows Squaw Creek down the old Long-X Trail, then returns eastward along the river bottom.

In its 4 miles, *Upper Caprock Coulee Trail* rises to uplands and bentonite breaks surrounding Cedar Canyon. Unfamiliar names? Cedars really are junipers. A coulee is a dry canyon—the same thing as a gully, or an arroyo in the Southwest. Caprocks crown mushroom-shaped pillars of soft clay, protecting them from collapse for a time.

South of the River. With extensive views, upland prairie, lively badlands, a spring, and two river crossings, the *Achenbach Trail* offers as much variety as any trail in the park. This walk leads about 9.6 miles from Squaw Creek to where it rejoins the rim at Sperati Point. Another mile's walk and you reach Oxbow parking area. Ranch roads provide access to the trail at the southeastern park boundary. In the Achenbach Hills grows the park's greatest concentration of aspen.

The Little Missouri River

The "Little Mo" flows through the South Unit for 9 miles and through the North Unit for 14 miles. For a unique view of the badlands, canoe either stretch. Or spend at least three days running the 120 river miles between the two units. The gradient is tiny: the river enters the South Unit at 2,266 feet and leaves the North Unit at 1,958 feet.

Take care to pick the right season. Canoeing usually is possible between mid-April and mid-July; but flow can vary wildly, from a near trickle to 65,000 cubic feet per second. The frozen winter river channel has been designated a snowmobile trail.

In March, the ice begins to break up. This was the season of Roosevelt's famous boat chase. One March day in 1886, T.R. found his boat missing from the Elkhorn. Sewall and Dow built a new boat for the pursuit, and Deputy Sheriff Roosevelt and his two companions caught up with the three thieves almost 100 miles downstream, 12 miles past today's North Unit.

Roosevelt marched the culprits—"Redhead" Finnegan and his two sidekicks—45 miles at gunpoint. He finally delivered them to jail in Dickinson. In the process, he blistered his feet, finished a volume of poems by Matthew Arnold as well as *Anna Karenina*, and took delight both in justice done and in thinking what a good story it would make.

He was right about the story.

Opposite: Haze at sunrise softens the colors of Painted Canyon in the South Unit.

WIND CAVE NATIONAL PARK

About 38 miles of passageways have been explored in one of the world's longest caves.

WIND CAVE NATIONAL PARK
HOT SPRINGS, SOUTH DAKOTA 57747
TEL.: (605) 745-4600

Highlights: The Temple □ The Elk's Room □ Pearly Gates □ Garden of Eden □ Black Hills □ Rankin Ridge □ Bison Herd □ Prairie Dog Town □ Pronghorn Bands

Access: From Hot Springs, take hwy. 385 north 11 miles. From Custer, take hwy. 385 south 23 miles.

Hours: All year, 24 hours daily. Cave closed Thanksgiving, Christmas, and New Year's Day.

Fees: Entrance, none; Camping, $6/unit.

Gas, food, lodging: Food service available during summer. Full service at Hot Springs and Custer.

Parking: Enough for 100 cars and 50 campers.

Visitor Center: In Headquarters area. Sales area for publications.

Museum: At Visitor Center.

Gift shop: Open during summer at Visitor Center.

Pets: Permitted on leashes, except in backcountry, on trails, in public buildings, or in cave.

Picnicking: Just north of Headquarters area.

Hiking: Throughout park. Carry water. Beware of bison.

Backpacking: Permitted with permit. Carry water. No open fires.

Campgrounds: 100-unit area; fires only in pits; no showers. Trailers, 80 sites at Elk Mountain; no ice, electricity, or gas.

Tours: Cave tours in English.

Other activities: Various interpretive activities available.

Facilities for disabled: Cave not accessible, Visitor Center has elevator.

For additional information, see also Sites, Trails, and Trips on pages 198–199 and the map on pages 182–183.

MOTORISTS ON U.S. HIGHWAY 385, WHICH WINDS among grassy hills dotted with buffalo and pronghorn in southwestern South Dakota, might never guess what geological marvel lies within a short distance. From the road one can see the eastern flank of the Black Hills, once the target of a gold rush, where gold is now mined from the pockets of tourists. Out of sight, just east of the highway, Wind Cave, one of the largest caverns in the world, snakes through limestone beds formed millions of years ago after great numbers of tiny creatures died and drifted to the bottom of an inland sea. The Dakota, or Sioux, believed the Black Hills to be sacred. According to one of their legends Wakan Tanka, the Great Spirit, sent the buffalo out from the center of the earth through the mouth of the cave to darken the northern Great Plains. For white people, the cave has been a place of mystery and, for some, a place to exploit. For several years late in the nineteenth century, men competed for the right to lead visitors inside the cave and to extract its minerals. Fortunately, before much irreparable damage was done, the federal government protected the premises, creating a national park. Today, everyone can enjoy Wind Cave.

A prairie of long- and short-stemmed grasses at sunset.

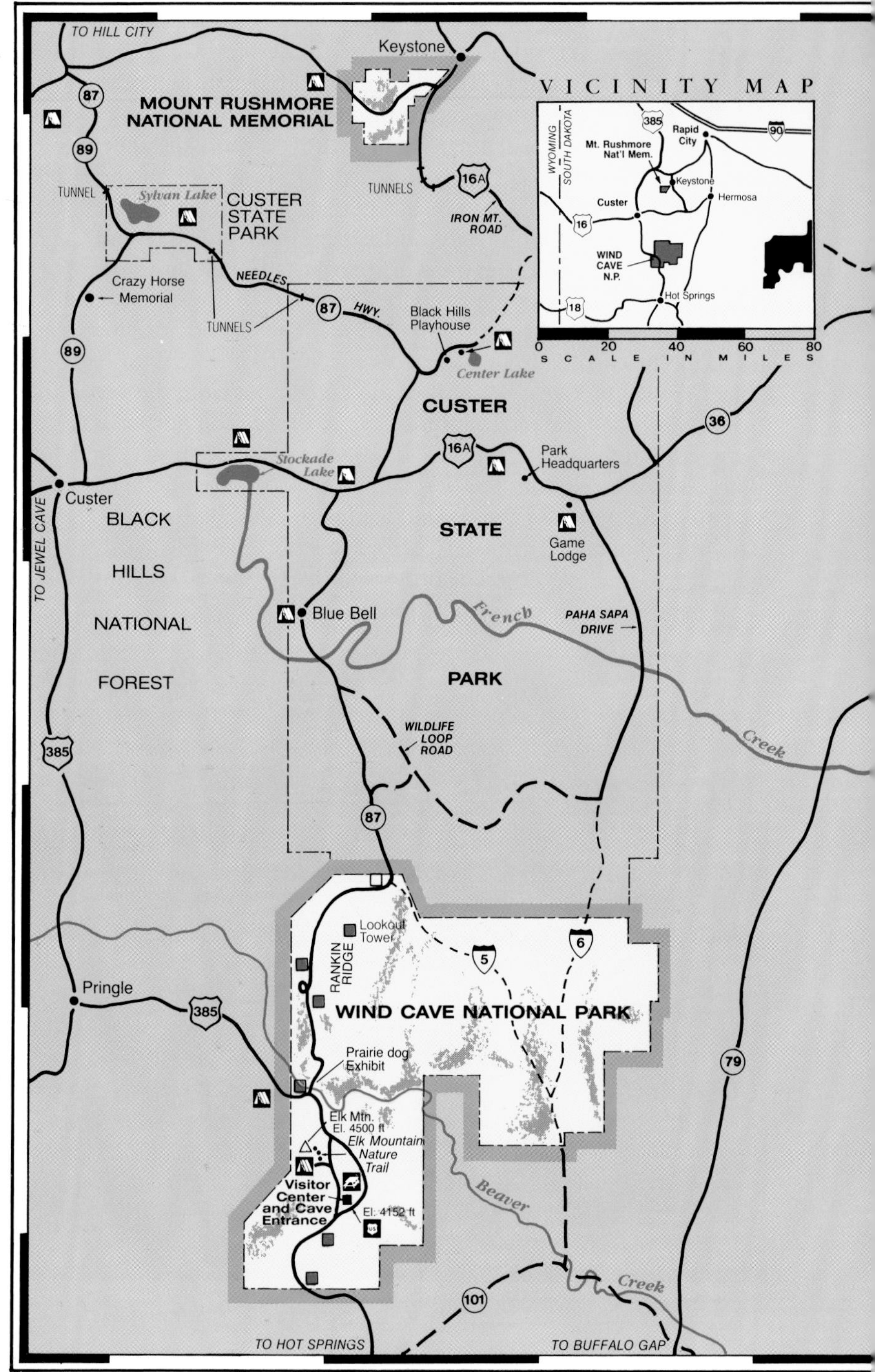
TO HILL CITY
Keystone
MOUNT RUSHMORE
NATIONAL MEMORIAL
VICINITY MAP
WYOMING
SOUTH DAKOTA
Rapid City
Mt. Rushmore Nat'l Mem.
Keystone
Hermosa
Custer
WIND CAVE N.P.
Hot Springs
0 20 40 60 80
SCALE IN MILES
TUNNEL
Sylvan Lake
CUSTER STATE PARK
TUNNELS
IRON MT. ROAD
NEEDLES
HWY.
Crazy Horse Memorial
TUNNELS
Black Hills Playhouse
Center Lake
CUSTER
Stockade Lake
Park Headquarters
Custer
TO JEWEL CAVE
BLACK HILLS NATIONAL FOREST
STATE
Game Lodge
Blue Bell
French
PAHA SAPA DRIVE
PARK
Creek
WILDLIFE LOOP ROAD
Lookout Tower
RANKIN RIDGE
Pringle
WIND CAVE NATIONAL PARK
Prairie dog Exhibit
Elk Mtn. El. 4500 ft
Elk Mountain Nature Trail
Visitor Center and Cave Entrance
El. 4152 ft
Beaver
Creek
TO HOT SPRINGS
TO BUFFALO GAP

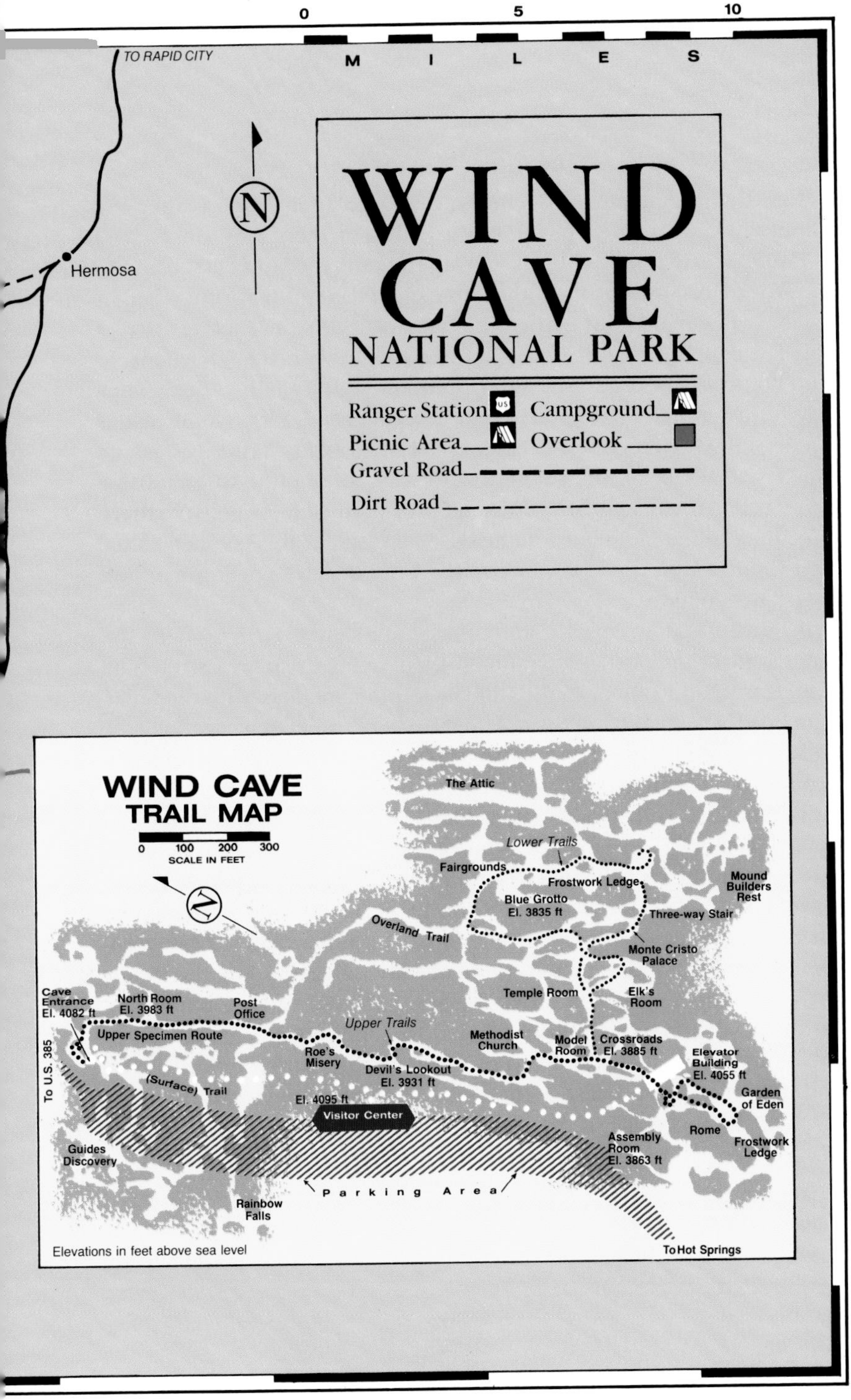

0 5 10
MILES

TO RAPID CITY

Hermosa

N

WIND CAVE NATIONAL PARK

Ranger Station
Campground
Picnic Area
Overlook
Gravel Road
Dirt Road

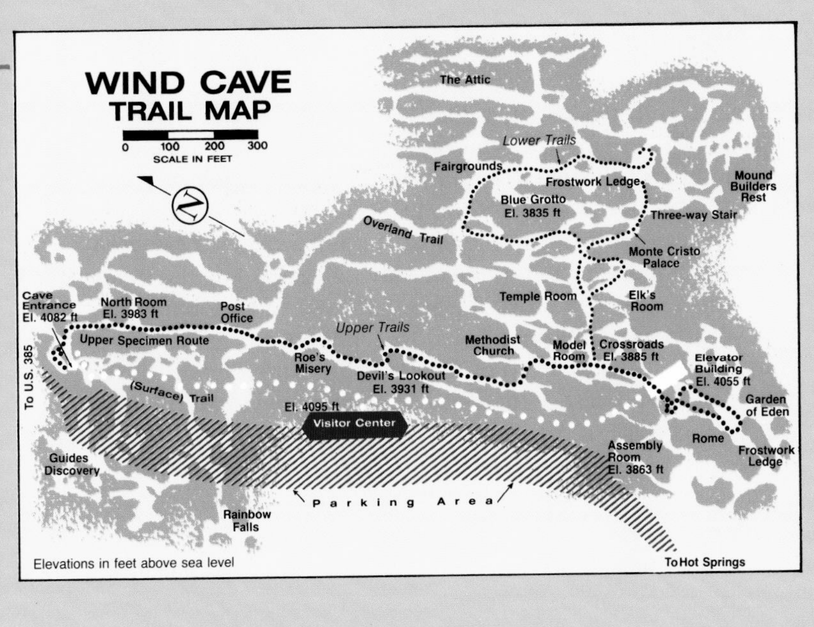

The Sioux Paha Sapa

Before the mid-nineteenth century, the Dakota, or Sioux as they are popularly known, lived in the Black Hills. For them it is a holy land —*Paha Sapa*, or "hills of black." From the time the Sioux first came to the Black Hills—probably in the late eighteenth century—they fought valiantly to defend it. At Battle Mountain, near the present-day town of Hot Springs, they clashed in a fierce struggle with the Cheyenne to gain control over the warm water bubbling to the surface there. They fought just as fiercely against the new settlers and, for a while, just as successfully. When gold was discovered in Montana in the 1860s, the Sioux waged war on the soldiers who were attempting to establish a route called the Bozeman Trail from Fort Laramie up through northern Wyoming to the Montana gold fields. As a result of this conflict, called Red Cloud's War, the Sioux forced the United States government into treaty negotiations.

In April 1868 at Fort Laramie, the Sioux signed a treaty with the federal government that guaranteed their rights to an area stretching from the Missouri River to the Bighorn Mountains, and from the Canadian border to the Platte River. At the heart of this area were the Black Hills, declared by the treaty to be "unceded Indian territory" and forbidden to settlement. Unfortunately for the Sioux, however, the Black Hills contained gold; this greatly valued resource was discovered by an aide to General George Custer during the latter's military reconnaissance of the Black Hills in 1874. The word spread, triggering a gold rush in 1875, a direct violation of the 1868 treaty. The U.S. Army was unable to prevent the rush into the hills. The Sioux rejected a government offer of $6 million for settlement rights. Disregarding the treaty, the government sought to move the Sioux to reservations, but Sitting Bull's refusal to comply ultimately led to a military campaign against the Sioux, the defeat and death of Custer at the Little Bighorn River, and the subsequent defeat of the Sioux. Redrafting the treaty, the government took control of the Black Hills from the Sioux.

The Fight Over Wind Cave

The credit for the discovery of Wind Cave is given to two brothers, Jesse and Tom Bingham. According to their story, Tom was pursuing a

Opposite, top: In the 1890s, a log house was built over the cave entrance. Bottom: Future presidential nominee William J. Bryan (front, with child) joined an 1892 cave tour.

wounded buck up a ravine one day in 1881 when he heard a loud whistling noise. Getting down from his horse, he discovered a hole in the rocks. When he leaned over to inspect it, the wind issuing forth struck him with such force that it knocked off his hat.

Within the next few years the Binghams and others explored the cave for short distances. In 1889, the South Dakota Mining Company filed a mining location-certificate and hired Jesse McDonald to manage the property. McDonald and his two sons, Elmer and Alvin, guided only by candles and balls of twine, began the first serious exploration of the cave. In January 1891, Alvin started to keep a log of his trips into Wind Cave. He developed a consuming interest in the cave, and named many of the passageways and rooms that he discovered. Once, when forced by illness to stay out of the cave for a few days, Alvin wrote in his diary, "Am getting homesick after staying out of the cave so long." Stricken by typhoid fever and pneumonia, Alvin died in 1893 at the age of 20. A bronze plaque marks the site of his grave on a hill near the cave entrance.

John Stabler settled in Hot Springs in 1891 to manage the Hotel Parrott. He was attracted by the commercial possibilities of the cave. Jesse McDonald, who had little money, offered Stabler half interest in the cave. The men filed claims, began joint management of the property, and conducted tours for visitors who arrived from Hot Springs by stagecoach. The McDonald and Stabler families formed the Wonderful Wind Cave Improvement Company in 1892. A log house was constructed over the cave entrance and a two-story hotel was built on a nearby hill. In 1893 the South Dakota Mining Company took legal action, asking for back rents and profits. The legal snarl became more complex when growing differences between Stabler and McDonald led to a court fight between them for full control of the cave. The General Land Office in Rapid City, South Dakota, declared in 1898 that neither party had a valid claim.

Establishment of the Park

The U.S. government directed its attention to the cave in 1900 when the General Land Office ruling was appealed to the Department of the Interior. The decision to create a national park was based on data provided by scientists from the South Dakota School of Mines. After another report established that there were no legitimate mining claims, the Department of the Interior recommended that the cave and lands above it be protected by the federal government. A bill to create a national park was approved by both houses of Congress in 1902 and signed into law by President Theodore Roosevelt on January 9, 1903.

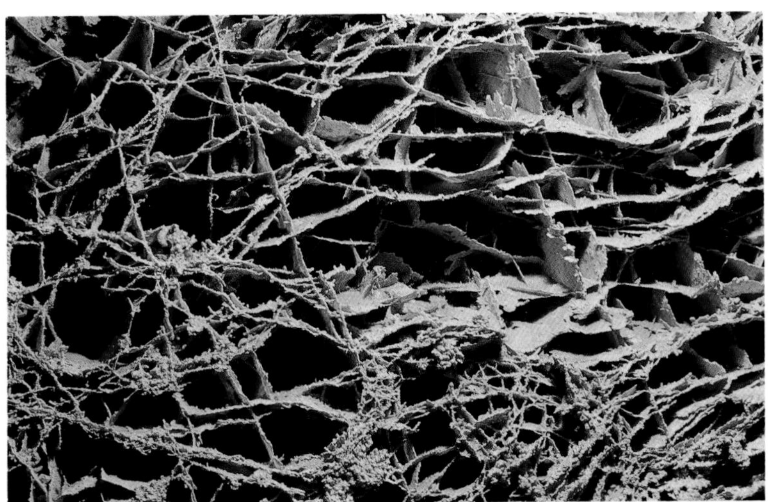

The intricate boxwork formation was created when calcite filled cracks in limestone and then remained after the limestone dissolved.

G E O L O G Y

Wind Cave is one of the longest and most complex caves in the world. Although more than 38 miles of passageways to depths of 613 feet have been explored, many areas remain unexplored. Unlike most limestone caves, which have been formed at much shallower depths, Wind Cave was formed hundreds of feet below the surface. Its decorations include much more than stalactites and stalagmites. It is also one of the oldest caves in North America, dating back millions of years. The name of the cave derives from the strong currents of air that blow alternately in and out of the cave. When the atmospheric pressure outside the cave drops below that of the cave's interior, wind blows outward. When outside pressure rises, wind blows into the cave.

Jewel Cave, a national monument, 21 miles northwest of Wind Cave, is still being explored. It is already one of the longest caves in the world, with more than 70 miles of passageways.

Pahasapa Limestone

During the middle of the Mississippian period, roughly 340 to 330 million years ago, a shallow, continental sea covered South Dakota. North America was then located at the earth's equator, and the climate throughout most of the continent was tropical. Near the close of the Mississippian period, the sea level dropped, and the accumulation of Pahasapa deposits ceased. The layer of sediment, in which all Black Hills caves were subsequently formed, attained a thickness of between 300 and 600 feet. Another sea inundated the region at the start of the Pennsylvanian period, about 320 million years ago. These deposits formed a layer several hundred feet thick on top of the Pahasapa.

Uplift of the Black Hills

Some 70 million years ago, during the late Cretaceous period, the Rocky Mountains and the Black Hills began to be uplifted as a result of the westward drift of the North American continent, which, as it pushed against parts of the earth's hard outer crust, became subject to buckling and wrinkling. The sedimentary layers that had been deposited millions of years earlier were thrust upward by metamorphic action into a huge, flattened dome. Erosion subsequently removed several of these domed layers; the remnants of their edges now form the ridges, or "hogbacks," that encircle the Black Hills. Today, the center of the Black Hills is composed of the granite remains of the metamorphic action. The lower slopes, where Wind Cave is located, are made up largely of limestone layers, warped and buckled by the violent uplift. Over the millennia, both the core and the surrounding slopes have been worn down by erosion.

Cave Formation

The labyrinthine network of passages that composes Wind Cave was tunneled out of the Pahasapa Limestone some 30 to 50 million years ago. As the layer uplifted to form the Black Hills, a network of cracks was created. Acidic ground water percolated down through the cracks. Over thousands of years, this water dissolved numerous passageways through the rock. The cave finally drained when streams on the surface cut their beds below the water table. Today, little water passes through Wind Cave.

Cave Decoration: Popcorn, Frostwork, and Boxwork

Wind Cave has few stalactites and stalagmites, which makes it different from most caves. Instead of emerging through wide openings and eventually depositing its minerals in thick columns, surface water seeps through cracks and pores in the Pahasapa limestone, appearing as a thin film and as tiny droplets on the walls and ceilings and floors. Once it mixes with the air, the water deposits minerals instead of dissolving them, thus forming the unusual encrustations that decorate Wind Cave.

Two prominent formations are popcorn and frostwork. Popcorn is a knobby growth that resembles coral. Frostwork, crystals of calcite

Popcorn is one unusual formation resulting from the seepage of mineral-laden water.

and aragonite, varies in size and appearance, from small, hair-like strands to large, snowball-like formations.

No other cave in the world possesses as much boxwork as Wind Cave. Boxwork is the result of both weathering and water seepage. Before the cave was hollowed out, cracks in the limestone were filled with percolating water from the surface. As it seeped down through the ground, the water absorbed carbon dioxide from decaying vegetation, thus forming carbonic acid, which is capable of dissolving limestone. Saturated with dissolved limestone, the ground water leaked into the cracks and fissures, where it crystallized into calcite. As the calcite accumulated in the interlacing cracks, the limestone separating the calcite dissolved, forming the cave and leaving only the calcite "fins" standing out in delicate relief. These fins, intersecting one another at right angles, form openings that resemble post-office boxes or honeycombs.

Boxwork is common in such chambers as the Post Office, the Temple, the Elk's Room, and the Pearly Gates—all of which are open for tours by the public.

Aboveground, the 28,056 acres of Wind Cave National Park combine elements of three ecosystems. Creeping down from the higher elevations of the Black Hills are dense forests, composed primarily of ponderosa pine. On the margins of these forests, clustered along creeks that wind out into the prairie, are woodland ravines that feature a mixture of eastern and western vegetation and animals. Beyond the ravines, reaching all the way to the gaps in the ridge that circles the Black Hills, are the grasslands, the most extensive surface ecosystems in the park.

Grasslands

With an annual precipitation level of 16 inches, Wind Cave is predominantly a prairie park. The grasses are of a mixed variety, featuring both short- and long-stemmed species. The most abundant grasses include blue grama, western wheatgrass, and little bluestem. These grasses produce extensive root systems that enable them to withstand icy winters and parching summers. So dense are the root systems that 1 square yard of prairie soil 4 inches deep may contain up to 20 miles of grass roots!

Many wildflowers dot the prairie in the spring and summer. The more prominent examples include the mariposa lily, prairie coneflower, pasqueflower, and star lily. To withstand the rigors of freezing weather, the early spring bloomers tend to grow close to the ground and send out disproportionately large flowers.

Forests and Ravines

At the point where the woodland ravines extend onto the prairie, a silent struggle is taking place between the trees and the grasses. Each invades the other's domain: tawny grasses surround and isolate individual trees; trees march out like soldiers from the edge of the forest to encroach upon the grasslands. Actually, in the last 100 years, the forest has been slowly winning the battle. Since the Black Hills were first settled by white people, the number of forest fires—the grasslands' greatest protector—has diminished considerably. As a result, the forested area has enlarged by one-third.

Wind Cave National Park is a meeting ground for a diverse collection of eastern and western life forms. In the woody groves along the creeks can be found the bur oak and the American elm, as well as the

Opposite: Beaver Creek flows through a wooded area near the Black Hills.

Badgers may be seen on the open prairie or in shallow water on hot days.

eastern phoebe and the eastern bluebird—flora and fauna more commonly situated in the forests to the east of the hundredth meridian. Higher up, on the rocky slopes of the foothills, are found the ponderosa pine and the Rocky Mountain juniper. Because of the dry climate, neither tree achieves maximum growth; despite this, both have achieved a tenacious hold on the landscape.

Larger Animals

With few places to hide, the larger animals of Wind Cave National Park have to rely on speed. The graceful pronghorn is one of the fastest creatures on earth. Gifted with long, muscular legs, a large heart, and phenomenal eyesight, it moves effortlessly across the prairie in small herds.

In 1900, there were fewer than 1,000 buffalo left on the continent, a pitiful remnant of what once had been a concentration of more than 60 million. One column observed in 1839 covered 1,350 square miles —an area larger than the state of Rhode Island! Today, a herd of 350 lives at Wind Cave National Park. Although buffalo are fascinating to watch, visitors should observe them from a distance. Early plainsmen regarded buffalo as more dangerous than grizzly bears. They can run very fast, and are unpredictable.

The best time for observing the American elk is early morning or late evening. Shy creatures, they prefer to stay back in the trees during the day. September and October is their rutting season, at which time the bull elk makes his distinctive bugling call. Wind Cave National Park supports a herd of approximately 350 American elk. Mule deer are also common in the park, as is the coyote.

Smaller Animals and Birds

In the woods, the prickly porcupine trundles slowly between the trees. The badger, despite its short legs and chunky body, successfully hunts a variety of small mammals. Quite fierce, the badger, when cornered, bares its teeth and digs furiously into the ground with its sharp claws.

Cottontails are plentiful, along with ground squirrels and chipmunks. The most likeable rodent in the park is the black-tailed prairie dog. Highly social animals, prairie dogs live in complex "towns" that are easily observed from the roadside. Their value to the ecosystem of the Great Plains is enormous. The buffalo once roamed the plains in such immense herds that millions of trampling hooves compacted the soil into a dense mass, threatening to shut off the vital flow of moisture and air to the roots of grasses and plants. Burrowing animals like the prairie dog helped to keep the soil open and fresh, thus aiding significantly in the yearly renewal of forbs and grasses. It has been estimated that the activity of these rodents was equivalent to a deep plowing of the prairie every twenty years.

Two of the most frequently seen birds are the black-billed magpie and western meadowlark. Some of the larger birds, occasionally observed in the summer, are the golden eagle, Swainson's hawk, crow, and turkey vulture. In the forested sections of the park dwell the hairy woodpecker, western tanager, and horned owl.

The long, loud trill of the red squirrel is often heard in the wooded areas of the park.

Above: Sharp eyes are an asset to the turkey vulture in its search for carrion. Opposite: A red-headed woodpecker perches on a branch to watch for flying insects.

SITES, TRAILS, AND TRIPS

The main routes through Wind Cave National Park are South Dakota 87 and U.S. 385. South Dakota 87 enters the park from Custer State Park to the north. Halfway through, near the Visitor Center, it joins U.S. 385, which continues south for another 4 miles to the park boundary. A few miles beyond is the town of Hot Springs.

Surface Trails

Off-trail hiking is permitted and encouraged at Wind Cave National Park; visitors are free to go anywhere they please. There are a couple of things to remember, however. Try to avoid walking through prairie-dog towns; feet trample the grass, the animals' main source of food. Also, please refrain from feeding the prairie dogs; their digestive systems are not used to human food, and they can become very sick.

Watch out for buffalo. Observe them at a safe distance of at least 100 yards. When a buffalo looks at you and raises its tail, it may be time to look for a tree to climb or for some other avenue of escape.

There are two designated aboveground trails in the park.

Elk Mountain Nature Trail. Elk Mountain Nature Trail is located .5 mile north of the Visitor Center. The trail, a 1-mile loop around the west end of Elk Mountain Campground, swings out across sloping prairie before slipping into ponderosa pine forest. It is an excellent way to experience both the grassland and the forest ecosystems that are found in the park.

Rankin Ridge Trail. Rankin Ridge Trail is located near the park's northern boundary. A .5-mile spur road leads from South Dakota 87 to a parking area. There is a limited turn-around area, so trailers are not permitted.

The hike itself is moderately strenuous. The 1.25-mile trail ascends through a ponderosa pine forest along the northwest face of Rankin Ridge to the summit. There, at an elevation of 5,013 feet (the highest point in the park), is a lookout tower that is staffed in summer and open to the public. The view from the summit is superb: to the north lies Harney Peak, the tallest peak of the Black Hills; to the east, rolling prairies cascade down the foothills, beyond which lies the expanse of the Great Plains.

Preceding overleaf: A spider web on a damp morning in the prairie grassland.

Cave Trips

Walking tours inside Wind Cave are moderately strenuous, and there are several things to consider before going on one. Sandals or high heels should not be worn; the trail surface may be slippery, and low-heeled walking shoes are preferred. The cave maintains a steady temperature of 53° F year-round, and a light sweater or jacket might be in order. People with heart conditions should think twice or three times before entering; the cave is a totally different environment from the surface, and some people are afflicted by acute claustrophobia. Please remember that there are no restroom facilities inside the cave.

An elevator goes down 220 feet into an area of the cave called the Assembly Room. Disabled visitors who are unable to take the regular walk-in tour may be able to visit this one room if personnel are available to take them into the cave. Inquiries should be made at the Visitor Center information desk.

The exhibit rooms in the Visitor Center are accessible to wheelchairs.

There are four cave trips, all conducted by park rangers. The *Half-Mile Tour* accommodates up to 40 people and takes approximately 1 hour. The *Mile Tour* also accommodates 40 people and takes approximately 2 hours. Both tours are offered from mid-June to mid-August. The passageways are dimly lit, and ascent from one level to another is by means of sturdy steps that sometimes are provided with handrails. Many interesting examples of boxwork are visible along the way.

The *Candlelight Tour* covers approximately 1 mile; some of the tour follows an undeveloped trail. Ten people, carrying candles, are guided through passageways by a park ranger. The aim of the tour is to give the visitor a taste of what it must have been like to explore the cave in the days before electric lights. The tour is offered daily from mid-June to mid-August. Reservations made 1 month in advance are preferred.

For the truly adventurous there is the *Spelunking Tour*. This trip takes approximately 3.5 hours. There are no developed trails and no electric lights. A hard hat and kneepads, furnished by the National Park Service, are required, along with old clothes and sturdy shoes. Ten people make the trip at a time, accompanied by a ranger. No one younger than fourteen years of age is permitted to go. The trip is quite strenuous, and requires a great deal of crawling, some climbing, and much squeezing through small spaces. A sense of adventure is necessary, along with limber appendages and flexible joints.

Overleaf: Rainbow over Bison Flats.

YELLOWSTONE NATIONAL PARK

Old Faithful has never been known to miss its 33-to-120-minute eruption schedule.

YELLOWSTONE NATIONAL PARK
P.O. BOX 168, YELLOWSTONE NATIONAL PARK, WYOMING 82190, TEL.: (307) 344-7381

Highlights: Gallatin Range □ Animal Herds □ Two Ocean Plateau □ Upper Geyser Basin □ Old Faithful □ Fort Yellowstone □ Mammoth Hot Springs □ Norris Geyser Basin □ Yellowstone Lake

Access: From Gardiner or Cooke City, Montana; from Jackson, Wyoming.

Hours: Open to cars from about May 1 to October 31. Also open between mid-December and mid-March for snowmobile traffic; auto traffic from Cooke City, Montana, to North Entrance only throughout year.

Fees: Entrance, $2/car; Camping, up to $6/unit.

Parking: Throughout park; Old Faithful area crowded during summer.

Food, gas, lodging: At Mammoth Hot Springs, Roosevelt Lodge, Old Faithful, Grant Village, Lake, Canyon, and Tower Falls (food only).

Visitor Centers: At Mammoth Hot Springs, Lake, Norris, Old Faithful, Canyon, Fishing Bridge, and Grant Village.

Museum: At Mammoth Hot Springs, Fishing Bridge, Canyon, Grant Village, Norris, and Madison (self-service).

Gift shops: Mammoth Hot Springs, Grant Village, Roosevelt, Old Faithful, Lake, Canyon, and Fishing Bridge.

Pets: Permitted on leashes, except in geyser basins, in backcountry, on trails, or in public buildings.

Picnicking: Along roads throughout park. No open fires.

Hiking: Trails throughout park. Restrictions in some backcountry areas, check at ranger station. Carry water.

Backpacking: In designated backcountry campsites; permit required. Carry or boil water.

Campgrounds: 11 areas; 2 only for RVs, the rest for tents too. Fishing Bridge RV park has hookups. Showers available.

Tours: Ranger- and concessioner-led tours throughout park. In English, other languages sometimes available. Self-guided tours in other languages.

Other activities: Horseback riding, cross-country skiing, and boating and fishing (permits required).

Facilities for disabled: All hotels, eating establishments, and public areas. Some interpretive areas have ramps. Accessibility guidebook available.

For additional information, see also Sites, Trails, and Trips on pages 228–244 and the maps on pages 206–207 and 231.

A bull elk, one of thousands of large animals in this major wildlife sanctuary.

ALTHOUGH IT HAS REVEALED ITS MAJESTY AND DIVERSITY to more than 60 million visitors since it was established in 1872, Yellowstone National Park is still a surprise to many people. They come expecting Old Faithful, a few bears, a little fishing; they find 2,219,823 acres of Rocky Mountain wilderness, most of it pristine. Yellowstone is so rich in biological, geological, and scenic attractions that its most common nickname before 1920 was "Wonderland."

The center of the park, known informally as the Yellowstone Plateau, is rolling and heavily forested; most elevations are between 7,000 and 7,800 feet. The plateau, which occupies the northwestern corner of Wyoming, is surrounded by ranges of the Rockies, mountain walls that thwarted some early explorers and helped to keep the area unknown after the surrounding lowlands had been mapped and settled. To the northwest is the Gallatin Range, with several peaks that rise above 10,000 feet; to the north stretch the broad Absarokas; to the northeast, the Beartooth Plateau, with several peaks higher than any in the park; to the east, the Abasaroka Range forms a natural boundary and drainage divide (the park shares its highest point, Eagle Peak's 11,358 feet, with Shoshone National Forest to the east); to the south, Two Ocean

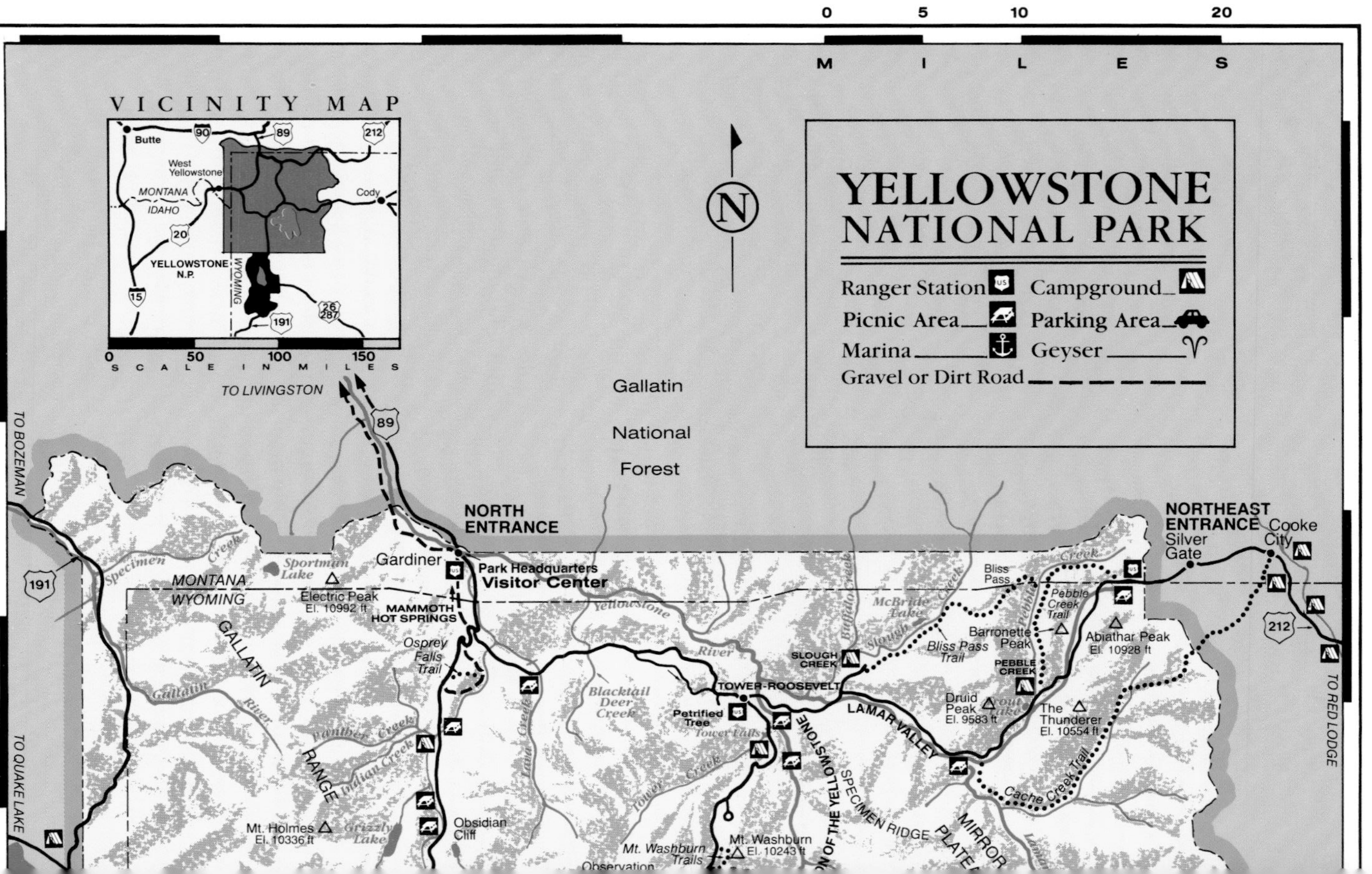
YELLOWSTONE NATIONAL PARK
Ranger Station
Campground
Picnic Area
Parking Area
Marina
Geyser
Gravel or Dirt Road
0 5 10 20
MILES
VICINITY MAP
Butte
West Yellowstone
MONTANA
IDAHO
Cody
YELLOWSTONE N.P.
WYOMING
0 50 100 150
SCALE IN MILES
TO LIVINGSTON
Gallatin National Forest
NORTH ENTRANCE
Gardiner
Park Headquarters
Visitor Center
MAMMOTH HOT SPRINGS
Osprey Falls Trail
Electric Peak El. 10992 ft
Sportman Lake
MONTANA
WYOMING
GALLATIN RANGE
Gallatin River
Panther Creek
Indian Creek
Mt. Holmes El. 10336 ft
Grizzly Lake
Obsidian Cliff
Blacktail Deer Creek
Lava Creek
Yellowstone River
Petrified Tree
TOWER-ROOSEVELT
Tower Falls
Tower Creek
Mt. Washburn El. 10243 ft
Mt. Washburn Trails
Observation
SLOUGH CREEK
Slough Creek
Buffalo Creek
McBride Lake
Bliss Pass
Bliss Pass Trail
Barronette Peak
Pebble Creek Trail
PEBBLE CREEK
Druid Peak El. 9583 ft
Trout Lake
LAMAR VALLEY
The Thunderer El. 10554 ft
Cache Creek Trail
Abiathar Peak El. 10928 ft
NORTHEAST ENTRANCE
Silver Gate
Cooke City
TO RED LODGE
SPECIMEN RIDGE
MIRROR PLATEAU
Specimen Creek
TO BOZEMAN
TO QUAKE LAKE

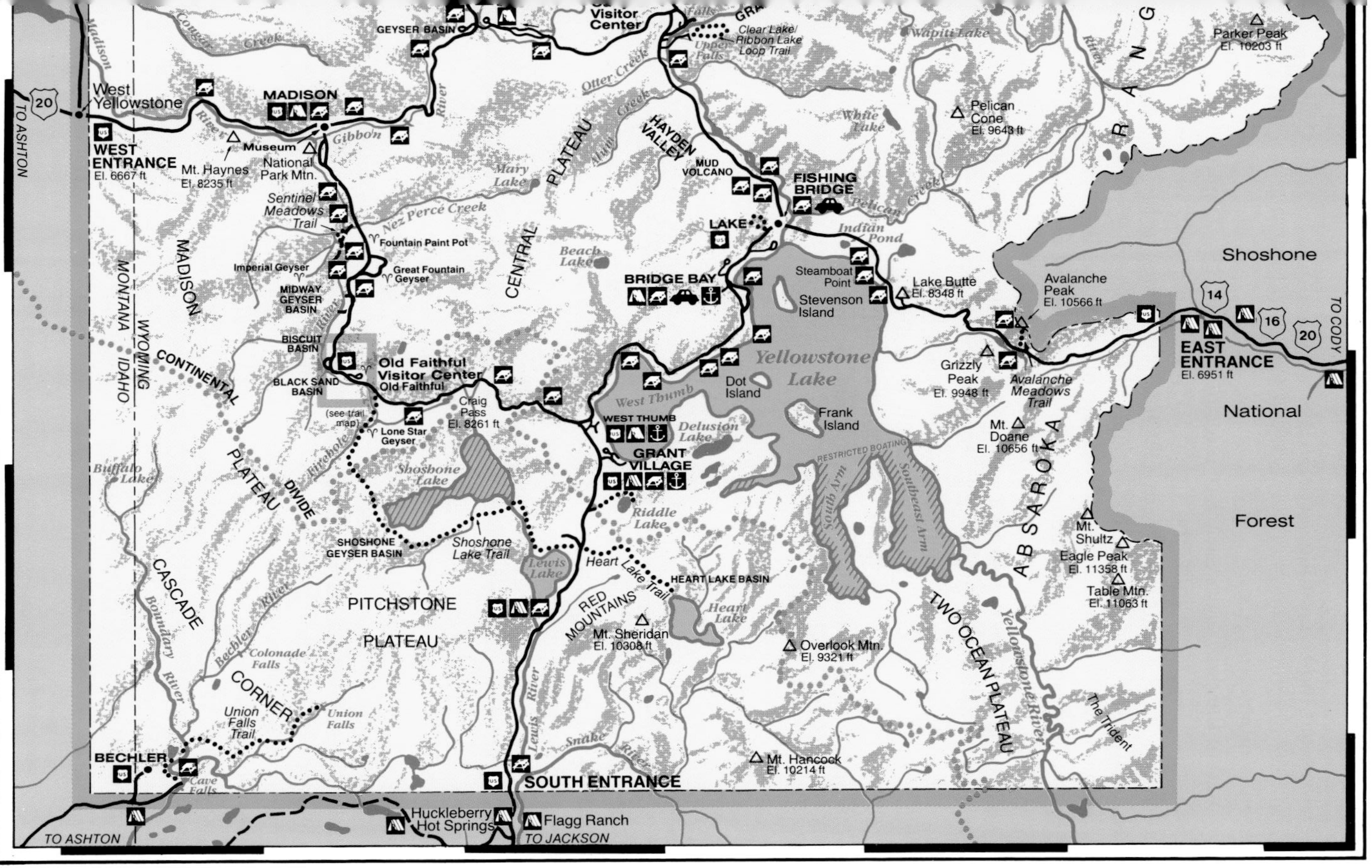
Visitor Center
GEYSER BASIN
Clear Lake/ Ribbon Lake Loop Trail
Upper Falls
Wapiti Lake
Parker Peak
El. 10203 ft
West Yellowstone
MADISON
Otter Creek
Alum Creek
HAYDEN VALLEY
White Lake
Pelican Cone
El. 9643 ft
Gibbon
River
Museum
National Park Mtn.
WEST ENTRANCE
El. 6667 ft
Mt. Haynes
El. 8235 ft
Mary Lake
PLATEAU
MUD VOLCANO
FISHING BRIDGE
Pelican Creek
Sentinel Meadows Trail
Nez Perce Creek
LAKE
Indian Pond
Fountain Paint Pot
Beach Lake
Shoshone
Imperial Geyser
Great Fountain Geyser
CENTRAL
BRIDGE BAY
Steamboat Point
Stevenson Island
Lake Butte
El. 8348 ft
Avalanche Peak
El. 10566 ft
MIDWAY GEYSER BASIN
MONTANA
WYOMING
IDAHO
MADISON
BISCUIT BASIN
EAST ENTRANCE
El. 6951 ft
TO CODY
CONTINENTAL
Old Faithful Visitor Center
Old Faithful
BLACK SAND BASIN
Yellowstone Lake
Dot Island
Grizzly Peak
El. 9948 ft
Avalanche Meadows Trail
West Thumb
(see trail map)
Craig Pass
El. 8261 ft
Lone Star Geyser
WEST THUMB
Delusion Lake
Frank Island
National
Mt. Doane
El. 10656 ft
GRANT VILLAGE
RESTRICTED BOATING
Firehole
Shoshone Lake
Buffalo Lake
PLATEAU
DIVIDE
Riddle Lake
South Arm
Southeast Arm
ABSAROKA
Forest
Mt. Shultz
Eagle Peak
El. 11358 ft
Table Mtn.
El. 11063 ft
SHOSHONE GEYSER BASIN
Shoshone Lake Trail
Lewis Lake
Heart Lake Trail
HEART LAKE BASIN
CASCADE
PITCHSTONE
PLATEAU
RED MOUNTAINS
Mt. Sheridan
El. 10308 ft
Heart Lake
Overlook Mtn.
El. 9321 ft
TWO OCEAN PLATEAU
Yellowstone River
Bechler River
Colonade Falls
Boundary River
CORNER
Union Falls Trail
Union Falls
Lewis River
Snake River
The Trident
Mt. Hancock
El. 10214 ft
BECHLER
Cave Falls
SOUTH ENTRANCE
Huckleberry Hot Springs
Flagg Ranch
TO ASHTON
TO JACKSON

Plateau and Big Game Ridge separate the park from the Jackson Hole country; and to the southwest, the Teton Range and the Madison Plateau complete the ring.

Within the park major points of interest are linked by a figure-eight loop road 142 miles long; the Grand Loop Road is joined to outside highways by five entrance roads that total 100 miles in length. The roads are the primary—and 1,000 miles of trails are the secondary—avenues to an immense dynamic vignette of primitive America that is inhabited by, among other things, 10,000 thermal features; more than 20,000 elk; 2,000 bison, hundreds of bear, deer, bighorn sheep, moose, and pronghorn; a waterfall twice the height of Niagara; several large canyons; a handful of rangers; and thousands of visitors.

Yellowstone is also home to some remarkably complex ideas and ideals that have evolved far more rapidly than the natural setting. It is more than wilderness. Yellowstone is home and birthplace of many of the principles by which the national parks are managed.

H I S T O R Y

The First Visitors

One of the most charming and enduring myths about Yellowstone is that Native Americans avoided the area because its strange thermal features made them think of hell. Popularized by early historians and travel writers, the myth has endured despite its internal contradiction: Native Americans did not learn about hell until they met and were to some degree Christianized by missionaries.

The Yellowstone region has been used steadily by Native Americans since the ice of the most recent period of glaciation left the land more than 8,500 years ago. The climate has undergone several major changes since the glaciers retreated, so Yellowstone's natural bounty has varied, at times providing mammalian riches for hunters, at times only marginal subsistence for gatherers of seeds, berries, insects, and roots. Numerous archeological sites suggest that some seasonal influxes of humans were sizable, and that the migrants came not only for food but also for weapons. Points and other devices made from Yellowstone obsidian (a hard, glasslike volcanic rock) have traveled, as trade items, as far east as Ohio.

By 1800, three tribes were most prominent in the Yellowstone area: Crow, Blackfoot, and Shoshone. All seem to have made some use of the

Opposite: Descriptions of Yellowstone by Ferdinand Hayden and members of his government surveying party of 1871 led to the creation of the first national park.

park area, but the only steady residents were a small group of Tukudikas, whose heritage seems to have been a blend of Shoshone and Bannock. The Tukudikas were known as Sheepeaters, and had no horses and very few European weapons; they were regarded as backward and shy by the first trappers to see them. In the late 1860s and early 1870s, when other tribes in the northern Rockies were being placed on reservations, the Yellowstone Sheepeaters were not recognized as a distinct tribal body and so did not conclude settlement treaties with the federal government. No claim to the Yellowstone area seems to have been made on their behalf, and even before the park was established, in 1872, they moved to a reservation. During the 1870s, a large group of Bannocks occasionally traveled across the northern part of the park to and from hunting grounds to the east. In a few places near the Mammoth Hot Springs–Tower Road, ruts carved by the dragging ends of their travois can still be seen. In 1877, Chief Joseph led his band of Nez Percé through the park with the cavalry in pursuit. The Nez Percé, a peaceful tribe driven to warfare by the pressures of land greed, seized several tourists, whom they released later.

Rumors of Wonderland

The first explorer to see the Yellowstone area was probably John Colter, a member of the Lewis and Clark Expedition until August 1806, when he was permitted to leave the eastbound explorers to prospect for furs. In the winter of 1807/08, Colter may have crossed portions of the present-day park and seen at least a few of the thermal features. Colter was followed by many other wandering trappers and, later, prospectors over the next sixty years. Although Yellowstone remained officially unexplored and unmapped until after the Civil War, it was crossed, trapped, or panned more or less annually after 1820.

Rumors of the area's peculiar character and stunning scenery, spread mostly in the form of trappers' fireside yarns and second- or third-hand narratives, finally led to three formal expeditions by "respectable" citizens whose reports would be believed by most: Folsom, Cook, and Peterson (1869); Washburn, Langford, and Doane (1870); and Hayden (1871). The Hayden Geological and Geographical Survey, part of the federal government's efforts to map and evaluate the western public domain, added enough solid information to the earlier reports to pique public interest.

Establishment and Definition of the Park

With strong backing from the tourism-minded Northern Pacific Railroad, members of the 1870 and 1871 expeditions launched a cam-

Visitors arrive by stagecoach at Mammoth Hot Springs Hotel about 1890.

paign to preserve the region's wonders. Yellowstone National Park was established by act of Congress and signed into law on March 1, 1872, by President Ulysses S. Grant.

Early efforts to preserve, protect, and manage Yellowstone were halting, even fumbling. Vandalism, poaching, and campfire carelessness threatened the park from within, while commercial interests sought to develop and control the main attractions (the Northern Pacific Railroad fought hard until almost 1900 to gain rights-of-way for tracks within the reserve). In 1886, an underfunded civilian administration was replaced by the cavalry, which provided basic legal order and developed many management practices and philosophies. The National Park Service was created in 1916, but did not assume complete control of Yellowstone until 1918, when rangers replaced the last soldiers.

Yellowstone was established primarily for geological reasons: to protect the geyser and hot-spring areas and the Grand Canyon of the Yellowstone River from private exploitation and ruin. The act that set up the park made it clear that forests and wildlife were not to be wasted, but they were not given the protection they now have in wil-

The steamship Zillah *was a turn-of-the-century attraction on Yellowstone Lake.*

derness legislation. Respect for the wholeness of ecosystems was virtually unheard of at that time, and many lessons were learned (and many mistakes were made) in the process of figuring out how best to manage the park. "Protection" was defined very aggressively by the army, whose top officers were important early conservationists. Grazing animals were "protected" from predators (the army and the National Park Service killed 132 wolves, 121 cougars, and 4,352 coyotes between 1904 and 1935 in Yellowstone). They were further protected by winter feeding programs that concentrated hundreds of elk and deer unnaturally and that short-circuited winter's natural culling process.

There gradually dawned an awareness, not only of the checks and balances by which nature "manages" itself, but also that Yellowstone provided an extraordinary opportunity to preserve an entire primitive setting, not perfectly, but more nearly whole than anywhere else in the country on such a grand scale. Hunting, necessary to provision early visitors before hotels and restaurants were built, became illegal in 1883 after much wasteful slaughter and market hunting had occurred. Fishing was considered harmless (fish generally being thought of as second-class citizens of the animal world), so many waters were thoughtlessly and indiscriminately stocked, diluting or destroying pure native strains. A hatchery program was established and fish populations were subjected to devastating exploitation until the late 1960s, when fishermen were asked under new regulations to release most fish instead of eating them. Wildfires, which had maintained a diverse and productive "mosaic" of vegetative types and wildlife habitats in the park area, were suppressed whenever possible. Only slowly, after such well-intentioned interference with the natural setting backfired, did managers permit various parts of the wild setting to manage themselves. Over the years, each management issue, be it fisheries, elk, grizzly bears, mountain pine beetles, or fire, has been the subject of strong, even furious debate as we have tried to determine just how far we can go in "letting it be." The process continues today, fueling an occasional controversy and made even more urgent by the damaging press of millions of visitors.

Visitors in Yellowstone today see two dynamic processes at work. The first is the wilderness itself, which for the most part is free to act upon itself as it will. The second is the even faster-paced process of evolution of park management and philosophy, which changes steadily as we seek to determine exactly why the park is here.

G E O L O G Y

Hot Water

It is somehow appropriate that Yellowstone, with its complex and surprising life forms and the equally complex human ideals that protect it, should have a geologic foundation that is both dynamic and unusual. The geysers and hot springs are the giveaway, the leading hint that something strange has been going on here; to exist, they need heat, and here they get it—enough to give Yellowstone more than half the world's geysers.

They get heat because the earth's crust is unusually thin in the Yellowstone area. In most places, the solid crust is 15 to 30 miles thick and rests, apparently rather loosely, on a mantle of softer, hotter material that makes up the bulk of the earth's mass. The mantle contains great amounts of molten rock, called magma until it appears on the surface of the earth, at which point it becomes lava. Geologists have determined that an upwelling of magma, known as a magmatic plume, occurs beneath the Yellowstone area. In places, molten rock may be less than 2 miles down. It heats the earth above it, which in turn heats the water in the geysers and hot springs.

Geyser function is fascinating and not yet fully understood. Unlike hot springs, in which ground water is more or less simmered constantly, geysers have complicated underground "plumbing." Water, flowing in from precipitation, snow melt, and interconnected subterra-

Overleaf: Water from a hot spring deposits dissolved minerals, forming tiny terraces.

nean channels, seeps deeply into the rock of the adjacent volcanic plateaus. It follows open cracks in the rocks, and enters the vertical tubes of geysers. A natural geyser can occur only if the water is moving relatively slowly and if the heat is unusually intense. As water heats, it becomes lighter in weight. Therefore, the hot water heated by the magma rises above the incoming cooler water, and is pushed up the tube. Deep in the tube, water is unable to boil, even at temperatures of 500° F, because of the tremendous depth and water pressure. But as it rises toward the surface, the water boils and some of it is converted into steam. When the water flashes into steam, it expands greatly in volume. Continuing to rise, it pushes before it water that has entered the main vertical tube from side channels. This water and steam erupt from the ground. After an eruption subsides, a recovery period follows, during which subsurface channels and open spaces in the reservoir fill with water.

Obviously nature does not construct precise tubes and tunnels, and each system is unique and even unpredictable. Some small geysers erupt every few minutes, or constantly, and some big ones are quiet for months or years at a time. Each has a character, almost a personality, that serious geyser gazers become familiar with, even fond of.

Geysers are not the whole story. Hot springs, mudpots, fumaroles, and explosions are also features of Yellowstone's thermal landscape. Hot springs differ from geysers in that in most cases water and steam are discharged in a relatively steady and noneruptive manner. In some hot springs the water wells up quietly, but others boil violently and release clouds of vapor. Mudpots occur when a limited supply of water mixes with clay and other undissolved mineral matter. These are called "paint pots" if tinted pale pink or red by iron compounds. When the mudpot expels pellets of thick viscous mud, a circular cone or mound called a "mud volcano" is created. Fumaroles, commonly called "steam vents," discharge only water vapor and other gases, including hydrogen sulfide and carbon dioxide.

Here and there, craterlike depressions ranging in size from 30 to 5,000 feet in diameter suggest that thermal explosions occurred in bygone years. Many of the depressions, which are surrounded by rims of rock fragments blown from the craters, date from the Pinedale Glaciation of 15,000 years ago. The underground design of these thermal systems was similar to those of geysers, except that the energy remained bottled up until the explosion occurred. At Pocket Basin in the Lower Geyser Basin, for example, the ground above the explosion sites may have been weighted down by the water of lakes formed in melted pockets of glacial ice. With rapid drainage of such a lake, the very hot

Deposits of travertine, a form of limestone, on Minerva Terrace at Mammoth Hot Springs.

water at shallow depths could flash into steam—just as would happen if the lid of a pressure cooker was removed before cooling.

The geysers tell more about the subsurface conditions than just their temperatures. They bring up dissolved minerals and spread them across the basin. The deposits that build up around the vents of geysers and hot springs in the basins are a type of silica called siliceous sinter (the water passes through other minerals, as demonstrated by the sulfurous "rotten-egg" fumes given off by many features). Sinter, also called geyserite, builds up very slowly, usually adding less than 1 inch in 100 years. In this way, ledges, terraces, and mounds are created. In some cases, tree trunks, branches, or rocks are coated and added to the general architecture of the formation.

The final dressing of the hot-water features is provided by plant life, mostly algae and filamentous bacteria, that is adapted to live in the hot water. The plant life can become quite dense in the cooler runoff channels, which are also bordered, even in winter, by unusually thick beds of grasses and herbs that luxuriate in the hothouse climate.

Old Rock, Young Mountains

Like much of the Rockies, Yellowstone's face has been shaped and reshaped countless times. In Yellowstone can be found metamorphic rocks 2.7 billion years old and sedimentary deposits from 500 million years ago, but most of the landscape in Yellowstone is the result of more recent geological activity. About 75 million years ago, in an event with the delightful name of the Laramide Orogeny (mountain-building), the region of the modern Rocky Mountains was raised to far greater than its present height. Numerous cracks and faults appeared in the earth's surface as it was contorted and lifted, so that deep layers of rock were exposed as they were raised free of neighboring lands. Since that original event, there have been enough periods of volcanism, glaciation, and slow erosion that the Laramide formations are echoed in the modern landscape only here and there.

About 55 to 50 million years ago, the Yellowstone region experienced extensive volcanic activity that poured several new mountain ranges over the area. Most significant of these are the Absaroka Range, its smaller neighbor the Washburn Range, and part of the Gallatin Range. Volcanoes are not tidy architects, and during the eruptions (some violent, some rather subdued), surface rocks of many types mixed with the outpouring lava as it flowed and settled across the land. The combination of flowing lava, cinders, ash, and displaced surface material eventually covered much of the older Laramide landscape in a jumble of rock types that charms geology students. During the 20 million or so years of this volcanism, the earth sometimes quieted down long enough for plant and animal life to move in; in some northern parts of the park these plants have been revealed, trunks and stumps of trees that were buried and petrified under mudflows and ash falls and have become exposed on steep ridges.

After the volcanism, the Yellowstone area remained fairly quiet until about 10 million years ago. Then began an uplifting process that squeezed and pressed huge blocks of land against one another, causing some to slide up, some down (the incredibly steep eastern face of the Teton Range to the south of Yellowstone was the result of an especially spectacular slippage). Some of these raisings were remarkable even in the scale of those great mountain-building times; the entire Gallatin Range was lifted thousands of feet, along faults that border it on each side, as a single great block more than 20 miles long.

The great uplifting was its own undoing. The steepened, jagged new peaks and ridges generated wild, powerful streams that immediately began to wear them down. Geologists imagine the park area 5 million years ago as a maze of ragged crests, precipitous canyons, and isolated tablelands. And, inconceivable as this scale of landscape creation is to

Opposite: Basalt columns above Yellowstone River were formed as lava cooled and contracted.

us today, it was—all 75 million years of it—mere prelude for the grand finale, the great Yellowstone Caldera.

Fire and Ice

About 600,000 years ago, two magma chambers beneath the park area rose to within a few thousand feet of the surface. As the land bulged and cracked over the chambers, lava reached the surface, flowing out through the cracks in small amounts at first. Then, in a series of explosions, pumice, ash, and rock debris spewed upward and spread across the land. Ash and dust in huge quantities were blown into the air and carried by the wind. The incandescent pumice, ash, and rock particles flowing on the ground filled in valleys and settled into wide horizontal sheets. The cooling material welded into compact rock called ash-flow tuff. With the removal of hundreds of cubic miles of material, the surface of the land collapsed into the empty chambers, creating the Yellowstone caldera, a rough crater possibly more than half a mile deep and about 30 by 45 miles in extent. The caldera, now partly buried by lava flows, is no longer so dramatic a feature.

Geologists know that the Yellowstone Caldera was only the most recent of three similar events; the earlier two were farther to the south and west. In geological terms we are about due for another one, because they have been 600,000 to 800,000 years apart. The next caldera should occur near the northeast corner of the park, judging from the northeasterly progress of the previous three. Scientists estimate that the land in the center of the park is now rising on the order of 14 millimeters a year.

Smaller local eruptions have occurred since the main caldera event; but more recently, the biggest shaper of the land has been ice. At least three glaciations, during each of which the park was almost or totally covered with deep layers of ice, have occurred in the past 300,000 years. Each carved and polished the land as it came and went; each pushed, carried, and dumped its gravel and silt as it moved. When the final ice retreated, leaving the park open for company, it was only 8,500 years ago. Company was quick to arrive.

N A T U R A L   H I S T O R Y

The Big Piney Woods

Yellowstone's plant communities range from Great Basin desert type (near the North Entrance, at Gardiner, Montana) to alpine tundra (areas

Opposite: A 50-million-year-old stump on Specimen Ridge petrified under volcanic ash.

above 10,000 feet), but most of the park is fairly simple to describe. Early wanderers characterized this kind of country, with its monotonous (to them, at least) rolling forests, as "big piney woods."

Admitting that the glacial legacy of the past 300,000 years has softened and obscured many of the boundaries, we can still generalize and identify certain forests with certain bedrocks. Lodgepole pine forests are found on volcanic rocks from the various eruptions related to the Yellowstone Caldera; about 75 percent of the park is forested, and about 75 percent of the trees are lodgepole pines. Spruce and fir forests—a mixture of lodgepole pine, Engelmann spruce, and subalpine fir with heavy concentrations of whitebark pine above 8,400 feet—are found on the richer soils of the older Absaroka volcanics. Douglas fir forests, which in the park are often more sagebrush than fir, grow at elevations between 6,000 and 7,600 feet in the open river valleys of northern Yellowstone, where they rest on glacial till that has spread from the granite and Absaroka volcanic bedrocks upstream (aspen groves are scattered, primarily on hillsides, in this zone). There are numerous other small plant communities, including two enormous meadow grasslands, Pelican Valley and Hayden Valley, both of which are north of Yellowstone Lake; they are the result of sediments that blanketed and enriched this area from ice-age lakes.

In country so recently scoured by glaciers, the soil is quite thin, limiting the types of large vegetation that can thrive. Look for upturned lodgepole pines and notice how flat and shallow their root systems are.

Snowfall has a more immediate influence on life in the park. In the Douglas fir zone, associated with the Yellowstone and Lamar rivers in northern Yellowstone, precipitation averages less than 20 inches a year; by contrast, within this same zone but near streams and ponds, specialized plant communities, especially willows, may develop. Curiously, some of the park's best wildflower shows occur above 8,000 feet (the steep meadows near Dunraven Pass, between Canyon and Tower, are perhaps the best roadside example) because precipitation is heaviest there. Huge field-size bouquets of Indian paintbrush, monkey flower, aster, pentstemon, and lupine blossom during the brief mountain summer.

Because of the park's mission to preserve natural settings as nearly primitive as possible, Yellowstone's plant communities are subject to natural predation, even destruction, by insects—most notably the mountain pine beetle and the western budworm—and by wildfire.

Unharvested Wildlife

Yellowstone National Park is, of course, world famous for its wildlife, especially the large "glamour animals" that grace the covers of the

Everts (or elk) thistle, named for an early explorer who survived by eating it.

wildlife magazines. Smaller animals get much less attention but are just as deserving. Insects, the neglected treasures of the animal world, are seasonally common; there are twenty-nine varieties of mosquitoes in the park. Relatively few reptiles and amphibians make their homes here; visitors sometimes see bullsnakes, rubber boa, or garter snakes, and once in a great while, near the North Entrance, a rattlesnake. Salamanders occasionally make mass migrations on warm summer nights, crossing roads in northern Yellowstone in great numbers as they move from one pond to another.

There are at least eighteen species of fish in the park, six of which were introduced around the turn of the century. After nearly a century of overharvest and waste, the fishing in the park is managed strictly to limit harvest. The quality of fishing has improved markedly, as has the condition of fish populations. Although many people are uncomfortable with fishing as an appropriate use of the park (the National Park Service does not, for example, allow similar tampering with mammal or bird populations), the regulations have allowed the growth of a new activity, fish-watching. Every summer, from Fishing Bridge on the

Overleaf: Cutthroat trout and other fish may be caught in the park in limited numbers.

Yellowstone River and from several other easily accessible locations, thousands of visitors can see trout and other species in their wild state —feeding, preying and being preyed upon, mating, and dying—as integral parts of the Yellowstone wilderness.

Park birdlife offers enduring lessons in both the worth and the ultimate limitations of national parks as wildlife protectors. On the success side of the ledger is the trumpeter swan, regularly seen on the Madison and Yellowstone rivers and on several lakes; the trumpeter exists in the lower forty-eight states largely because of protection given it fifty years ago in Yellowstone and in another refuge in Idaho. And osprey, which are seen soaring above and fishing in many park waters, are recovering in numbers because fewer pesticides are being used today in Central America, far south of the park's sanctuary.

The park's other large birdlife includes great blue herons, sandhill cranes, ravens, bald eagles, golden eagles, Canada geese, and white pelicans (Yellowstone has, on Yellowstone Lake, the only white pelican breeding colony in a national park). Among the other birds that seem especially to appeal to visitors, because they either appear to be out of place or are somehow unusual, are magpies, yellow-headed blackbirds, killdeer, dippers, and harlequin ducks.

The mammals are of greatest interest to most visitors, and Yellowstone is the largest sanctuary for western large mammals in the lower forty-eight states. The most common large mammal is the elk, with a summering population in excess of 20,000; at that time of the year, however, they are least visible, scattered about the high meadows. In the winter, many move north, down the Yellowstone River valley, or south, into the Jackson Hole region; as snow and cold drive the elk downhill, as many as 1,000 can be seen at once in the Lamar River and Yellowstone River valleys in northern Yellowstone. After many years of human manipulation, the elk population has in the past fifteen years been allowed to restore itself to whatever level it prefers. The availability of food in winter, rather than predators, seems to be the chief regulating factor that controls herd size; in an exceptionally severe winter, as many as 15 percent of the population may die. And their numbers are also reduced by hunters when the elk leave the park in cold weather. Most of the other large animals have only natural hunters to contend with: the 2,000 bison and several hundred each of bighorn sheep, deer, pronghorn, and moose exist at levels that their environment has established; population, therefore, varies with food supply and other environmental conditions.

The park's large predators, which were unmercifully persecuted before 1930, are now respected for their role in the dynamics of a wild ecosystem. Except for the wolf, which was probably eliminated from the park in the early days, Yellowstone predators hunt and kill much as they did prehistorically. The largest is the grizzly bear (whose diet is 90 percent vegetation), whose future has been the focus of anguished controversy since the late 1960s. Most scientists agree that the grizzlies (which range in great part beyond park boundaries onto less protected lands) are in some jeopardy. Estimates of population size for the park and adjacent lands is 200, and the total number seems to be declining. Black bears are no longer found begging at roadsides. Since 1969, those who feed bears have been fined (it has been illegal to feed the bears since 1905, but rangers looked the other way because it was so popular), and bears have been taken from the roads; now black bears are seen only rarely, under natural circumstances. Again, there are considerable differences of opinion and judgment over population size, but park biologists have estimated that there may be 500 to 650 black bears in the park. Other predators include an occasional cougar, coyotes (common throughout the park and regularly mistaken for wolves), and a number of smaller mammals: wolverine (always quite rare), mink, fox, weasel, marten, lynx, and otter.

Yellowstone's wild inhabitants, both plant and animal, are for the most part interacting as they always have. Seeing an elk grazing alone

Trumpeter swan.

Male yellow-headed blackbird.

in a meadow, or a group of pelicans herding trout into shallow water, is seeing a primitive vignette. Feeding a bear, chipmunk, raven, or trout is violating the fragile integrity of that vignette. Disturbing the setting unnecessarily is also a violation, although you may be doing nothing technically illegal. If you are watching an animal and get close enough that it stops what it was doing and watches you instead (or moves away), you are too close. Large mammals, bison in particular, may *charge*, too, if you get too close. The natural setting—elk, trees, wind, and water—benefits us most when we affect it least.

SITES, TRAILS, AND TRIPS

The most frequent complaint of visitors to Yellowstone is that they do not have time to do the park justice. There is just too much to see and do. Unless your time is unlimited, the best approach may be to concentrate on a few points of interest. Rather than racing the entire Grand Loop Road for a quick glimpse of every major attraction, pick a few representative areas and enjoy them leisurely. Get to know one of the geyser basins instead of sprinting through four or five. Take your time on one or two trails rather than seeing how many miles you can log.

At the same time, know that the park's road system works for visitors in many ways. Even the most devoted off-road travelers must accept the logic that the best chance of seeing wildlife is not on a hike, but along the roads, especially at dawn and dusk, because much more territory can be covered by car than on foot. As well, the road can get hikers to any trail head, and they may find more of interest in three or four short hikes than in one long one.

Museums and Visitor Centers

Yellowstone has the most elaborate system of visitor centers and museums in the national park system. The Horace Albright Visitor Center at Mammoth Hot Springs specializes in the history of Yellowstone as a park; the Norris Museum concentrates on park geology and on the Norris Geyser Basin; the Canyon Visitor Center, on the Grand Canyon of the Yellowstone River; the Old Faithful Visitor Center, on the Upper Geyser Basin; the Madison Museum, on evolution of the park concept; the Fishing Bridge Museum, on birds; and the Grant Village Visitor Center, on the wilderness around Yellowstone Lake. Most have ranger-naturalists on duty, and all can help you plan your stay. You will have to visit one of them if you are going to hike overnight or use a boat (both require permits). Information on everything from firewood to campfire talks to nature walks to bear safety is free for the asking.

Historical Surprises

Yellowstone's pre-establishment history left little evidence of human occupation, but more than a century as a park has left a considerable architectural heritage. Perhaps most significant is Fort Yellowstone, the large collection of wood and stone buildings that now serve as National Park Service headquarters at Mammoth Hot Springs. When cavalry was sent to the park to protect it, the army built this fort, the only permanent military post in a national park. The army turned it over to the National Park Service when that agency was created in 1916. Most of the buildings are now used for administration, storage, or residence, but a walk down the front street ("Officers' Row") is worth the time (the Albright Visitor Center was the bachelor officers' quarters); living-history walks, with a ranger dressed in 1915 soldier costume, are given several times a week during the summer.

After many years of use, many buildings take on new value. Such is the case with the grand old hotels in the park. They are relics of a more relaxed and flamboyant era in American tourism. Had we the chance to do it over now, we probably would prefer not having so many large buildings in the park, but their presence does not materially diminish the quality of a visit.

Morning Glory Pool, one of the park's 10,000 thermal features.

Trails of Yellowstone National Park

The following trails are but a representation of the more than 1,000 miles of trails in Yellowstone; each of these is considered particularly outstanding by experienced hikers. *Yellowstone Trails, A Hiking Guide*, by Mark Marschall, is recommended.

Shoshone Lake Trail: Starts at the Lone Star trail head, just south of Kepler Cascades on Old Faithful–West Thumb Road, and ends at the Lewis trail head, about 7 miles south of West Thumb Jct. on South Entrance Road; 22 miles one way; best done as a two-day trip; leads through the finest backcountry geyser basin in the park.

Clear Lake/Ribbon Lake Loop Trail: Starts and ends at trail head in parking area just east of Chittenden Bridge on road to Artist Point; 6 miles round trip; 3 hours; easy, level trail leads by Clear, Lilypad, and Ribbon lakes in the backcountry; opportunity to see wildlife, perhaps moose, bison, and grizzly; be alert.

Osprey Falls Trail: Starts at trail head on Bunsen Peak Road, about 3 miles from the road's southern end, and ends at Osprey Falls on the Gardner River; 3 miles round trip; 3 hours; steep trail loses 700 feet in elevation down a series of switchbacks to bottom of Sheepeater Canyon and along the river to the 150-foot falls.

Mt. Washburn Trails: From south, trail starts at Dunraven Pass Picnic Area; from north, trail begins at parking area on Chittenden Road; both trails end at Mt. Washburn; both are 3 miles one way; allow 4–5 hours for trip from road to summit and back; this is the one hike in the park to take if time is limited; both trails climb about 1,400 feet, but it is not strenuous if pace is gradual and steady; excellent opportunity to see bighorn sheep; abundant wildflowers and a tremendous view of Yellowstone Lake, Grand Canyon, the Teton Range, Hayden Valley, Electric Peak, and the steam rising from geysers along the Firehole River.

Bliss Pass Trail: Starts at Pebble Creek Campground on the northeast entrance road, and ends at Slough Creek trail head; 21.5 miles from one trail head to the other; 10–15 hours—best done in 2 days; trail fords Pebble Creek (calf deep in late summer; knee deep in June), ascends 2,700 feet steeply through a meadow and forest to pass, then descends to Slough Creek Trail and on 8 miles to trail head; magnificent mountain scenery; pass blocked by snow until late summer in most years.

Cache Creek Trail: Starts at Lamar River trail head on northeast entrance road, crosses Republic Pass, and continues to Cooke City; 25 miles one way; allow 2–3 days; trail parallels Cache Creek, then climbs away toward Republic Pass nearly 2,300 vertical feet for a magnificent view, then down on a U.S. Forest Service trail to Cooke City.

The southwest corner of the park, known as the Bechler area, is often subject to extremely wet conditions and high insect populations through much of the summer. Most routes require fording of rivers. Inquire at the Bechler Ranger Station before attempting hikes in this part of park.

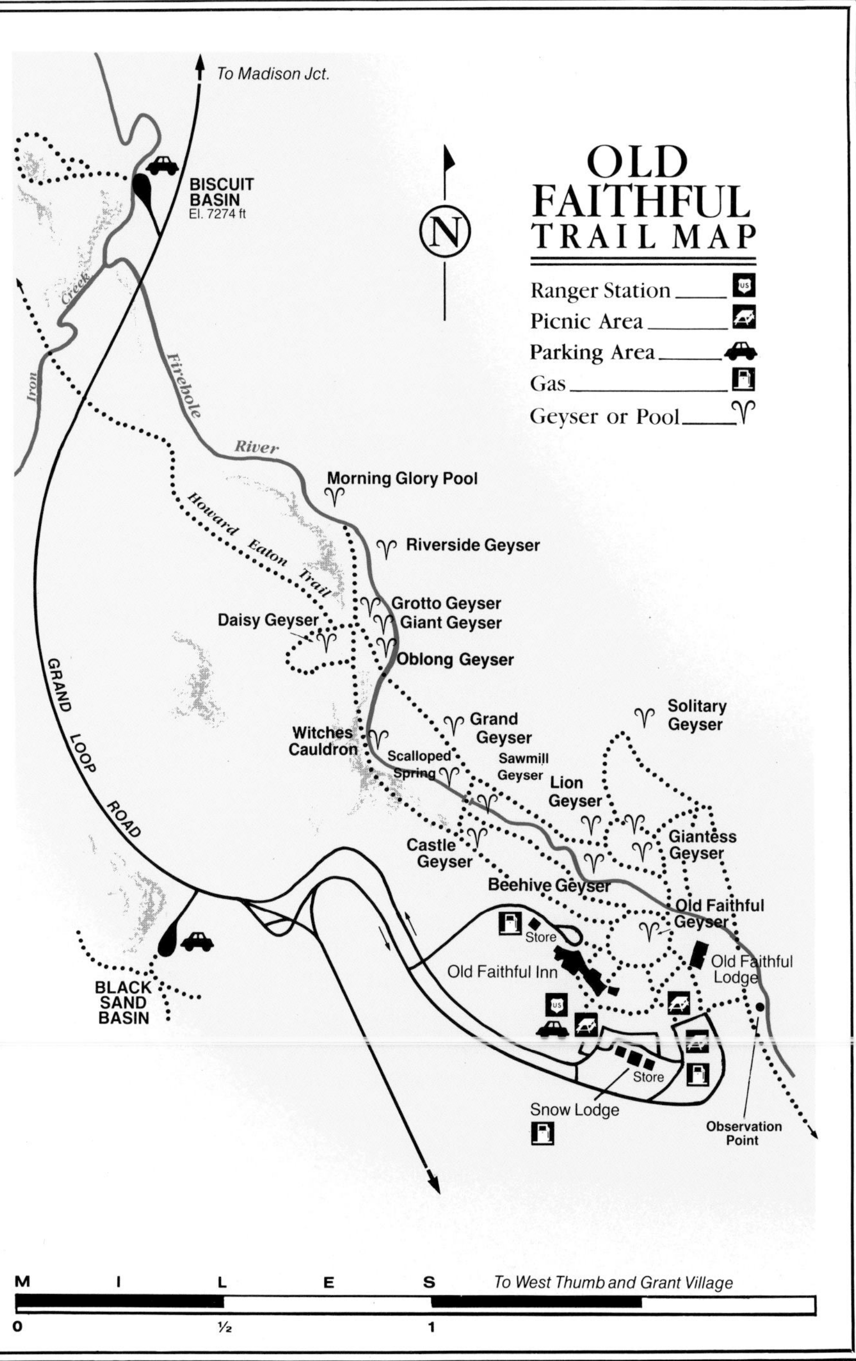
OLD
FAITHFUL
TRAIL MAP
Ranger Station
Picnic Area
Parking Area
Gas
Geyser or Pool
N
To Madison Jct.
BISCUIT
BASIN
El. 7274 ft
Iron
Creek
Firehole
River
Howard Eaton Trail
GRAND LOOP ROAD
Morning Glory Pool
Riverside Geyser
Grotto Geyser
Giant Geyser
Daisy Geyser
Oblong Geyser
Witches
Cauldron
Grand
Geyser
Solitary
Geyser
Scalloped
Spring
Sawmill
Geyser
Lion
Geyser
Giantess
Geyser
Castle
Geyser
Beehive Geyser
Old Faithful
Geyser
Store
Old Faithful Inn
Old Faithful
Lodge
Store
Snow Lodge
Observation
Point
BLACK
SAND
BASIN
M I L E S
To West Thumb and Grant Village
0
½
1

Geyser Gazing: The Basins

There are several major concentrations of thermal activity, as well as scores of lesser known ones. The best-known are on roads, but there are a number of fascinating backcountry thermal areas that are only lightly visited.

Mineral deposits from the geysers and hot springs are incredibly fragile, and so are the delicate growths of algae and other plants that grace the runoff channels. For the sake of their beauty and for your own safety, stay on the designated trails when visiting the geyser basins. Serious or fatal burns await anyone who breaks through crusts.

Upper Geyser Basin. Upper Geyser Basin is easily the most visited, since it is the home of Old Faithful. The basin straddles the Firehole River, radically altering that stream's temperature and chemical content with the runoff from dozens of thermal features. In this small space, barely 1 square mile, are one-quarter of the world's geysers; well over 130 are currently active. Old Faithful erupts on an average of every 70–80 minutes, but varies from 33 to 120 minutes. It is neither the most frequent nor the most consistent of the park's geysers, but has assumed a personality of international fame.

Trails in the Upper Geyser Basin lead to the various concentrations of geyser and hot-spring activity, known locally as "groups." Old Faithful and Geyser Hill are closest to the Visitor Center. Geyser Hill provides a good cross section of geyser types, including some quite dainty and two—Beehive and Giantess—among the world's largest. A paved path with frequent boardwalk side trails goes down the Firehole River to the Castle and Grand groups (more than three dozen geysers here, including Grand, now called the "largest frequently active geyser in the world"), the Giant and Daisy groups, the Riverside and Morning Glory Pool groups, the Cascade group, and, finally, about 1.5 miles from Old Faithful, the Biscuit Basin (so named for the peculiar roundish geyserite formations once common to the area). In other directions, closer to Old Faithful, are the Myriad group and the singular Black Sand Basin.

Midway Geyser Basin. Midway Geyser Basin, about 6 miles down the Firehole River (north) from the Upper Geyser Basin, is small but contains a few magnificent features. Grand Prismatic Spring, more than 100 yards across, is the largest hot pool in the park. Excelsior Geyser

Opposite: Norris Geyser Basin, which is about 14 miles north of Madison Junction, contains the park's hottest and most active thermal area.

Crater is all that remains of one of the world's largest geysers. When it was active, until 1888, Excelsior erupted as high as 300 feet. It evidently erupted so violently that it blew its plumbing apart, and it can no longer establish adequate pressure to erupt. Even in retirement it is impressive, overflowing at the rate of several thousand gallons per minute into the nearby Firehole River.

Lower Geyser Basin. Lower Geyser Basin, a few miles downstream from the Midway Geyser Basin, is actually several areas of thermal activity spread across the Firehole River valley. A one-way loop drive leaves the main Old Faithful–Madison Road and meanders for 3 miles among active thermal areas, including the Great Fountain Group, the White Dome Group, the Pine Cone Group, and the Firehole Lake Group. Most appealing to the majority of visitors are the Great Fountain Geyser, among the most predictable of the truly large geysers, erupting 100 to 150 feet every 9 or 10 hours; White Dome Geyser, a shining white and pink mound of mineral about 25 feet high with a small geyser spouting at irregular intervals from the top; and Firehole Lake, an extremely large hot pool with a self-guiding nature trail designed especially for sightless people.

Norris Geyser Basin. Norris Geyser Basin, about 14 miles north of Madison Junction, is the hottest thermal area in the park. There are two areas of activity: Porcelain Basin, so named for the expanse of grayish geyserite that covers it; and Back Basin, which contains Steamboat, the world's largest geyser (eruptions to 400 feet have been reported). There are numerous regular and frequent geysers at Norris Geyser Basin, so the visitor is assured of several eruptions in any 2-hour period.

Mammoth Hot Springs. Mammoth Hot Springs is unlike the geyser basins in that the hot water is depositing travertine rather than the harder geyserite. Because of limestone's greater solubility and softness, it is laid down much faster—as much as 2 feet per year—and it cannot maintain the pressures required for geyser action. Mammoth Hot Springs is a great pile of limestone, known as travertine, just west of the settlement of Mammoth Hot Springs. As much as 200 feet of deposition exists in some areas. Most of the settlement, which is park headquarters, rests on long-extinct travertine deposits that have been overgrown with vegetation; a few old spring holes are fenced off on the flat plain in front of the hotel and restaurant. There are dozens of springs of all sizes, most reachable either by boardwalk around the lower terrace

Grand Prismatic Spring, 370 feet in length, is the largest hot pool in Yellowstone.

area or by the one-way 1.5-mile Upper Terrace Drive. In the lower terraces, the most outstanding springs in recent years have been Minerva and Jupiter terraces. The amount of flow can change rapidly, and frequently a spring will choke itself off with its own deposition. The water must find another outlet, and a new spring can start anywhere. As in the geyser basins, hot water could be only a few inches below the surface, so stay on the designated trails and boardwalks. If there is anything uglier than a footprint in a delicate limestone terrace, it is a badly scalded foot.

Other thermal areas abound in Yellowstone. There are smaller areas of hot-spring or geyser activity at the West Thumb of Yellowstone Lake, at several points along the Gibbon River, at the Mud Volcano area just south of Hayden Valley, and dotted here and there across the park's backcountry. Most popular among the backcountry basins are the Lone Star Geyser, a few miles south of Old Faithful; the Shoshone Geyser Basin, about 9 miles by foot from Old Faithful; and the Heart Lake Basin, about 8 miles by foot from the Grant Village–South Entrance Road.

Yellowstone River, Lake, and Canyon

Yellowstone Lake is not the headwaters of the Yellowstone River—the river starts high in the wilderness area just south of the park—but the portion of the river that most people know as the Yellowstone is born in the lake. Yellowstone Lake was once more than twice its present size, and geological evidence of the ancient shoreline is unquestionable. Even now it is the largest lake at its elevation (7,733 feet) in North America; its shoreline is over 100 miles in length, and its average depth is 137 feet. The deepest spot is 320 feet. More than 1 million acre-feet of water flow out under Fishing Bridge every year; but it still takes eleven years for the water in the lake to completely replace itself, thus slowing, settling, and warming the Yellowstone River, which enters the lake a brawling and relatively barren mountain stream and leaves it a mature and stable river.

The lake is too cold for swimming, but excellent for fishing, boating (boats are not allowed on park rivers), and general lakeside enjoyments. Moose are frequently seen near the north shore, especially along the Yellowstone River downstream from Fishing Bridge and in the valley of Pelican Creek, a few miles to the east of Fishing Bridge.

After leaving the lake, the river travels north-northwest for about 25 miles, paralleled most of the way by road. It passes the Mud Volcano thermal area, then enters Hayden Valley, the park's largest meadowland and home to bison, elk, and bears. Swans, pelicans, eagles, and an assortment of ducks and shore birds are seen regularly along the river, as are moose.

When it leaves Hayden Valley, the Yellowstone River plunges over two waterfalls, the Upper Falls (109 feet) and the Lower Falls (308 feet, twice as high as Niagara), into a 20-mile-long canyon that is as deep as 1,500 feet in spots. Looking deceptively like the sandstone canyons of the American Southwest, the Grand Canyon of the Yellowstone River is actually volcanic rock, the rhyolite that was spread across the park area after the caldera eruption. Once again Yellowstone's subterranean heat source has been at work; through hundreds of centuries of hydrothermal activity near the surface in the canyon area, the usually dark rhyolite has been chemically altered to its present yellows, oranges, and whites. A few active hot springs can be seen near the river at the bottom of the canyon.

Visitors first seeing the canyon recognize a good reason for calling the river "Yellowstone," but the river was not named for this yellow stone. Indians who lived many miles downstream named the river for the long sandstone bluffs that line much of its lower course.

There are roads along both rims of the Grand Canyon of the Yellowstone, with frequent turnouts. A steep, .5-mile trail descends to the lip of the *Lower Falls*. Among the other canyon trails, the most popular is probably the walk down into the canyon to *Red Rock Point*.

Pelican Creek flows to Yellowstone Lake, the largest North American lake at this altitude.

For the well-conditioned and ambitious, the *Seven-Mile Hole Trail* goes clear to the river. The last 1.5 miles of the 5.5-mile trail drop 1,250 feet to the river, and the climb back up is considered "grueling."

Trails

Yellowstone National Park has 1,000 miles of trails, enough to occupy the better part of a summer. With the aid of a good topographical map and trail guides available locally, hikers can narrow their choices considerably. In order to control public impact, as well as to ensure the safety of visitors who may not be familiar with the park's unusual features (especially hot springs, grizzly bears, and high country weather), all overnight hikers are required to get a permit at a ranger station or Visitor Center. For practical purposes, trail descriptions are generally offered by dividing the park into regions.

The Gallatin Range. The Gallatins are approached by a series of east–west trails that cross the range at a few passes. Viewed from the Mammoth Hot Springs–Norris Road to its east, the range seems big but featureless—a single line of mountains. Once the passes are approached, the range loses its two-dimensional appearance, and the rugged steep valleys between the peaks offer some of the park's most spectacular scenery. There is a trail to the fire lookout tower on *Mount Holmes* (10,336), and most of the other peaks can be reached by hikes

Overleaf: The Firehole River receives geyser flow, but fish still thrive in its waters.

At Mammoth Hot Springs, two tons of travertine are added to the terrace each day.

(rather than climbs). Two well-established trails, over *Fawn Pass* and *Bighorn Pass*, cross the range and take hikers the 20 or so miles from the Mammoth Hot Springs–Norris Road to U.S. 191 near the west boundary of the park. The Gallatins are excellent grizzly country, and at times hiking is restricted or prohibited to avoid conflicts with bears. There is no overstating the importance of knowing the risks and etiquette of grizzly-country hiking; grizzlies are one of the most exciting elements of the Yellowstone experience, but they must be taken seriously.

The North and Northeast. Most popular trail in this part of the park is the *Yellowstone River Trail*, which follows the river its last 20 miles before it leaves the park at Gardiner, Montana. The trail and the river pass through the Black Canyon, a wild backcountry gorge that is home to bighorn sheep, elk, and an occasional cougar. The trip is worth it just for the sight of so large a river without a road next to it.

Farther east, trails up *Hellroaring Creek* (a tributary of the Yellowstone River) and *Slough Creek* (a tributary of the Lamar River) lead to the Buffalo Plateau region, a rugged and relatively unvisited part of the park. The chances of seeing elk and pronghorn are good, and the scenery is outstanding. Much of the plateau is outside the park, and for some miles hikers follow trails that originally were established by poachers working the north boundary of the park years ago (some still do).

In the northeast corner of the park, the trail up Slough Creek goes to a catch-and-release angler's paradise, a dozen miles of mountain meadows and serpentine trout stream. Three miles from the north boundary a trail leaves Slough Creek and climbs east over *Bliss Pass* (9,350 feet) and down into the Pebble Creek drainage, a much tighter valley than Slough Creek's, with the sheer faces of Mount Hornaday and Barronette Peak rising on either side.

The East. The Absaroka Range, a jumble of imposing peaks along the east side of the park, provides numerous long hikes. The range is drained by the *Lamar River*, up which the main trail to this area runs. Side trails go east from the river up *Cache Creek*, 16.5 miles to the east boundary at Republic Pass (10,000 feet), and up *Miller Creek*, 12.5 miles to the east boundary at Bootjack Gap (9,200 feet), or, a few miles farther south, to the weird pinnacle formations known as the Hoodoos, certainly one of Yellowstone's least visited geological eccentricities.

There are few trails up the steep drainages to the west of the Lamar River; the country between the Lamar and the Grand Canyon of the Yellowstone is most often entered from the south, up *Pelican Creek* (the trail head is on the Lake–East Entrance Road). Perhaps most popular in this great wedge of wilderness is Specimen Ridge, which forms the divide between the Yellowstone and Lamar rivers just east of Tower. Specimen Ridge is littered with petrified wood, including several standing stumps, all the result of that period of intermittent volcanism 50 million years ago. There are day hikes conducted by rangers to the most prominent trees, or you can visit them on your own. Remember that collecting any object—be it stone, flower, or antler—is prohibited in the park.

The high ridge directly west of the Lamar River and south of Specimen Ridge is the Mirror Plateau, a heavily forested region with very few trails. To its south is the Pelican Creek drainage, a lush region of small lakes, unnamed thermal areas, and trout-rich streams. It is possible to reach the Pelican Creek drainage from the upper Lamar River valley, over *Mist Pass*, but most hikers go up Pelican Creek. The Pelican Creek Trail branches in several directions, all in good country for moose and grizzlies; the bears use this area heavily because its vegetation stays moist and fresh when much of the park has dried up.

The Canyon Area. There are good short trails just east of the Grand Canyon of the Yellowstone, to *Ribbon Lake* and *Clear Lake* as well as farther east to the *Pelican Valley*. Directly west of the canyon, within a few miles of one another, are *Cascade, Grebe, Wolf,* and *Ice lakes*, all reachable by hikes of only a few miles. One of the park's most beautiful creatures, the Montana grayling, can be seen in Grebe Lake, and osprey are frequently seen fishing there. A few miles north of Canyon, at

Storm clouds gather over Mammoth Hot Springs.

Dunraven Pass on the Canyon–Tower Road, is the trail head for the *Mount Washburn* hike, a 3-mile trip (there is another trail head a few miles farther north on the same road) that climbs 1,400 feet to the fire lookout at 10,243 feet. Mount Washburn provides a breathtaking and windy view of most of the park and beyond: the Tetons far to the south, the Gallatins to the west, the Beartooth Plateau to the northeast, the Absarokas to the east, and Yellowstone Lake to the southeast. Any map of the park means much more after you have stood on Mount Washburn. Bighorn sheep are seen regularly near the summit during most of the summer.

The Central Plateau. The Central Plateau, between Old Faithful and Canyon, has very few trails. In much of it no overnight camping is permitted because of the frequency of grizzly activity. The main trail, the 20-mile *Mary Mountain Trail*, starts from the Old Faithful–Madison Road a few miles north of Old Faithful at Nez Percé Creek (the Nez Percé traveled up this creek during their flight across the park). The trail moves up the creek through lodgepole pines and meadows to Mary Lake, then down the Alum Creek drainage across Hayden Valley to the Canyon–Lake Road. This is good bison and elk country, and is part of the Yellowstone Caldera.

The Thorofare and South. The region to the east and south of Yellowstone Lake is the park's most remote country. The Yellowstone

River originates in the high country just south of the park, and snakes through the southeast corner of the park, known as the Thorofare region, to its mouth in the Southeast Arm of Yellowstone Lake. Since it is a 20-mile hike along the east shore of the lake just to get to the mouth of the river, the sense of solitude in the Thorofare is unmatched anywhere else in the park.

Two Ocean Plateau is a long, gradually rising, north–south highland to the west of the Thorofare. The only trail across it is the *South Boundary Trail*, which joins the *Snake River Trail* at the park boundary. The other trail that leads west from the Thorofare skirts the south end of Yellowstone Lake. By either trail, hikers can reach Heart Lake, a large backcountry lake with a reputation for huge lake trout. From there, it is only 8 miles to the Grant Village–South Entrance Road. The country between the Thorofare and the road, a large block of high terrain split by the Continental Divide, is the Yellowstone wilderness at its least disturbed.

The Southwest Corner. Only a few miles to the south of the Old Faithful–West Thumb Road lies Shoshone Lake, Yellowstone's second largest lake, perhaps the largest lake in the lower forty-eight states without road access. Dense forests surround it on most sides, with occasional breaks such as the Shoshone Geyser Basin at its west end. Canoeists on the lake see big lake or brown trout finning slowly along 20 or 30 feet below in the clear water. To the south of Shoshone Lake, along the Grant Village–South Entrance Road, sits smaller Lewis Lake, also good fishing.

Southwest of Lewis Lake is a subalpine meadow more than 6 miles across: the Pitchstone Plateau. Most of the plateau, dotted with stands of spruce and fir, is above 8,700 feet, part of a massive flow of lava that spread following the main caldera event. The flow reaches to within a few miles of the southwest corner of the park, giving that region numerous sudden dropoffs and earning for it the name of Cascade Corner. It is also known as the Bechler region, so-called after the largest of the rivers to flow off the Pitchstone Plateau and out of the park. Many trails cross the Bechler region, and access is easiest on the Cave Falls Road from Ashton, Idaho; the road leads to the park boundary, where a spur road goes to the Bechler ranger station and the trail head.

The Madison Plateau. The heavily forested area west of the Firehole River and south of the Gallatin Range is also made of the rhyolite flows that occurred during and after the Yellowstone Caldera eruption. There are only a few trails here. A 7.5-mile walk from the Biscuit Basin, near

Old Faithful, leads to *Summit Lake*, near several backcountry hot springs; and a 9.5-mile hike from the same basin goes to 200-foot *Fairy Falls*. Most hiking in this part of the park is best invested in the geyser-basin trails.

There is little hope that Yellowstone's trails can be summarized so briefly. Many unmentioned details come to mind—the fossil forests of the northwest corner, the imponderable rumble of a backcountry earthquake, trout rising on Grizzly Lake at the foot of the Gallatins, Tower Falls shrouded in ice—that cannot be shared here. There are two excellent trail guides to the park—Butch Bach, *Hiking the Yellowstone Backcountry*, and Mark Marschall, *Yellowstone Trails*—but even these only hint at what you will find. No book can tell you what awaits you at Yellowstone, or how it will affect you.

No wilderness can survive except through the sufferance of our own species, and Yellowstone, even today, more than a century after it was "preserved," is clouded by a variety of dangers. In the mid-1980s, decisions were pending on 200 applications to explore the Island Park Geothermal Area just west of the park. The drilling of deep wells, which scientists believe might well destroy the geysers within the park, could begin within thirteen miles of Old Faithful and within two miles of some of the park's lesser known thermal features. Major geyser fields in New Zealand, Iceland, and Nevada were snuffed out forever by similar activities. Today, only two of the world's ten most outstanding geyser basins remain essentially undisturbed.

Yellowstone provides a case study of how a park can be threatened. Because grizzly bears, elk, and some other large mammals use areas outside the park, they are subject to poaching and elimination of critical habitat. Powdered elk antler is worth more than $40 an ounce in the Far East as an aphrodisiac. In certain countries, gourmets regard bear paws as delicacies. Trophy hunters have paid up to $30,000 for a bighorn sheep. Poachers have killed animals outside the park boundaries and even inside the park. Former Yellowstone Superintendent John Townsley asserted, "It's blatantly clear that the grizzly bear can't survive if Yellowstone Park is its only refuge. It also needs portions of the five adjacent national forests." Yet these forests are also the "home" of oil, gold, copper and platinum deposits and they contain prime candidates for ski slopes. The Yellowstone story underscores the truth that no part of the natural world is ever saved permanently—it must be defended anew by each succeeding generation.

Opposite: A bison in winter; hunters and poachers are still a threat to migrating animals.

ANIMALS & PLANTS
OF THE ROCKY MOUNTAINS AND THE GREAT PLAINS

This appendix provides a sample of animals and plants commonly found in the national parks of the Rocky Mountains and the Great Plains. The codes indicate in which parks these animals and plants are most often seen.

BL	Badlands	RM	Rocky Mountain	YS	Yellowstone
GL	Glacier	TR	Theodore Roosevelt		
GT	Grand Teton	WC	Wind Cave		

MAMMALS

AMERICAN RIVER OTTER
BL, GT, YS

The river otter is one of the largest members of the weasel family, measuring 3–4.25 ft., and weighing up to 30 lbs. Seeing it is really a chance occurrence, but when seen it is a major attraction, distinguished by clownlike actions—floating on its back in the water, sliding in the snow, and generally frolicking about. The river otter has a dark-brown coat, lighter belly, silver-gray throat, and whitish whiskers. Its long tail is thick at the base and tapers to a point, and its feet are webbed. It feeds mainly on fish, but also eats mice.

BADGER
BL, GL, GT, RM, TR

The nocturnal badger is seldom seen in heavily visited areas. Generally a little over 2 ft. long, including a 5-in. tail, it has a flattish body, with short, bowed legs. Its coat is gray to yellow and brown, with a white stripe running from the nose over the top of the head, white cheeks, black patches in front of the ears, and black feet. Its burrow has an 8–12-in. elliptical opening, and is marked by a large mound of earth and debris; the badger can bury itself faster than a person can dig with a shovel. It feeds on rodents.

BEAVER
BL, GL, GT, RM, TR, YS

The beaver is North America's largest rodent; dark brown, it generally is up to 4 ft. long, including a 1-ft., flat, scaly tail, and weighs 45–60 lbs., but can weigh up to 100. Mainly nocturnal, it is seldom seen; but there is evidence of its work in the dams of small streams. The beaver lives in lodges formed by logs; on major rivers, it lives in dens along the bank. The beaver's diet is mainly the bark of trees, although in summer it feeds on water vegetation.

BIGHORN SHEEP
BL, GL, RM, TR, YS

It is also known as the "mountain sheep" or the "Rocky Mountain bighorn sheep." Rams are 3–3.5 ft. in height, 127–316 lbs., and with a horn spread of 33 in. (the horns curve up and back over ears); ewes are 2.5–3 ft. in height and weigh 74–200 lbs. Color varies from dark brown to pale tan; generally the belly, rump patch, backs of legs, muzzle, and eye patch are white. The bighorn's diet is mostly grasses, sedges, and woody plants, and its habitat is rugged terrain, including mountain slopes. As rutting season approaches, rams competing for ewes charge each other at great speed and butt heads.

BISON
BL, GT, TR, WC, YS

The largest land animal in North America, also known as the buffalo; weighs as much as 2,000 pounds and stands up to 6 ft. at the shoulder. Its large, broad head, humped shoulders, short horns, and shaggy mane and beard make it easily recognizable. Systematically exterminated as a government policy in the mid-19th century, the bison was down to less than 1,000 by 1900. Today, more than 30,000 live in protected areas. Most active in the morning and late afternoon, they can be seen in herds, but should not be approached.

BLACK BEAR

GL, GT, RM, YS

The black bear may be a brownish or cinnamon color, but it can easily be distinguished from the grizzly and brown bear by its straight-profiled face, rather than the dished face of the others, and by its comparatively smaller size (3 ft. at the shoulder, 4.5–6.25 ft. long, 203–595 lbs.) and humpless shoulders. The black bear feeds on grasses, buds, leaves, berries, nuts, bark, insects, rodents, the fawns of deer and elk, and fish, particularly salmon; a scrounger by nature, it will forage near campsites. This is a powerful and potentially dangerous animal, despite its clown-like antics; although primarily nocturnal, it may be seen during the day.

BOBCAT

BL, GL, TR

The bobcat is North America's most common wild cat; nocturnal and secretive, it is seldom seen. It is tawny in color, with indistinct black spots, a pale or white belly, and a short, stubby, or "bobbed," tail with 2 or 3 black bars. It weighs 14–68 lbs. and measures 2.3–4 ft. long; the males are larger than the females. In the late winter, the male may be heard yowling at night, much like a domesticated cat. Kits are born in a den, usually in thickets or under rocks and logs. The bobcat feeds on rodents and especially ground-nesting birds.

COYOTE

BL, GL, GT, RM, TR, WC, YS

The coyote is the smallest species of wild dog; although it resembles a domestic dog, it is often mistaken for a wolf. The coyote is seen fairly regularly in the western parks; its evening "howl" has made it legendary. It weighs about 75 lbs., stands about 2 ft. at the shoulder, and is 3.5–4 ft. long, including a tail of 12–15 in. Its fur is brownish- to reddish-gray— at the lower altitudes more tan and red, at the higher altitudes more gray and black. The coyote has a varied diet of deer, elk, rabbit, rodents, snakes, birds, and insects. A typical den is a wide-mouthed earthen tunnel, 5–30 ft. long, which may be the former residence of a fox or badger.

DEER MOUSE

BL, GL, GT, RM, TR, WC

Of the 70 species of rats or mice in North America, one of the most common is the deer mouse. A grayish to reddish-brown mouse about 5–8.75 in. long, including a 2–5 in. tail, it feeds on seeds, nuts, small fruits, berries, and insects. It usually burrows in the ground, but may nest in trees or stumps.

DESERT COTTONTAIL

BL, TR, WC

The buff-brown desert cottontail is 13–16.5 in. long and can be seen at night sitting on a stump or log watching for prey; during the day, it scampers about feeding on grass and plants. Cottontails usually hop, but they can leap up to 15 ft., and, like all rabbits, they freeze when threatened and then abruptly flee.

ELK

GL, GT, RM, WC, YS

The elk, or wapiti, is second in size only to the moose in the deer family. Males may weigh 600–1,100 lbs. and stand 5 ft. at the shoulders (their graceful antlers may reach another 5 ft.); females weigh 450–650 lbs. They are tan or brown above with darker underparts and yellowish tail and rump patch. Mostly nocturnal, elk can be seen at dusk or dawn grazing in meadows on grasses and woody vegetation. Mating season is the fall, when the legendary fights with clashing antlers occur.

FISHER

GL, GT, YS

The fisher closely resembles but is larger than both the marten and the mink. Its long, thin body is dark brown with a broad grayish head and a bushy tail. The male may measure up to 40 in. and weigh 18 lbs.; the female is smaller. It preys mostly on snowshoe hares, porcupines, squirrels, and mice. Fishers tolerate one another only during the mating season; for the most part they are loners and thus are rarely seen. Their fur is considered valuable, and for this reason the population has dropped in recent years.

LONG-TAILED WEASEL

BL, GL, GT, RM, TR

Entirely carnivorous, the long-tailed weasel feeds on rats, rabbits, birds, and even other weasels when its killing instincts are triggered by the smell of blood. The animal's name is derived from a 3–6 in. brown tail with a black tip. The body is brown with a white chest. During the winter the long-tailed weasel is completely white, except for its black nose and eyes and the black tip of its tail.

MEADOW VOLE

GL, GT, TR, WC

The meadow vole, or field mouse, varies in color from yellowish- or reddish-brown peppered with black, to blackish-brown above, and generally gray below. It measures 5.5–7.75 in. in length, including a 2 in. tail. While they scoot about fast and are hard to spot, grass cuttings piled in the form of "runways" usually indicate burrows. Diet is mostly green vegetation.

MOOSE

GL, GT, YS

The largest member of the deer family, the moose is at once a majestic animal and an unpredictable and dangerous beast viewed best from a distance. The male weighs up to 1,400 pounds and stands up to 7.5 ft. at the shoulder. Its antler spread is 4–5 ft., but the record is 81 in. Moose, identified by an overhanging snout and pendent "bell" on the throat, live in spruce forests, swamps, and aspen and willow thickets, where they feed on willows, aquatic vegetation, and, at streams, the leaves of water lilies.

MOUNTAIN GOAT

GL

Not a true goat, this mammal belongs to a group known as goat-antelopes; its distinctive smooth, black, daggerlike horns are unlike the corkscrewlike horns of goats. Compact and short-legged, it has a yellowish-white coat, long and shaggy in winter, shorter in summer. The mountain goat is not conspicuous, but with patience, good field glasses, and a little guidance from park rangers, it can be found. Active in morning and evening hours, sometimes in moonlight, on sheer cliffs and rocky ledges, it feeds on green vegetation in summer, woody plants and mosses in winter. The male is generally 3.5 ft. tall and weighs up to 300 pounds. The female is about 15% smaller.

MULE DEER

BL, GL, GT, RM, TR, WC, YS

The mule deer is a common species of the deer family seen in the western parks, particularly in the early morning and late evening. It is characterized by its large, mulelike ears (hence its name) and white rump, although it should not be confused with the white-tailed deer—also seen in some western parks. It weighs up to 400 lbs., and stands 3–3.5 ft. at the shoulder. The male loses its antlers in the late winter and is generally solitary. The mule deer eats acorns, berries, cactus fruits, twigs, buds, grasses, herbs, tree bark, and mushrooms.

MUSKRAT

BL, GL, GT, RM, TR

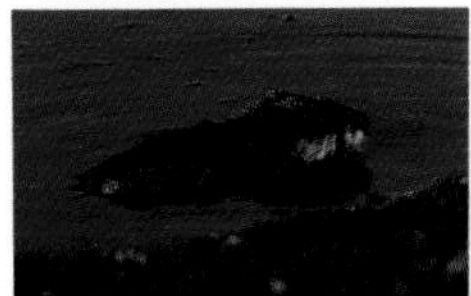

A large, volelike rodent with dense, glossy brown fur, the muskrat can be seen at any time, but especially at night. It measures 16–24.5 in. in length, including a 7–12 in. scaly tail, and weighs about 4 pounds. Muskrats live in multi-chambered structures made of plants, roots, and mud in marshy areas along streams and lakes, similar to those of the beaver. It eats nearby vegetation—cattails, sedges, water lilies, rushes—on a specially built eating platform.

PIKA

GL, GT, RM, YS

Sometimes called the "whistling hare," this small furry mammal, which closely resembles the guinea pig, has a pudgy brownish body, is 6.5–8.5 in. long, has short, rounded ears, and lacks a discernible tail. It feeds mostly on green plants and burrows among rocks. It may spread plant cuttings to dry in the sun, then store them in its den.

PORCUPINE

BL, GL, GT, RM, TR

Contrary to legend, porcupines *cannot* throw or "shoot" their quills, although the quills are rather loosely attached and may shake off if the porcupine thrashes its tail about in self-defense. Classified as a rodent, it is the only quilled mammal. About 3 ft. long, 1 ft. high, and 35 lbs., it lives mostly in coniferous forests, but may also inhabit brushy areas of the Southwest. It survives mostly on a diet of the wood directly beneath tree bark, although it also eats buds and twigs.

PRONGHORN

BL, GT, TR, WC, YS

The pronghorn is neither goat nor antelope, although called the "American antelope," but instead is the sole survivor of an ancient *Antilocapridae* family dating back 20 million years. Its upper body and the outside of its legs are pale tan or reddish-tan, while its sides, chest, inner legs, and rump patch are white. Black horns are 12–20 in. fully grown. It stands 35–41 in. at the shoulder and can be up to 6 ft. long. Conspicuous in scattered bands, the pronghorn grazes on grasses and moist green plants. When frightened it will flee, with a buck usually in the rear guard. It is the fastest animal in the Western Hemisphere with speeds of 45 mph or more—30 mph is "cruising speed" for distances of up to 15 miles.

RED FOX

BL, GL, TR

Although this fox goes through color phases—black and silver—it is primarily reddish with white underparts, chin, and throat. Its tail is 13–17 in. long, bushy with a white tip. Doglike in size, it measures 15–16 in. high and 15–40 in. long. Though common, the red fox is difficult to spot in the parks; it is shy and primarily nocturnal. Red foxes feed on whatever is available, from corn and apples to birds and mice, crickets and crayfish. Dens are usually "remodeled" or enlarged marmot or badger dens along stream banks, slopes, or rock piles, but are always high for a full view of the surrounding area.

RED SQUIRREL

GL, GT, TR, WC, YS

A small tree squirrel, rust-red to grayish-red above to white or grayish-white below, the red squirrel nests in a hollow tree or a hole in the ground and eats a wide assortment of nuts, seeds, birds' eggs, and even the deadly (to man) amanita mushroom. Its tail is the same color as its back, but with a broad black band edged in white, and in the winter its ears have large tufts of fur. It measures about 15 in. in length.

SNOWSHOE HARE

GL, GT, RM

Small and shy and mostly nocturnal, the snowshoe hare rests in hollow logs or the burrows of beavers and woodchucks during the day. In the summer its coat is dark brown, but in winter it changes to white or white mottled with brown. The snowshoe hare measures 15–20 in. in length and weighs 2–3 pounds. Its ears are 2.5–3.25 in. and black-tipped, and in winter its large hindfeet are well-furred. When frightened, it can run up to 30 mph.

STRIPED SKUNK

BL, GL, RM, TR

The striped skunk is found almost everywhere in the U.S. except Alaska. It has a narrow stripe of white down its nose, and a V-shaped, white configuration down its back; males weigh 6–14 lbs. and measure 20–31 in., including a 7–15 in. bushy tail. The striped skunk feeds on insects, small mammals, amphibians, and eggs of small ground-nesting birds. Notorious for the scent of the musk that it may spray at potential enemies, it can hit a victim from a distance of up to 12 ft.

BIRDS

AMERICAN KESTREL

BL, GL, GT, TR, YS

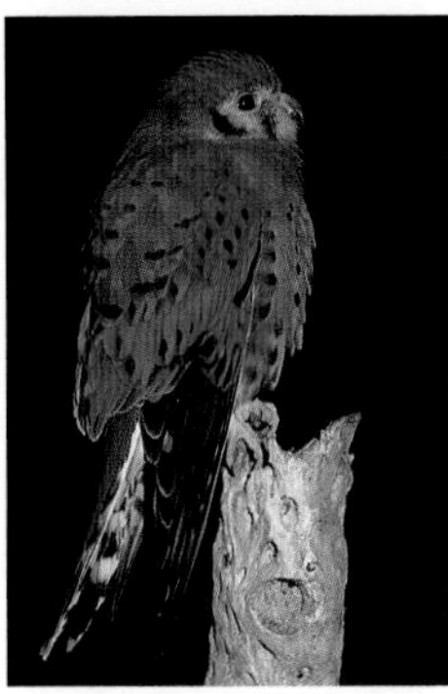

Until recently, this small falcon was known as the "sparrow hawk." The kestrel measures 9–12 in. from bill to tail and has a wingspread of 22–23 in. It has blue-gray wings and head with a buff breast and nape. The kestrel does not build a nest of its own, but lays its eggs without nesting or borrows another bird's nest in tree holes or building niches. It can be seen perched on trees and telephone poles, from which it swoops rapidly upon its grasshopper and rodent prey.

BALD EAGLE

GL, GT, WC, YS

The adult bald eagle, over 5 years old, has a snow-white head, neck, and tail; the rest of the body is brownish-black. The immature eagle is brown except for some white wing linings and whitish blotches on underparts; a white head and tail comes gradually with each molt. The U.S. national bird, it measures 30–43 in. from head to tail with a wingspan of 78–96 in. Primarily a fish eater, it also eats carrion and catches crippled waterfowl. Hunting and poaching have diminished their numbers, but they can occasionally be seen nesting in tall trees.

BARN SWALLOW

BL, GL, GT, RM, TR

The barn swallow lives in the open country, often near water, but draws its name from nesting under eaves of houses and on bridges, rarely away from man-made structures. It is 5.75–7.75 in. long, with a long, deeply forked tail, and is blue-black above with light cinnamon-rust below. It feeds on insects.

BREWER'S BLACKBIRD

BL, GT, TR, WC, YS

The male Brewer's blackbird has an iridescent purple-black head, glossy green-violet body, and yellow eyes; the female is a light gray-brown with brown eyes. It is 8–10 in. long and is a very social bird, mixing with other blackbirds, such as the red-winged. Its range is wide, from British Columbia to northern Baja California and east to the Great Lakes, and it feeds primarily on seeds and insects.

BURROWING OWL

BL, TR, YS

Classified as a small owl, measuring 9–11 in., the burrowing owl is earth brown with white spots, whitish eyebrows, and white throat with a dark collar. It has long legs and a short tail and stands upright whether perching or on the ground. The burrowing owl nests in ground squirrel or prairie dog burrows; the stories that it shares a nest with rodents or rattlesnakes are only legend. When agitated, it bobs and bows.

CANADA GOOSE

BL, GL, GT, YS

This majestic waterfowl, with its long black neck, black head and bill, white cheek patches, and grayish-brown body, measures up to 36 in. in length and weighs up to 13 pounds. It will nest in a marsh or on a haystack, sometimes on lake shores. It breeds across North America from Alaska to Labrador, migrates south to the mid-Atlantic states, Kansas, and California, and each spring it returns to its ancestral breeding grounds.

COMMON FLICKER

BL, GT, RM, TR, WC

The common flicker is a large woodpecker with barred cinnamon-brown back and white rump, measuring 12.5–14 in. in length. It has a brown head and a gray face and neck, and the male has a red mustache separated from boldly black-on-white spotted underparts by a black crescent on its breast. The flicker nests in a hole excavated in a tree, post, or cactus. It feeds on ants and other ground insects.

COMMON NIGHTHAWK

BL, GL, GT, TR, WC, YS

A slim-winged gray-brown bird, with ample tail, large eyes, tiny bill, and short legs, the common nighthawk measures 8.5–10 in. from bill to tail. Male has white throat patch and white subterminal tail bar. It feeds on nocturnal insects, and by day sits on tree limbs in a "dead-leaf" camouflage.

COMMON RAVEN

BL, GL, GT, RM, TR, YS

Considered to have an intelligence matching a dog's, applying reason to new situations, the raven is the largest of the crows; it is 21.5–27 in. from bill to tail. It is black, with thick bill and wedge-shaped tail. The raven nests in a large collection of sticks, bones, and soft material on a cliff face or in a tree, and feeds on almost anything.

GOLDEN EAGLE

BL, GL, TR, WC, YS

The golden eagle, the most majestic of North America's birds, is 2.5–3.5 ft. from bill to tail and has a wingspread of 7–8 ft. It is shaped like a hawk, but with a much greater wingspan when flying. It is dark brown with a "golden" nape visible only at close range, and its legs are feathered down to the talons. Its nest is generally a large mass of twigs or sticks on a crag or rocky ledge or high in a tree. The golden eagle's primary diet is rodents and rabbits.

GREAT BLUE HERON

GL, GT, YS

This is a large heron, some 42–52 in. in length, with blue-gray back and wings and underparts whitish with black streaking. The head is white with a black stripe ending in black plumes behind the eye. It nests in trees but is seen more often standing in water or on banks feeding on fish.

GREAT HORNED OWL

GL, GT, TR, YS

The great horned owl is common to all of North America, from Mexico to the tree line in Canada. It is 1.5–2 ft. from tail to top of head, gray-brown above, with a fine dark-gray horizontal barring below, large yellow eyes, and ear tufts set far apart. It nests in trees, crevices, or cliffs, often in a nest once occupied by a hawk. The owl hunts rabbits, rodents, ducks, crows, and other owls.

HAIRY WOODPECKER

GL, GT, RM, TR, YS

A medium-size woodpecker, but larger than the downy, the hairy woodpecker has a white head with black crown, eyemask, "whiskers," and white back. Male has red patch at base of crown, and black tail with white outer feathers; female has no red patch. Both are 8.5–10.5 in. from bill to tail. It feeds by pecking a hole in tree bark and, with long, flexible tongue, extracting grubs; it nests in tree cavities.

HORNED LARK

BL, GL, TR, WC, YS

This bird is faithful to its birthplace and so each population adapts to the color of its habitat. It is generally pale brown with a black bib, yellow wash on its throat and face, and black whisker marks and black "horns." North America's only true lark, it is about 7.5 in. long and feeds mostly on seeds.

KILLDEER

BL, GL, GT, TR, WC, YS

The killdeer is grayish-brown above, white below, with two black breast bands, and a long tan tail which is evident in flight. It measures 9–11 in. long. It lays its eggs in a scrape on bare ground in plowed field, gravel shore, roadway, or bald spot in pasture, and is conspicuous for its means of distracting predators from young—by dragging itself along the ground, as though it has broken a wing, until it has led danger away. It feeds on worms and insects.

MALLARD

BL, GL, GT, YS

The mallard is the ancestor of America's domestic duck, with which it frequently interbreeds. It measures 20.5–28 in. The male has a green head, white collar, and chestnut breast. The female is a mottled brown, with a purplish-blue speculum bordered in front and back by a black-and-white stripe. The male's bill is yellow, the female's, orange. They feed on grain and on plants and small animals found at the bottom of shallow waters.

MOURNING DOVE

BL, GL, GT, YS

The mourning dove's name comes from the melancholy cooing of the male, generally "sung" from a prominent perch and followed by a courtship flight. The bird measures 11–13 in. from bill to tail; it is light brownish-gray, with a pale buff chest, darker wings with black spots along the inside edge, and an iridescent, light violet neck shield. The central tail feathers are quite long, with sharply tapered, white-tipped outer feathers. Like other species of doves, it feeds primarily on seeds, and nests in trees and bushes.

RED-TAILED HAWK
BL, GL, GT, RM, TR, YS

The red-tailed hawk is one of the larger hawks, measuring 19–25 in. tall, with a wingspan of 48–54 in. It has a dark-brown back, a light-brown chest with a dark belly band, and a finely streaked grayish tail. Frequently seen perched atop fence posts or telephone poles, the bird will sit inordinately still for a long time, then suddenly swoop down on a squirrel or a rabbit.

SANDHILL CRANE
BL, GL, GT, TR, YS

This "dancing" crane is 3–4 ft. in length, with a wingspan of 6.5–7 ft., and is gray or ash. Adults have a red cap on the forehead. They eat amphibians, reptiles, small mammals, insects, as well as fruits and grain. The sandhill crane bows, droops its wings, hops, and leaps as high as 20 ft. in a "dance" during courtship, as well as at other times and sometimes in large groups. It nests on mounds of vegetation surrounded by water.

SHARP-TAILED GROUSE
BL, TR, WC

The sharp-tail resembles but is smaller than the female pheasant, measuring 15–20 in. A narrow tail shows white on outer feathers in flight. It is mottled buff overall, with slightly lighter underparts; the male has a violet neck patch. Males perform an elaborate mating dance, with erect tail, puffed breast, inflated air sac on the neck, and much hopping and stamping. This grouse nests in tall grass brush.

SWAINSON'S HAWK
BL, GT, WC, YS

Common to the Great Plains, the Swainson's hawk is about 22 in. long, with a wingspan of 48–56 in. when it soars on thermal air currents. It is smaller than the red-tailed hawk. The typical adult is dark brown above with a white throat, dark breast band, and white lower chest. The tail is finely barred with a broad band near the tip. It feeds on insects and rodents and nests on the ground as well as in trees and on cliffs.

WESTERN MEADOW-LARK
BL, TR, WC, YS

Lewis and Clark first noticed the difference between the eastern meadowlark and this beautiful songbird, and Audubon gave it its Latin name, *Sturnella neglecta*, "neglected meadowlark." The birds look very much alike, but the western meadowlark is superior in song. It measures 8–10.5 in., and is chunky and brown with a bright yellow breast crossed by a black V. The tail feathers are white, streaked with brown, and the top of the head has black and white stripes. It feeds on seeds and insects.

WHITE-TAILED PTARMIGAN
GL, RM

This open-country grouse is almost pure white in the winter. In summer it has a mottled-barred brown head, breast, and back, with white wings, belly, and tail. It measures about 13 in. and nests in a scrape lined with grass, leaves, and feathers.

AMPHIBIANS AND REPTILES

BULLSNAKE

BL, TR, WC, YS

Large and powerfully built, the bullsnake measures 4–8 ft. and has a small head. The yellowish snake has at least 40 black, brown, or reddish-brown blotches on back and sides. Active during the day, it consumes large numbers of rodents.

COMMON GARTER SNAKE

GL, GT, RM, TR, YS

This is one of the snakes seen most often in North America, but its colors and identification marks vary from one region to another. It can best be recognized by three stripes, one on the back and one on each side; the side stripes occupy the second and third rows of scales above the belly. The area between stripes often has a double row of black spots and red blotches. The common garter snake can range between 1.5 and 4 ft. in length and generally lives near the water or in moist vegetation where it feeds on frogs, salamanders, earthworms, mice, and occasionally small fish.

GREAT PLAINS TOAD

BL, TR

Like other "true" toads, this one has large cranial crests that converge to a bony hump on the snout; it also has conspicuous, puffy glands behind the eyes. Gray to olive to brown, it has large, light-bordered dark blotches all over the body. The plains toad lives in grasslands and drier bushy areas and feeds on insects. It measures 2–4.5 in. in length.

NORTHERN LEOPARD FROG

BL, TR, RM, WC

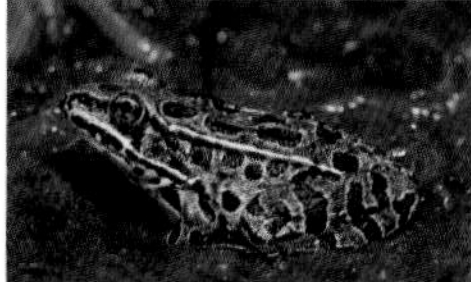

Also called the "meadow frog," the northern leopard frog may wander far from water. Brown or green in color, it is 2–3.5 in. in length. Its dark spots are round or oval with light borders, and adjacent spots may run together. Two or three rows of spots, irregularly spaced, lie between the dorsolateral ridges, and more spots appear on the sides.

PLAINS SPADEFOOT TOAD

BL, TR, WC

This 1.5–2 in. toad is gray or brown, often with a green tint, and has dark markings. It prefers open grasslands in areas of low rainfall on the Great Plains. It has a prominent boss, or bump, between the eyes, and it uses the sharp-edged black spade on each hind foot to burrow vertically down into sandy or other loose soil. A swift flick of its sticky tongue captures insects, many of which are regarded as agricultural pests.

PRAIRIE RATTLESNAKE

BL, TR, WC

The prairie rattler is a subspecies of the western rattlesnake and has cousins called Hopi, Grand Canyon, Arizona black, and Great Basin, among others. The size varies from 16–64 in., but the prairie's colors are generally greenish or brownish above, with well-defined brown blotches. Feeding on small mammals, this species finds its home in prairie dog towns and rocky outcrops.

SAGEBRUSH LIZARD

GT, TR, YS

This spiny lizard measures 5–6 in. and lives in sagebrush areas or gravelly soils, never far from the shelter of rock outcroppings, crevices, or animal burrows. Occasionally one can be seen climbing a tree in pursuit of an insect. The sagebrush lizard is grayish-green to brown with four longitudinal rows of brown spots. Males usually have blue patches on the belly that do not meet the blue of the throat. The sides of the female may be reddish-orange behind the forelegs.

TIGER SALAMANDER

GL, TR, WC

The tiger salamander is the world's largest land-dwelling salamander; it is 6–13 in. long. It has a broad head and small eyes. Often seen at night after heavy rain, the tiger salamander lives beneath debris near water. It feeds on earthworms, large insects, small mice, and amphibians.

WESTERN CHORUS FROG

BL, GT, TR

The rasping voice of this little creature has often been likened to the sound of someone running a fingernail across the teeth of a comb. In the evenings at breeding time, males gather around ponds and produce a "chorus" of near-deafening sound. The western subspecies has three dark stripes down the back. Its skin is smooth and greenish-gray to brown and it measures .75–1.5 in. The western chorus frog feeds on insects.

WESTERN PAINTED TURTLE

BL, GL, TR, WC

The painted turtle is the most widely distributed turtle in North America and the most familiar. It measures 4–9.75 in. and can be identified easily by its fondness for basking in the sun. The carapace, or shell, is olive to black; the western subspecies' back is laced with a network of light lines and patterns. The young are carnivorous, but as they mature they eat mostly green leafy plants.

WESTERN TERRESTRIAL GARTER SNAKE

GT, YS

There are four subspecies of this snake, so the colors and marks vary. This garter has a narrow, dull yellow or brown back stripe that fades toward the tail; the light areas are marked with small dark spots that are sometimes enlarged, sometimes absent altogether, and at other times fused and mottled. It measures 1.5–3.5 ft. in length. This snake feeds on tadpoles, frogs, fish, mice, and small birds.

WESTERN TOAD

GT, RM

The western toad is slightly larger than its plains cousin. The western is gray to green, with a light-colored stripe down the middle of the back. Its warts are reddish, surrounded by black blotches. Generally active at dusk, it may be seen during the day at high elevations. It feeds on insects and lives in housing borrowed from rodents.

FLOWERS, SHRUBS, AND TREES

AMERICAN ELM
BL, TR, WC

This graceful tree has been ravaged by a fungus disease in the past several decades. The elm grows to 100 ft. and the trunk sometimes is larger than 4 ft. in diameter. Its branches spread and droop at the ends, forming a broad crown sometimes wider than high. The leaves are dark green and elliptical. The Indians conducted council meetings under the tallest elms.

BEAR GRASS
GL

Growing thickly in clearings and open fields, bear grass may reach a height of 5 ft. Rising from basal leaves that resemble coarse blades of grass, a strong stalk is topped by a long dense raceme of small cream-colored flowers. Bear grass is also called Indian basket grass, and the leaves were used by Indians to weave garments and baskets.

BLAZING STAR
BL, TR, WC

This member of the stickleaf family is called blazing star because of barbed hairs on its leaves that stick to fabric. Many large, starlike blooms are on branches at the top of a stout, satiny, white stem: flowers 2–5-in. wide bloom from June to September; 4–12-in. leaves are very rough, with large, irregular teeth. It grows 1–3 ft. high.

BLUE GRAMA
BL, TR, WC

The most important range grass on the Great Plains, primarily because it withstands droughts so well, blue grama provides good feed for range animals in both summer and winter. It attains a height of 3 ft. and has narrow, curly leaves and one-sided seed spikes.

BOX ELDER
BL, TR, WC

Classed with maples, the small to medium-size box elder has a short trunk and a broad, rounded crown of light-green foliage. It grows to a height of 30–60 ft. and a trunk diameter of 2.5 ft. Its leaves are 2.4 in. long: flowers are .2 in., with small, yellow-green calyx of five lobes. Plains Indians made sugar from box elder sap.

CHOKECHERRY
BL, GL, TR, WC

The name comes from the astringent meat of the fruit, especially when immature. The tree, or shrub, is small, perhaps to 20 ft. tall and 6 in. in diameter, and is one of 2,000 species in the rose family. The egg-shaped leaves are 2–5 in. long and sharply saw-toothed; the white flowers are up to 5 in. long.

DOUGLAS FIR

GL, GT, RM, YS

This tree is found primarily in the loamy soils on mountain slopes, in pure or nearly pure stands. It grows 80–200 ft. tall and the trunk measures up to 10 ft. in diameter. The evergreen needles are about .75–1.25 in. and quite flexible; cones measure 2–3.5 in. long and are light brown and egg-shaped. The foliage is eaten by grouse, deer, and elk; the seeds are eaten by birds and mammals.

FREMONT COTTONWOOD

GT, RM, TR

Named for its discoverer, John Charles Fremont, this cottonwood is a tall tree, with a broad, flattened, open crown of large, widely spreading branches. It is 40–80 ft. high, 2–4 ft. in diameter, with 2–3-in. leaves. The cottonwood grows in wet soil and indicates permanent water. Hopi Indians carve kachina dolls from cottonwood roots.

INDIAN PAINTBRUSH

GL, GT, WC, YS

The flower resembles a crimson or scarlet paintbrush, thus the name Indian paintbrush. Usually found in clumps of several stems in sagebrush areas, it grows to 1–3 ft. and flowers from May to September.

KINNIKINNICK (BEARBERRY)

GL, RM, WC

Kinnikinnick is an Indian word that applies both to the mixture of dried leaves, herbs, and bark they called "tobacco" and to any of the plants used in that mixture, especially the bearberry. This plant is a low, spreading, woody-stemmed perennial, whose fruits bears do in fact eat. The fruit is a bright red berry about .5 in. wide. The flower is small, pink, and lantern-shaped, and about .25 in. long.

LIMBER PINE

GL, GT, RM

This medium-size tree has a short trunk and broad crown of stout branches. It grows on dry, rocky ridges and peaks. "Limber" refers to tough, flexible twigs that can be twisted without breaking. The height is 40–50 ft. and the diameter of the trunk is 2–3 ft. Cones measure 4–8.5 in. and are egg-shaped and yellow-brown. The needles are slender and about 3 in. long.

LODGEPOLE PINE

GL, RM, YS

This tall, slender, straight tree may attain a height of 150 ft., growing slowly over a life span of up to

600 years. Very hot days or forest fires cause cones to shed their seeds, which quickly establish themselves on burned-over sites. The needles, two per bundle, are long, stiff, and usually twisted. The bark, orange-brown or grayish, forms small, thin, close scales.

LUPINE

GL, GT, RM, YS

This species of lupine blooms from May to August. The leaf blades are divided into 7–9 splayed, or palmate, segments; leaves are silvery-silky on upper surfaces. The plant rises 8–20 in., with the purple blossoms occurring on a long raceme of 4–6 in. The cup-shaped flowers are typical of the pea family to which lupines belong.

PASQUE FLOWER

BL, GL, TR, WC

South Dakota's state flower, the pasque flower blooms in the early spring before any of its surrounding vegetation turns green and continues to bloom through August. The plant is covered with silky hair. "Petals" are really sepals, or a part of the main flower stem, and vary in color from white to lavender.

PONDEROSA PINE

BL, GT, RM, TR, WC

The most widely distributed and common pine in North America, the ponderosa pine is a large evergreen with a broad, open, conical crown of spreading branches. It is 60–130 ft. high, and the trunk is 2.5–4 ft. in diameter, with stiff dark-green needles and 2–6 in. cones. It is the most commercially valuable western pine.

PRICKLY PEAR

BL, TR, WC

The prickly pear is a flat, nearly oval cactus, 3–6 in. high. Its bright yellow or bright magenta many-petaled flowers are 2–3 in. wide and bloom in late spring.

QUAKING ASPEN

GL, GT, RM

The most widely distributed tree in North America, the quaking aspen grows to a height of 40–60 ft. or more. Its leaves are 1.25–3 in. long and nearly round. Shiny green above, dull green beneath, the leaves turn golden yellow in autumn before dropping. The "quaking" comes from leaves that tremble in even a light breeze. The bark is a favorite of beaver and rabbits; deer and elk feed on twigs and foliage.

ROCKY MOUNTAIN JUNIPER

BL, GL, GT, RM, TR, WC

Growing on ridges, cliffs, and dry, rocky hillsides, this evergreen tree stands 20–50 ft. tall, with a 1.5 ft.-diameter trunk. Its small cones are .25 in. in diameter and berry-like. Bright blue with a whitish coat, the cones are eaten by wildlife. Wood is used for cedar chests and lumber.

SAGEBRUSH

BL, GL, GT, WC, YS

There are several species of sagebrush in the western U.S. All have an aromatic, almost pungent, odor. They are silvery shrubs, with persistent leaves, whose heads are small and yellow, green, or white when in bloom.

SEGO LILY

BL, TR, WC

The sego lily is a showy flower with three waxy petals of white or magenta with a yellow base, or it is often all yellow. It flourishes in dry soil on plains, with sagebrush, and in pine forests. When food was scarce, Mormon pioneers ate the bulbs of the sego lily, which taste something like potatoes when boiled.

SHRUBBY CINQUEFOIL

BL, GL, RM, TR, WC, YS

A small, low-growing shrub with reddish-brown bark and yellow flowers, the shrubby cinquefoil is a member of the rose family. The flower has five petals about 1 in. long. Some plants grow to 36 in., and sometimes the flowers are white.

SUBALPINE FIR

GL, GT, YS

This is the most widespread western true fir, growing to a height of 50–100 ft., with a trunk diameter of 2.5–6 ft. Its evergreen needles spread at right angles to the twig in two rows and are 1–1.75 in. long. Cones are 2.25–4 in. long. Wildlife feed off the lower branches. When heavy with snow, lower branches will sometimes take root, sending up new shoots in the spring.

SUNFLOWER

BL, WC

The common sunflower is a tall, coarse, leafy plant with a hairy stem that grows to 2–13 ft. Its flower head has a central maroon disk surrounded by many bright yellow rays: it flowers from June to September. The head turns during the day to follow the path of the sun.

WESTERN WALLFLOWER

BL, RM, TR, WC

A member of the mustard family, the western wallflower has bright yellow (sometimes orange) flowers, whose four .75 in. petals are arranged in the form of a cross (the scientific name for mustard family is Cruciferae) The fruits mature into 4 in. pods. The unbranched stems have downy hair.

WHITEBARK PINE

GL, GT, YS

The whitebark pine, sometimes called a "scrub pine" or "white pine," is distinguished by its short, twisted, or crooked trunk and very irregular crown. It grows to 20–50 ft. in high mountains near the timberline, and has a trunk diameter of 1–2 ft. Cones are 1.5–3.25 in. long; they drop at maturity but do not open until decayed.

PHOTO CREDITS

Page 10: © Robert P. Carr
13: © Jim Brandenburg
17: © South Dakota State Historical Society
18–19: © Jim Rudnick
21: © Annie Griffiths/West Light
22, top: © Jeff Gnass; **bottom:** © Don & Pat Valenti
24–25: © Jim Brandenburg/West Light
26: © Rod Allin/Tom Stack & Assoc.
27: © John Cancalosi/Tom Stack & Assoc.
28: © David Muench
31: © Jim Brandenburg/West Light
33: © S.L. Eckert/Click, Chicago
34: © Sonja Bullaty
37: © Craig Blacklock
41, 43: © C.W. Buchholtz
45: © Ed Cooper
46: © Jeff Gnass
48: © Pat O'Hara
49, 51: © David Muench
52: © Jeff Gnass
53: © Tom J. Ulrich
55, both: © Robert C. Gildart
56: © Michael S. Sample
59: © Pat O'Hara
60–61: © Sonja Bullaty
64, 69: © David Muench
70: © D.C. Lowe
73: © David Muench
76–77: Grand Teton National Park
79: Grand Teton National Park
81: © Jeff Gnass
83: © David Muench
84–85: © Galen Rowell
87: © Pat O'Hara
88: © Manuel Rodriguez
89: © Stan Osolinski
90: © Barbara Von Hoffmann/Tom Stack & Assoc.
92–93, 94–95: © David Muench
99, 100: © Ed Cooper
101: © Alan D. Briere/Tom Stack & Assoc.
103: © Jeff Gnass
104: © D.C. Lowe
105: © David Muench
107: © Galen Rowell
108, 111: © David Muench
115, both; 116: Rocky Mountain National Park/National Park Service
119: © Rex Tefertiller
121: © Kent & Donna Dannen
123, 124: © Pat O'Hara
127: © Alan D. Briere/Tom Stack & Assoc.
128–129: © Jeff Gnass
131: © Ed Cooper
134–135: © David Muench
137: © D.C. Lowe
138: © Kent & Donna Dannen
140–141: © David Muench
143, top: © Kent & Donna Dannen; **bottom:** © Rex Tefertiller
145, 147: © David Muench
149: © Jeff Gnass
150: © Sonja Bullaty
153: © Stephen Trimble
158: Harvard Library Collections/Theodore Roosevelt National Park
158–159: Doug Ferris Collection/Theodore Roosevelt National Park
159: Harvard Library Collections/Theodore Roosevelt National Park
161, 163: © David Muench
164: © Stephen Trimble
165: © Robert C. Gildart
167: © Stephen Trimble
169: © David Muench
171: © Stephen Trimble
172–173: © James P. Rowan/Click, Chicago
174: © Wilford L. Miller
177: © Jeff Gnass
178: © David Muench
181: © Kent & Donna Dannen
185, both: Wind Cave National Park
187: © Ed Cooper
189: © Mike Crackel
191: © Gary S. Withey
192: © Kent & Donna Dannen
193, 194: © Don & Pat Valenti
195: © Robert P. Carr
196–197, 200–201: © Tom Bean
202: © Jeremy Schmidt
205: © Craig Blacklock
209, 211, 212: Yellowstone National Park/National Park Service
214–215: © Jeremy Schmidt
217, 219: © David Muench
221: © Kent & Donna Dannen
223: © Sonja Bullaty
224–225: © Laurance Aiuppy
227, left: © Stan Osolinski; **right:** © Craig Blacklock
229: © David Muench
233: © Barbara Von Hoffmann/Tom Stack & Assoc.
235: © Rex Tefertiller
237: © Alan D. Briere/Tom Stack & Assoc.
238–239: © Laurance Aiuppy
240: © Angelo Lomeo
242: © Paul Schullery
245: © Jeff Gnass

248, col. 1, top: © E.P.I. Nancy Adams/Tom Stack & Assoc., **bottom:** © Roy Murphy; **col. 2, top:** © Larry Thorngren/Tom Stack & Assoc., **bottom:** © G.C. Kelley/Tom Stack & Assoc.; **col. 3:** © John Cancalosi/ Tom Stack & Assoc. **249, col. 1, both:** © Roy Murphy; **col. 2:** © Roy Murphy; **col. 3, top:** © Joe McDonald/ Tom Stack & Assoc., **bottom:** © Roy Murphy. **250, col. 1, top:** © Roy Murphy, **bottom:** © Gary Milburn/ Tom Stack & Assoc.; **col. 2, top:** © C. Summers/Tom Stack & Assoc., **bottom:** © Rod Planck/Tom Stack & Assoc.; **col. 3, top:** © G.C. Kelley/Tom Stack & Assoc., **bottom:** © John Shaw/Tom Stack & Assoc. **251, col. 1:** © Rod Planck/ Tom Stack & Assoc.; **col. 2, top:** © Keith H. Murakami/Tom Stack & Assoc., **bottom:** © C. Summers/Tom Stack & Assoc.; **col. 3, top:** © William R. Eastman III/Tom Stack & Assoc., **bottom:** © G.C. Kelley/Tom Stack & Assoc.
252, col. 1: © John Shaw/ Tom Stack & Assoc.; **col. 2, top:** © Rod Planck/Tom Stack & Assoc., **bottom:** © Mark Newman/Tom Stack & Assoc.; **col. 3:** © Robert C. Gildart.
253, col. 1, top: © Christopher Crowley/Tom Stack & Assoc., **bottom:** © Tom Stack/Tom Stack & Assoc.; **col. 2, top:** © Leonard Lee Rue III/Tom Stack & Assoc., **bottom:** © Anthony Mercieca/Tom Stack & Assoc.; **col. 3:** © John Gerlach/Tom Stack & Assoc.
254, col. 1, top: © Gary Randall/Tom Stack & Assoc., **bottom:** © Alan G. Nelson/ Tom Stack & Assoc.; **col. 2, top:** © John Shaw/Tom Stack & Assoc., **bottom:** © G.C. Kelley/Tom Stack & Assoc.; **col. 3, top:** © Joe Branney/ Tom Stack & Assoc., **bottom:** © Robert C. Gildart.
255, col. 1, top: © Stephen Trimble, **bottom:** © Rod Planck/Tom Stack & Assoc.; **col. 2, top:** © Anthony Mercieca/Tom Stack & Assoc., **bottom:** © Rod Planck/ Tom Stack & Assoc.; **col. 3, top:** © John Shaw/Tom Stack & Assoc., **bottom:** © Roy Murphy.
256, col. 1, top: © C. Summers/Tom Stack & Assoc., **bottom:** © Richard P. Smith/Tom Stack & Assoc.; **col. 2, top:** © C. Summers/ Tom Stack & Assoc., **bottom:** © Anthony Mercieca/ Tom Stack & Assoc.; **col. 3, top:** © Robert P. Carr, **bottom:** © C. Summers/Tom Stack & Assoc.
257, col. 1, top: © C. Summers/Tom Stack & Assoc., **bottom:** © John Cancalosi/ Tom Stack & Assoc.; **col. 2, top:** © Robert C. Simpson/ Tom Stack & Assoc., **bottom:** © Rod Planck/Tom Stack & Assoc.; **col. 3, top:** © David M. Dennis/ Tom Stack & Assoc., **bottom:** © John Shaw/Tom Stack & Assoc.
258, col. 1, top: © Stephen Trimble, **bottom:** © Alan G. Nelson/ Tom Stack & Assoc.; **col. 2, top:** © Rod Planck/ Tom Stack & Assoc., **bottom:** © Milton Rand/Tom Stack & Assoc.; **col. 3, top:** © Jim Yuskavitch/Tom Stack & Assoc., **bottom:** © John Gerlach/Tom Stack & Assoc.
259, col. 1, top: © John Shaw/Tom Stack & Assoc., **bottom:** © Alan G. Nelson/ Tom Stack & Assoc.; **col. 2, top:** © Rod Planck/Tom Stack & Assoc., **bottom:** © Stephen Trimble; **col. 3, both:** © Stephen Trimble.
260, col. 1, top: © Jim Yuskavitch/Tom Stack & Assoc., **bottom:** © Roy Murphy; **col. 2, top:** © Roy Murphy, **bottom:** © Stephen Trimble; **col. 3, top:** © Jeff Gnass, **bottom:** © Laurance Aiuppy.
261, col. 1, top: © Alan G. Nelson/Tom Stack & Assoc., **bottom:** © Bob & Miriam Francis/Tom Stack & Assoc.; **col. 2, top:** © Stephen Trimble, **bottom:** © Michael Collier; **col. 3, top:** © Tom Stack/Tom Stack & Assoc., **bottom:** © Ed Cooper.
262, col. 1, top: © Stephen Trimble, **center:** © Bob & Miriam Francis/Tom Stack & Assoc., **bottom:** © D. Davidson/Tom Stack & Assoc.; **col. 2, both:** © Stephen Trimble; **col. 3, top:** © Stephen Trimble, **bottom:** © John Shaw/Tom Stack & Assoc.

INDEX

Numbers in italics indicate illustrations.